# Lecture Notes
# in Business Information Processing

**332**

Series Editors

Wil van der Aalst
*RWTH Aachen University, Aachen, Germany*
John Mylopoulos
*University of Trento, Trento, Italy*
Michael Rosemann
*Queensland University of Technology, Brisbane, QLD, Australia*
Michael J. Shaw
*University of Illinois, Urbana-Champaign, IL, USA*
Clemens Szyperski
*Microsoft Research, Redmond, WA, USA*

More information about this series at http://www.springer.com/series/7911

Robert Pergl · Eduard Babkin
Russell Lock · Pavel Malyzhenkov
Vojtěch Merunka (Eds.)

# Enterprise and Organizational Modeling and Simulation

14th International Workshop, EOMAS 2018, Held at CAiSE 2018
Tallinn, Estonia, June 11–12, 2018
Selected Papers

Springer

*Editors*
Robert Pergl ⓘ
Czech Technical University in Prague
Prague, Czech Republic

Eduard Babkin ⓘ
Higher School of Economics
National Research University
Nizhny Novgorod, Russia

Russell Lock ⓘ
Loughborough University
Loughborough, UK

Pavel Malyzhenkov ⓘ
Higher School of Economics
National Research University
Nizhny Novgorod, Russia

Vojtěch Merunka ⓘ
Czech Technical University in Prague
Prague, Czech Republic

ISSN 1865-1348 ISSN 1865-1356 (electronic)
Lecture Notes in Business Information Processing
ISBN 978-3-030-00786-7 ISBN 978-3-030-00787-4 (eBook)
https://doi.org/10.1007/978-3-030-00787-4

Library of Congress Control Number: 2018954927

This Springer imprint is published by the registered company Springer Nature Switzerland AG
The registered company address is: Gewerbestrasse 11, 6330 Cham, Switzerland

# Preface

The concept and the very essence of enterprises are currently undergoing significant change. The age of digital transformation implies new features in business activity investigation. Despite such a rapidly changing scenario, the engineering approach toward business studies remains valid and continues to deliver a more complete and versatile frameworks for enterprise analysis. This makes enterprise engineering a demanding discipline to master and creates new challenges for all spheres of business science: research, academic, and practical.

The International Workshop on Enterprise and Organizational Modeling and Simulation (EOMAS) represents a forum where researchers and practitioners exchange and mutually enrich their views, approaches, and results in the field of enterprise engineering and enterprise architecture. The EOMAS community has been working hard on various topics spanning from formal and conceptual approaches to enterprise modelling to highly practical problems such as IT-business alignment and the quality of business process modelling tools.

This year the 14th edition of EOMAS, as a traditional workshop in the frame of the Conference on Advanced Information Engineering Systems (CAiSE), was organized in Tallinn (Estonia) during June 11–12. Out of 22 submitted papers, 11 were accepted for publication as full papers and for oral presentation; each paper was carefully selected, reviewed, and revised.

This year we also introduced two new features, which we consider very promising: we extended the set of problems discussed in EOMAS by enterprise engineering teaching aspects and we organized a "workshop-inside-workshop" session dedicated to methods for evaluating the quality of process. The materials of this workshop are also included for you, dear reader, in this publication. These topics broadened the horizons of EOMAS topics and we really enjoyed the quality and the level of the presented contributions.

We would like to sincerely thank the entire EOMAS community: the authors, the Program Committee, and the chairs for their enthusiasm and devotion, as well as all participants for their contributions, which resulted in a high-quality event remarkable from both research and practical points of view. We are looking forward to the next 15th edition where we all meet again!

June 2018

Robert Pergl
Eduard Babkin
Russell Lock
Pavel Malyzhenkov
Vojtěch Merunka

# Organization

EOMAS 2018 was organized by the Department of Software Engineering, Czech Technical University in Prague, in cooperation with CAISE 2018 and CIAO! Enterprise Engineering Network

## Executive Committee

### General Chair

Robert Pergl      Czech Technical University in Prague, Czech Republic

### Program Chairs

| | |
|---|---|
| Eduard Babkin | National Research University Higher School of Economics, Russia |
| Russell Lock | Loughborough University, UK |
| Pavel Malyzhenkov | National Research University Higher School of Economics, Russia |
| Vojtěch Merunka | Czech Technical University in Prague, Czech Republic |

### Program Committee

| | |
|---|---|
| David Aveiro | University of Madeira, Portugal |
| Eduard Babkin | Higher School of Economics Nizhni Novgorod, Russia |
| Joseph Barjis | San Jose State University, USA |
| Anna Bobkowska | Gdansk University of Technology, Poland |
| Mahmoud Boufaida | Mentouri University of Constantine, Algeria |
| Peter de Bruyn | University of Antwerp, Belgium |
| Simona Colucci | Politecnico di Bari, Italy |
| Francesco Donini | Universitá della Tuscia, Italy |
| Samuel Fosso Wamba | NEOMA Business School, France |
| Sérgio Guerreiro | Técnico Lisboa, Portugal |
| František Hunka | University of Ostrava, Czech Republic |
| Petr Kroha | Czech Technical University in Prague, Czech Republic |
| Russell Lock | Loughborough University, UK |
| Pavel Malyzhenkov | Higher School of Economics Nizhni Novgorod, Russia |
| Vojtěch Merunka | Czech University of Life Sciences, Czech Republic |
| Martin Molhanec | Czech Technical University in Prague, Czech Republic |
| Maria Ntaliani | Agricultural University of Athens, Greece |
| Josef Pavlíček | Czech University of Life Sciences, Czech Republic |
| Robert Pergl | Czech Technical University in Prague, Czech Republic |
| Srini Ramaswamy | ABB Inc., USA |
| Victor Romanov | Russian Plekhanov University, Russia |
| Gustavo Rossi | Lifia, Argentina |

| | |
|---|---|
| Adrian Rutle | Bergen University College, Norway |
| Steven van Kervel | Formetis BV, Belgium |
| Ben Roelens | Ghent University, Belgium |
| Patrizia Ribino | ICAR Institute of National Research Council, Italy |
| Jan Verelst | University of Antwerp, Belgium |

# Contents

## Conceptual Modelling

Enterprise Ontology-Driven Development. . . . . . . . . . . . . . . . . . . . . . . . . 3
  *Jiri Matula and Frantisek Hunka*

Requirements Engineering for Model-Based Enterprise Architecture
Management with ArchiMate . . . . . . . . . . . . . . . . . . . . . . . . . . . . . . 16
  *Dominik Bork, Aurona Gerber, Elena-Teodora Miron,*
  *Phil van Deventer, Alta Van der Merwe, Dimitris Karagiannis,*
  *Sunet Eybers, and Anna Sumereder*

Towards OntoUML for Software Engineering: Optimizing Kinds
and Subkinds Transformed into Relational Databases. . . . . . . . . . . . . . . . . 31
  *Zdeněk Rybola and Robert Pergl*

## Enterprise Engineering

An Improved Way for Measuring Simplicity During Process Discovery. . . . . 49
  *Jonas Lieben, Toon Jouck, Benoît Depaire, and Mieke Jans*

IT-Business Alignment Problem Solution by Means of Zachman Model:
Case of Woodworking Enterprise . . . . . . . . . . . . . . . . . . . . . . . . . . . 63
  *Pavel Malyzhenkov, Tatiana Gordeeva, and Maurizio Masi*

The Simplified Enterprise Architecture Management Methodology
for Teaching Purposes. . . . . . . . . . . . . . . . . . . . . . . . . . . . . . . . . 76
  *Dmitry Kudryavtsev, Evgeny Zaramenskikh, and Maxim Arzumanyan*

Toward Development Tools for Augmented Reality Applications –
A Practitioner Perspective . . . . . . . . . . . . . . . . . . . . . . . . . . . . . . . 91
  *Ethan Hadar*

## Formal Methods

Enhanced Benchmark Datasets for a Comprehensive Evaluation of Process
Model Matching Techniques. . . . . . . . . . . . . . . . . . . . . . . . . . . . . . 107
  *Muhammad Ali and Khurram Shahzad*

Investigating the Applicability of the Normalized Systems Theory
on IT Infrastructure Systems. . . . . . . . . . . . . . . . . . . . . . . . . . . . . . 123
  *Geert Haerens*

The DEMO Co-creation and Co-production Model and Its Utilization . . . . . .   138
  *Frantisek Hunka, Steven J. H. van Kervel, and Jiri Matula*

The Intellectual Dimension of IT-Business Alignment Problem:
Alloy Application . . . . . . . . . . . . . . . . . . . . . . . . . . . . . . . . . . . . . . . .   153
  *Marina Ivanova and Pavel Malyzhenkov*

**Invited Workshop Notes**

Methods for Evaluating the Quality of Process Modelling Tools . . . . . . . . . .   171
  *Josef Pavlicek and Petra Pavlickova*

**Author Index** . . . . . . . . . . . . . . . . . . . . . . . . . . . . . . . . . . . . . . . . .   179

# Conceptual Modelling

# Enterprise Ontology-Driven Development

Jiri Matula[✉] and Frantisek Hunka

University of Ostrava, Ostrava, Czechia
{jiri.matula, frantisek.hunka}@osu.cz

**Abstract.** Most of the current techniques and approaches for user requirements specification have problems with capturing the appropriate context for development of enterprise information systems. Primarily, they are designed to capture the functional aspects of software rather than its relevancy to an enterprise. Transactions defined in the DEMO (Design & Engineering Methodology for Organizations) represent business activities in their existential essence without implementation details. Therefore, they are great candidates to be utilized for the initial development phase of enterprise information systems. The paper exemplifies how to specify software specification the using the DEMO transaction pattern and BDD (Behaviour-Driven Development) technique. This proposal resulted from a significant lack of direct utilization of ontology for enterprise information systems development. The major part of the paper gives a step-by-step explanation of how to integrate DEMO transaction patterns into initial BDD scenarios for the development of enterprise information systems. Such created scenarios provide a perfect guideline in the initial phase of information system development for enterprises. The created scenarios were verified using the domain specific language Gherkin and BDD framework Behat.

**Keywords:** DEMO methodology · Behaviour-Driven development
User requirements specification · Enterprise information system

## 1 Introduction

Information systems (IS) provide information for agenda fulfilment of many actors working in an enterprise. The goal of an information system, in general, is to support the business processes of an organization or even to automate them completely. This fact leads to investments into implementation of an information system with expectations of competitive advantages and saving the resources.

Nevertheless, the development of information systems is a continuous process and very prone to errors and challenges. Thus, it requires very careful decisions to which functionalities are worth developing or not. Understanding needs of businesses is the foundation stone of any successful enterprise system and almost every initial phase of development is accompanied by significant issues in terms of negotiating user requirements. Moreover, user requirements often tend to be uncertain, ambiguous and usually rely on one-way confirmation.

The agile community recommends several different techniques (e.g. Use Case, User story, BDD, etc.) for the definition of user requirements and stabilizing the

© Springer Nature Switzerland AG 2018
R. Pergl et al. (Eds.): EOMAS 2018, LNBIP 332, pp. 3–15, 2018.
https://doi.org/10.1007/978-3-030-00787-4_1

development process of software [1, 2, 12]. On the one hand, these techniques work well with the general user requirements. On the other hand, they have problems with linking the context of user requirements to business activities.

The transaction pattern defined in the DEMO methodology is a general pattern which captures the essential descriptions of every business process. Essentially, this pattern is potentially the missing describing part necessary for identification information system features which are relevant or not to business processes. Despite this fact, approaches which utilize ontology for software development exist [4, 8, 17], not many of them directly control the development process which gives an opportunity to utilize ontological enterprise descriptions and combine them with BDD technique into one coherent whole. Such a unique combination of DEMO methodology and BDD technique allows the following of the latest trends of project management in software development and directly utilize enterprise ontology within development process at the same time. BDD methodology works well with a declarative approach. Therefore, this paper tries to deal with user requirements using declarative semantic. Using a declarative approach to describe an enterprise can be also found in [5–7, 9]. Also, other research papers [10, 11, 13, 14] deal with the topic by formalization of techniques based on the best practices. Nevertheless, none of them combines ontological and best practice approaches for the definition of user requirements as it is presented in this paper.

The structure of the paper is as follows. Section 2 briefly describes the embedding of transactions into BDD scenarios. Section 3, the major part of the paper, shows step-by-step how to setup an initial guideline for the development of the enterprise information system. Section 4 deals with conclusion of the presented approach.

## 1.1 DEMO Methodology and Transaction Pattern

DEMO (Design Engineering Methodology for Organization) defines an organization as a composition of people (social individuals) that perform two kinds of acts - production and coordination acts [3]. By performing production acts, people fulfil the aims of the organization. An example of a production fact might be e.g. "checkout of order" or "customer payment". By performing coordination acts, human beings enter into and comply with commitments which initiate and coordinate production acts. The result of successfully performing a production act is a production fact. Coordination and production acts and facts are arranged into a transaction pattern.

The transaction pattern states that there are always two roles in a transaction, initiator (customer) and executor (producer). Initiator is someone who has a request and executor is responsible for fulfilling initiator needs. More detailed explanation of transaction pattern is depicted in Fig. 1. White boxes represent coordination acts, white rounded boxes are used for coordination facts. Production act is depicted as a grey box. Grey rounded boxes stand for production fact. Lifespan of every transaction has three phases – order (proposition), execution and result phase. In the order phase, the initiator and the executor work to reach an agreement about the intended result of the transaction, i.e., the production fact that the executor is going to create as well as the intended time of creation. In the execution phase, this production fact is brought about by the executor. In the results phase, the initiator accepts or rejects result (production fact) of the transaction [3].

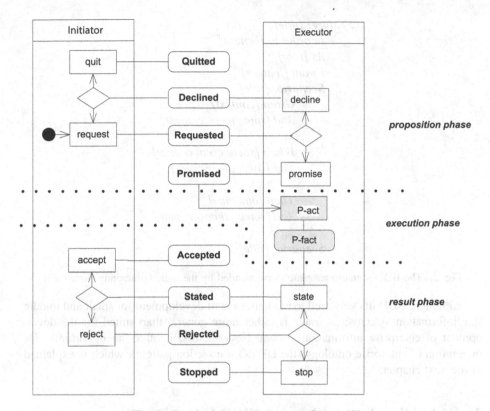

**Fig. 1.** Standard transaction pattern Source [3]

In simple terms, the transaction pattern provides a great opportunity of how to capture the main business processes of the enterprise in their existential essence. Usually, a business process is formed by one or more DEMO transactions arranged in a tree structure. Comparatively to other approaches which utilize ontology for business process modelling, the DEMO transaction pattern has as only one solid theoretical foundation [3].

## 1.2 Behaviour-Driven Development

Behaviour-Driven Development (BDD) is a set of software engineering practices designed to help teams build and deliver more valuable, higher quality software faster. It draws on Agile and lean practices including Test-Driven Development (TDD) and Domain-Driven Design (DDD). But most importantly, BDD provides a common language based on simple, structured sentences expressed in English (or in the native language of the stakeholders) that facilitate communication between project team members and business stakeholders [2]. These descriptions are called scenarios and they are being utilized for testing purposes (e.g. acceptance testing).

The BDD scenario consists of a feature title, an associated user story [1], and scenarios. Each scenario is defined by three keywords. *Given* describes context, *when* specifies actions or events and *then* states expected outcomes of the performed actions (Fig. 2).

*Feature:* *[title]*
        *In order to [benefit]*
        *As [role]*
        *I want [feature]*
        ***Scenario***: *[title]*
                ***Given*** *[context]*
                *And [some more context]*
                ...
                ***When*** *[some event occurs]*
                *And [some other event]*
                ...
                ***Then*** *[outcome]*
                *And [some other outcome]*
                ...
        ***Scenario:*** *[title]*

**Fig. 2.** The BDD scenario template recommended by the agile community Source [2]

Although, BDD fits very well to modern ways of development for small and middle size information systems; its usage is rather more general than suited for the development of enterprise information system. Nevertheless, it offers an opportunity for integration of enterprise ontology (the DEMO transaction pattern), which is explained in the next chapter.

## 2   Embedding Transactions into BDD Scenarios

An inevitable part of the BDD scenario is the user story, typically brief description told from perspective of the person who desires the new functionality. BDD scenario typically follows a simple template in Fig. 3.

*As a <type of user>, I want <some goal> so that <some reason>.*

**Fig. 3.** The user story template recommended by the agile community Source [2]

Previously published author's papers [15, 16] have presented how to map DEMO transactions to user stories and BDD scenarios. The template in Fig. 3 was modified into the form which fits for embedding the transaction pattern within a user story. The changes to the original template are as follows:

The type of user was replaced by either initiator or executor. The part defining user intentions was exchanged by coordination or production acts which are followed by either coordination or production facts (Fig. 4).

*As an <initiator/executor>, I perform a coordination/production act in <transaction> so that <coordination/production fact>.*

**Fig. 4.** The modified user story template utilizing DEMO transaction pattern Source [15]

In other words, the ontological origin of employee activities descriptions was utilized for formalization of user stories on the theoretical foundation given in the DEMO methodology. This is the significant difference between the before mentioned techniques (Use Case, User Story, BDD, etc.) that rely only on the best practices and do not use any kind of theoretical apparatus. Such a modified user story can be consequently integrated into BDD scenario. This is depicted in Fig. 5.

> **Feature:** *[title] - [transaction ID]*
> *In order to [production/coordination fact]*
> *As [initiator/executor]*
> *I want to perform [coordination/production act]*
> > **Scenario:** *[title]*
> > > **Given** *[context]*
> > > **And** *[some other context]*
> > > ...
> > > **When** *[some event occurs]*
> > > **And** *[some other event]*
> > > ...
> > > **Then** *[expected outcome or coordination/production fact]*
> > > **And** *[another outcome]*
> > > ...
> > **Scenario:** *[title] ...*

**Fig. 5.** The BDD scenario template for embedding of the DEMO transaction Source [15]

## 3  Example Case

The description of the existing company (located in Ostrava) was chosen as the explanatory case. The second, third, and the fourth steps comes from the DEMO methodology and its general elicitation method. Understanding of the below mentioned analysis and synthesis [3] from the DEMO methodology is necessary for the clear comprehension of the described apparatus. The following chapter describes each step of the procedure.

Procedure includes the following actions:

1. Gather text description of enterprise and business activities.
2. Perform the Performa-Informa-Forma analysis.
3. Perform the Coordination-Actors-Production analysis.
4. Perform the Transaction pattern synthesis.
5. Create BDD scenarios with embedded identified transactions.
6. Generate BDD test skeletons (optional).

### 3.1  The Performa-Informa-Forma and Coordination-Actors-Production Analysis

In the beginning it is necessary to gather text description, respectively descriptions of employee activities in the enterprise. Text descriptions should be discussed and confirmed by management and employees at the same time if possible. The true activities of employees might often differ from the expectations of the management board.

Gathering text description is followed by the second step – the Perfoma-Informa-Forma analysis. In this step, all available pieces of knowledge are divided in three sets according to the distinction axiom defined in [3]. This analysis can best be performed by colouring the appropriate parts of the descriptions: red for Performa items, green for Informa items, and blue for Forma items.

In the third step, the performa items are divided into C-acts/results, P-acts/results, and actor roles, according to the operation axiom. Actor roles are enclosed between square brackets "[" and "]", coordination acts/results between parentheses "(" and ")", production acts/results between the angular brackets "<" and ">". To avoid any confusion, the enclosed pieces of text are underlined. The result of first three steps is following:

The [company] <provides> the delivery of electricity and a "smart measuring" service which enables the monitoring of electricity consumption online. In addition, metering devices have the ability to save electricity. [Customer] <has to rent> a necessary device to <start monitoring> consumption. [Customers] have provided the [information systems] (IS) which reports electricity consumption and savings for each period. Measuring devices broadcast consumption data. These records are stored for further processing to a database.

In the beginning, a [client] (calls) the company and a [salesman] (meets) a customer and <offers> him a suitable subscription plan to them. The organization structure of the salesman is arranged as multi-level organization which is supported by another [IS] which allows a salesman to manage their colleagues.

Furthermore, the [IS] provides to [salesmen] overviews about ongoing contracts and paid commissions. When a <contract is signed> by a [client], its personal details are entered to the [IS]. Consequently, the manufacturing of devices is requested. The device manufactory department has their own employees and stock of material. Upon the signing of the contract, device arrangements are complemented.

Once devices are prepared for expedition, the service department is notified about the necessity of installation contracted devices. Firstly, an installation place is examined by a [technician] who (decides) whether an installation is feasible. After that, installations of devices are (planned). Planning of device installation is a complex process which considers the availability of company cars, booking of accommodation, skills of technicians etc. Once the device is installed, a customer signs the montage sheet. When the <installation> of the device is completed, a [new client] is entered into the information system, the device is registered to the IS and contracted services are started to be <billed>. [Customers] have to <settle payments> for contracted services monthly.

Moreover, the company operates with their own [IT department] which is responsible for development of information systems and management of internal IT services. The [IT department] closely cooperates with the development department and inform about quotas for client data. Moreover, the [IT department] <manages> their own servers and [branch manager] Charles, <rents> a professional server housing and third-party services.

## 3.2    The Transaction Pattern Synthesis

In the fourth step, identified C-acts/facts and P-acts/facts are clustered into transactions. Essentially, each transaction must be identified by its production fact, where the transaction name and id are assigned. When transactions are stated, then the belonging coordination and production acts need to be connected to transactions. Some transactions might have missing coordination acts. This is almost always the case because descriptions are typically very incomplete. A more detailed explanation of the transaction pattern synthesis is available in [3]. The result of the synthesis is as follows.

**Table 1.** Identified transactions and their associated production facts

| Transaction type | Associated production facts |
| --- | --- |
| T01 – service offer | *PF01 – A proper subscription plan was offered* |
| T02 – contract signing | *PF02 – A contract was signed* |
| T03 – appliance installation | *PF03 – A device was installed* |
| T04 – consumption monitoring | *PF04 – Monitoring of consumption started* |
| T05 – electricity delivery | *PF05 – Delivery of electricity started* |
| T06 – electricity subscription | *PF06 – A payment for the period was settled* |
| T07 – payments management | *PF07 – Services started to be billed upon the contract* |
| T08 – device rental | *PF08 – A device was rented for a period* |
| T09 – provision of IT services | *PF09 – Contracted services and housing were rented* |
| T10 – IT services management | *PF10 – IT department servers were managed* |

**Table 2.** Identified transactions and their associated production acts

| Transaction type | Associated production acts |
| --- | --- |
| T01 – service offer | *PA01 – Offer a proper subscription plan* |
| T02 – contract signing | *PA02 – Sign a contract* |
| T03 – appliance installation | *PA03 – Install a device* |
| T04 – consumption monitoring | *PA04 – Start monitoring of consumption* |
| T05 – electricity delivery | *PA05 – Provide delivery of electricity* |
| T06 – electricity subscription | *PA06 – Pay the monthly payment for electricity* |
| T07 – payments management | *PA07 – Initiate billing of contracted services* |
| T08 – device rental | *PA08 – Rent a device for consumption monitoring* |
| T09 – provision of IT services | *PA09 – Rent IT services and housing* |
| T10 – IT services management | *PA10 – Manage own servers* |

**Table 3.** Identified transactions and their associated coordination facts

| Transaction type | Associated coordination facts |
| --- | --- |
| T01 – service offer | *CF01 – A potential client met the salesman* |
| T02 – contract signing | – |
| T03 – appliance installation | *CF02 – A technician decided whether installation is feasible* |

*(continued)*

**Table 3.** (*continued*)

| Transaction type | Associated coordination facts |
|---|---|
| | **CF03** – *A device installation is planned* |
| T04 – consumption monitoring | |
| T05 – electricity delivery | – |
| T06 – electricity subscription | – |
| T07 – payments management | – |
| T08 – device rental | – |
| T09 – provision of IT services | – |
| T10 – IT services management | – |

**Table 4.** Identified transactions and their associated coordination acts

| Transaction type | Associated coordination acts |
|---|---|
| T01 – service offer | **CA01** – *Call the company to order* |
| T02 – contract signing | – |
| T03 – appliance installation | **CA02** – *Decide about feasibility* <br> **CA03** – *Plan the appliance installation* |
| T04 – consumption monitoring | – |
| T05 – electricity delivery | – |
| T06 – electricity subscription | – |
| T07 – payments management | – |
| T08 – device rental | – |
| T09 – provision of IT services | – |
| T10 – IT services management | – |

Previously, actor roles (text enclosed between square brackets in the company description) were identified in the third step. Roles were refined and generalized for modelling purposes. No person outside of a modelled domain would know who is, for example Charles, but almost everybody can understand who is branch manager in the IT department. In this way, each role is associated to a transaction which is depicted in Fig. 6. This diagram will be useful and will make the consequent preparation of BDD scenarios easier because it allows immediately finding out which actor role belongs to which transaction type.

## 3.3 Embedding Transactions into BDD Scenarios

Once coordination and production acts/facts are listed, the creation of BDD scenarios is straightforward. The created scenarios follow a template mentioned in Fig. 5. The "*In order to*" part can contain only coordination or production facts mentioned in Tables 1 and 3. Identified coordination or production acts defined in Tables 2 and 4 are placed into the "*I want to*" part of BDD specification. The actor role (initiator or executor) is attached to the "*As*" part. See results in Figs. 7 and 8.

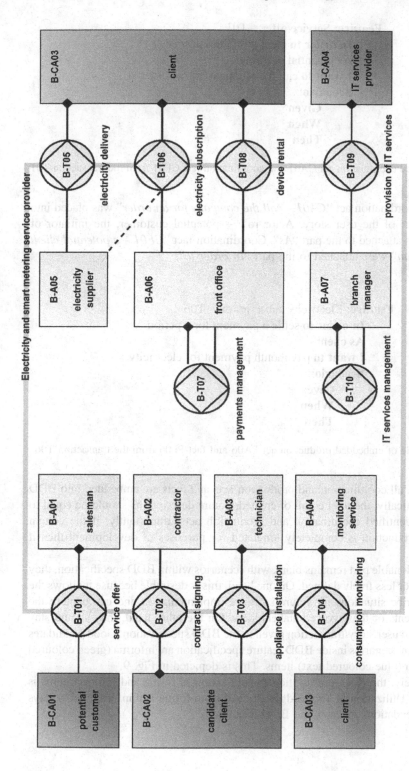

**Fig. 6.** The transaction diagram of the company

**Feature:** Service offer – T01
**In order to** meet with the salesman
**As** potential customer
**I want to** call the company for an order
**Scenario:**
    **Given**
    **When**
    **Then**

**Fig. 7.** Embedded coordination act CA01 and coordination fact CF01 from the transaction T01

In Fig. 7 coordination act "*CA01 – call the company for an order*" was placed into "*I want to*" part of the user story. Actor role – potential customer, the initiator of transaction, was attached to the part "*As*". Coordination fact "*CF01 – a potential client met the salesman*" were attached to the part "*In order to*".

**Feature:** Electricity subscription – T06
**In order to** settle a payment for a period
**As** client
**I want to** pay month payment for electricity
**Scenario:**
    **Given**
    **When**
    **Then**

**Fig. 8.** Example of embedded production act PA06 and fact PF06 from the transaction T06

In this way, all coordination and production acts and facts are embedded into BDD scenarios. Practically, the total count of created feature descriptions should be equal to the count of identified coordination and production acts. Importantly, if the certain coordination/production is completely unrelated for purposes of development then it can be omitted.

If the questionable part remains blank with scenarios within BDD specification, they might be more or less freely defined. On one hand, this is desirable because it allows the ability to describe situations for future software implementation and can capture the extra requirements of the involved stakeholders. On the other hand, they should stay coherent prior to user story/transaction given in the BDD specification. Good candidates for definitions of scenarios inside BDD feature specification are informa (green coloured text) and forma (blue coloured text) items. This is depicted in Fig. 9.

Unfortunately, the exact prescription for utilization of forma and informa items is missing so far. Utilization of knowledge retrieved from forma and informa items stays up to recommendations given in the BDD technique.

**Feature:** Payments management – T07
**In order to** start billing services upon the contract
**As** front office
**I want to** initiate billing of contracted services
**Scenario**:
    **Given** device is registered in IS
    **When** new client is entered into IS
    **Then** contracted services are started to be billed

**Fig. 9.** Example of utilization of performa and forma items within BDD scenarios (Color figure online)

### 3.4 Generating Test Skeletons (Optional Step)

Prepared BDD scenarios are compatible with Gherkin language syntax. Gherkin is a business readable, domain specific language often used by developers who practice BDD style of development. Gherkin serves two purposes, documentation and automated tests. The crucial condition for automated generation of test files skeletons is the definition of scenario steps within a BDD feature specification. The test class skeleton for Fig. 9 was automatically generated by Behat framework. Behat is an open-source Behaviour-Driven development framework for the PHP platform. The generated output is depicted in Fig. 10.

```
class PaymentsManagementContext implements Context {

    /**
     * @Given :device is registered in IS
     */
    public function deviceIsRegisteredInIS($device)
    {
        throw new PendingException();
    }

    /**
     * @When new client is entered into IS
     */
    public function newClientIsEnteredIntoIS ()
    {
        throw new PendingException();
    }

    /**
     * @Then contracted services are started to be billed
     */
    public function contractedServicesAreStartedToBeBilled()
    {
        throw new PendingException();
    }

}
```

**Fig. 10.** Generated test skeleton for the BDD scenario in Fig. 9

In this manner, it is possible to utilize ontological description directly for the definition of testing steps (in form of classes in the object-oriented paradigm) and thereby connect production codebase with the ontology of enterprise.

## 4   Conclusions

The main intention of the paper was to present the step-by-step process on how to integrate ontological enterprise description directly into a development process for small and middle size enterprise information systems. The proposed technique is derived upon the theoretical basis of DEMO methodology and follows one of the latest trends in the software development – BDD practices. Such a combination is different from other similar approaches e.g. Use Case, User Story, BPMN and others. These techniques usually rely only on the one-way confirmation of involved stakeholders.

The presented solution provides a solid guideline, emerging from existent business processes for the definition of user requirements in the initial phase of enterprise information system development. It enables simple observation of which business activities are involved in the information system. Another important benefit is a minimalization of potential between business needs and implemented information system in its beginning, facilitated by linkage of software specifications and ontological descriptions of enterprise.

The described procedure consists of several steps. At first, it is necessary to gather text descriptions of a modelled enterprise. Then identification follows of actors, coordination/production act and facts which is known as Coordination-Actors-Production analysis. This analysis is followed by the transaction pattern synthesis. After synthesis, it is possible to set an initial guideline for development in the form of BDD scenarios which has embedded identified transactions, respectively their coordination/production acts and facts. The whole procedure was demonstrated step-by-step in the existing company in Ostrava together with reference to book Enterprise Ontology, written by Dietz [3]. Usability of created scenarios for BDD testing was verified using Behat BDD framework, whereas test files skeletons for consequent implementation was possible to generate.

To summarize, the method offers a possibility of how to directly utilize ontological descriptions of business processes during the initial phase of enterprise information system development. Despite promising qualities, it would be appropriate to verify the method once again with an adequate case study, to eventually discover so far unknown further benefits and weaknesses. Also, another step would be a proper formalization of informa and forma items utilization for BDD scenarios. These mentioned facts will be an objective of further research.

**Acknowledgements.** The paper was supported by the grant provided by Ministry of Education, Youth and Sports Czech Republic, reference no. SGS05/PRF/2018 and the grant provided by city of Ostrava.

# References

1. Cohn, M.: User Stories Applied: for Agile Software Development, pp. 31–41. Addison-Wesley, Boston (2004)
2. Smart, J.F.: BDD in Action: Behavior-Driven Development for the Whole Software Lifecycle, pp. 3–32. Manning Publications Company, New York (2014)
3. Dietz, J.L.: Enterprise Ontology: Theory and Methodology. Springer, New York (2006). https://doi.org/10.1007/3-540-33149-2. pp. 16–160
4. Van Kervel, S.J.H.: Ontology driven enterprise information systems engineering. Doctoral dissertation, SIKS Dissertation series nr. 2012-50, Delft University of Technology (2012)
5. Pesic, M., Van der Aalst, W.M.: A declarative approach for flexible business processes management. In: Eder, J., Dustdar, S. (eds.) BPM 2006. LNCS, vol. 4103, pp. 169–180. Springer, Heidelberg (2006). https://doi.org/10.1007/11837862_18
6. Grosof, B.N., Labrou, Y., Chan, H.Y.: A declarative approach to business rules in contracts: courteous logic programs in XML. In: Proceedings of the 1st ACM Conference on Electronic Commerce, pp. 68–77 (1999)
7. de Leoni, M., Maggi, F.M., van der Aalst, W.M.: An alignment-based framework to check the conformance of declarative process models and to pre-process event-log data. Inf. Syst. **47**, 258–277 (2015)
8. Skjæveland, M.G., Giese, M., Hovland, D., Lian, E.H., Waaler, A.: Engineering ontology-based access to real-world data sources. Web Semant.: Sci. Serv. Agents World Wide Web **33**, 112–140 (2015)
9. Gigante, G., Gargiulo, F., Ficco, M.: A semantic driven approach for requirements verification. In: Camacho, D., Braubach, L., Venticinque, S., Badica, C. (eds.) Intelligent Distributed Computing VIII. SCI, vol. 570, pp. 427–436. Springer, Cham (2015). https://doi.org/10.1007/978-3-319-10422-5_44
10. Wautelet, Y., Heng, S., Hintea, D., Kolp, M., Poelmans, S.: Bridging user story sets with the use case model. In: Link, S., Trujillo, J. (eds.) ER 2016. LNCS, vol. 9975, pp. 127–138. Springer, Cham (2016). https://doi.org/10.1007/978-3-319-47717-6_11
11. Simões, D., Antunes, P., Cranefield, J.: Enriching knowledge in business process modelling: a storytelling approach. In: Razmerita, L., Phillips-Wren, G., Jain, L. (eds.) Innovations in Knowledge Management, vol. 95, pp. 241–267. Springer, Heidelberg (2016). https://doi.org/10.1007/978-3-662-47827-1_10
12. Maleki, N.G., Ramsin, R.: Agile web development methodologies: a survey and evaluation. In: Lee, R. (ed.) SERA 2017. SCI, vol. 722, pp. 1–25. Springer, Cham (2017). https://doi.org/10.1007/978-3-319-61388-8_1
13. Borgianni, Y., Cascini, G., Rotini, F.: Business process reengineering driven by customer value: a support for undertaking decisions under uncertainty conditions. Comput. Indus. **68**, 132–147 (2015)
14. Smit, K., Zoet, M., Berkhout, M.: Functional Requirements for Business Rules Management Systems (2017)
15. Zacek, J., Matula, J., Hunka, F.: Context definition for BDD scenarios upon DEMO methodology. In: 2nd International Conference on Theory and Practice, pp. 164–169. Sia Pacific Institute of Advanced Research, Melbourne (2016)
16. Matula J., Zacek J., Hunka F.: Relevant user stories by using DEMO analysis. In: Proceedings of the 11th Scientific Conference Internet in the Information Society, pp. 21–30. University of Dabrowa Górnicza, Cieplaka (2016)
17. Pan, J.Z., Staab, S., Aßmann, U., Ebert, J., Zhao, Y.: Ontology-Driven Software Development. Springer, Heidelberg (2012). https://doi.org/10.1007/978-3-642-31226-7

# Requirements Engineering for Model-Based Enterprise Architecture Management with ArchiMate

Dominik Bork[1]([⊠]), Aurona Gerber[2,3], Elena-Teodora Miron[1],
Phil van Deventer[2], Alta Van der Merwe[2], Dimitris Karagiannis[1],
Sunet Eybers[2], and Anna Sumereder[1]

[1] Research Group Knowledge Engineering, University of Vienna,
Waehringer Street 29, 1090 Vienna, Austria
{dominik.bork,elena-teodora.miron,dimitris.karagiannis,
anna.sumereder}@univie.ac.at
[2] Department of Informatics, University of Pretoria,
Hatfield, Pretoria 0083, South Africa
{aurona.gerber,phil.vandeventer,alta.vandermerwe,sunet.eybers}@up.ac.za
[3] CSIR Center for AI Research (CAIR), Brummeria, Pretoria, South Africa

**Abstract.** The role of information systems (IS) evolved from supporting basic business functions to complex integrated enterprise platforms and ecosystems. As a result, enterprises increasingly adopt enterprise architecture (EA) as a means to manage complexity and support the ability to change. We initiated a study that investigates the pivotal role of enterprise architecture management (EAM) as an essential strategy to manage enterprise change and within this larger context, specifically how the ArchiMate modeling language can be enhanced with capabilities that support EAM. This paper reports on the evaluation of an EA modeling tool (TEAM) which has been enhanced with EAM capabilities. The evaluation was performed by a focus group of enterprise architects that attended a workshop and applied the tool to an EAM case study. The evaluation results, requirements as well as a conceptualization for further development are presented and are of value for both, enterprise architecture researchers and enterprise architects.

**Keywords:** Enterprise architecture management · ArchiMate
Requirements engineering · Focus group

## 1 Introduction

*"The digitization of our society changes the way society work, communicate and collaborate."* [1] Similarly, digitization or digital transformation changes the way enterprises create value. Traditionally, enterprises created value by selling products or by providing services to customers with direct and simple business models. The digital transformation significantly changed these business models

© Springer Nature Switzerland AG 2018
R. Pergl et al. (Eds.): EOMAS 2018, LNBIP 332, pp. 16–30, 2018.
https://doi.org/10.1007/978-3-030-00787-4_2

(e.g., toward platform ecosystems [2]), customer involvement (e.g., value co-creation [3]), and product/service systems [4]. These changes are either driven or supported by information systems and therefore directly influence the enterprise architecture (EA). Thus, it is of utmost interest for enterprises to manage their EA as well as to manage their enterprise using EA, collectively termed *enterprise architecture management* (EAM) [5,6].

The Open Group Architecture Framework (TOGAF) and the ArchiMate [7] modeling language are widely adopted EA standards. However, both have limited support for corporate EA management because of the sole focus on the methodological and modeling language aspects of EA, respectively. Supporting these standards with computerized modeling environments creates opportunities to support EAM by for instance exploiting conceptual models as knowledge base for advanced management support [8]. Our study therefore investigates how EA modeling with proper tooling supports enterprise architecture management.

Adopting the action design research paradigm that incorporates evolutionary design with short evaluation/feedback loops [9], we implemented a first prototype of the TOGAF-based Enterprise Architecture Management (TEAM) modeling tool[1] that implements the Archimate 3.0.1. standard [7]. This paper reports on an evaluation/feedback loop of TEAM that used a carefully designed focus group. The focus group introduced eight EA experts to both EAM as well as the TEAM tool using a case study in a workshop scenario. In depth feedback was collected from the EA experts on the functionality of the tool, as well as input on how a modeling platform could support the two focus areas of EAM namely: (1) managing the EA of an enterprise, and (2) managing the enterprise using EA. This feedback was consolidated into advanced requirement themes for the second prototype version of TEAM.

The remainder of this paper is structured as follows: foundations are presented in Sect. 2 and in Sect. 3 the research design for the evaluation of TEAM is discussed. Section 4 consolidates the results by means of a set of requirement themes for advanced EAM. Finally, Sect. 5 concludes the paper.

## 2  Foundations

### 2.1  Enterprise Architecture Management

Enterprise Architecture Management (EAM) is a relatively recent perspective within the domain of EA. EAM is broadly defined as *"management practice that establishes, maintains and uses a coherent set of guidelines, architecture principles and governance regimes that provide direction for and practical help with the design and the development of an enterprise's architecture in order to achieve its vision and strategy"* [6]. In the 80's John Zachman, often described as the father of EA, adopted a systems engineering approach to develop the Zachman Framework for Enterprise Architecture or Zachman Framework[TM] (ZFEA) [10]. The

---

[1] The tool is freely available on the OMiLAB TEAM project site at: http://austria. omilab.org/psm/content/team/info, last visit: 08.05.2018.

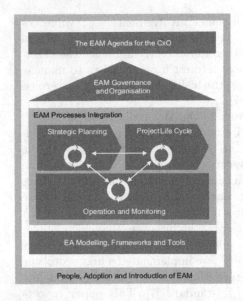

| | Passive structure | Behavior | Active structure | Motivation |
|---|---|---|---|---|
| Strategy | | | | |
| Business | | | | |
| Application | | | | |
| Technology | | | | |
| Physical | | | | |
| Implementation & Migration | | | | |

**Fig. 1.** EAM building blocks [6].       **Fig. 2.** ArchiMate 3.0 framework [7].

ZFEA had as primary goal the specification of a universal set of descriptive representations from different views for enterprises as socio-technical systems [10,11]. Originally, EAM was thus focused on the development of the enterprise architecture itself in an attempt to manage the complexity of modern enterprises [6, p. 13].

In the 90's the focus of EAM shifted from modeling the enterprise towards *alignment* of the different aspects within an enterprise [6, p. 14]. To assist with this alignment, several EA frameworks were proposed and EAM literature discussed various enterprise alignment aspects e.g. the execution of strategy through business-IT alignment [12–15]. Lapalme [16] summarized the EAM notions of the time by describing three schools of thought related to EA namely: (1) *Enterprise-wide IT platform (EIT)*, concerned with effective enterprise strategy execution and operation through IT-Business alignment; (2) *Enterprise (E)*, concerned with effective enterprise strategy implementation through execution coherency; and (3) *Enterprise-in-environment (EiE)*, concerned with fostering organizational learning by aligning the various facets of the enterprise such as governance structures and IT capabilities [16].

The most recent developments in EAM include the use of EA for strategic business management [6,17]. This strategic EAM standpoint incorporates all the previous EAM perspectives but specifically adopts the extended view that EA is a *management philosophy* and *executive management and governance function* that should, for instance, be used to manage holistic and sustainable enterprise transformation, alignment and integration [6, p. 57]. Given this perspective, EAM is a multidimensional function that influences all aspects of an enterprise, including its organizational culture, communication practices and operations. Ahleman et al. [6, p. 42] proposed a model that depicts the essential EAM building blocks. As is shown in Fig. 1, the main and outside container for EAM indicate the 'soft factors' that are important within an organization. Stakeholder buy in into EAM is crucial when, for instance, altering organizational culture and changing individual behavior. Figure 1 furthermore depicts the role of EAM as a chief executive officer agenda at the top. The EAM governance and organization role deals with the manner in which EAM is institutionalized within an organization. Furthermore, the integration of EA into organizational processes includes the embedding of EAM into strategic planning, project life cycles and organizational operations and monitoring, which all have to do with the day-to-day operations of an enterprise. EAM building blocks have to include EA frameworks, modeling and tools, which represent and include the existing body of knowledge and best practices regarding enterprise architecture [6, p. 42]. Since ArchiMate is one of the dominantly used EA languages, conceptual modeling methods in general and ArchiMate in particular are briefly introduced in the following to establish a theoretic foundation for the rest of the paper.

## 2.2   ArchiMate, TOGAF and Conceptual Modeling Methods

ArchiMate is a standard of the Open Group that describes an enterprise architecture modeling language [18]. ArchiMate was originally developed by a team from Telematica Institute in the Netherlands to model an EA within and across business domains [19]. ArchiMate adopts a layered view on an enterprise depicted in the ArchiMate Framework where the core entities of an enterprise are categorized along two dimensions (layers and aspects) as shown in Fig. 2. In addition, ArchiMate adopts a service-oriented model where each layer provides services to the layers above it. ArchiMate focuses on specifying a modeling standard for enterprise architecture. By contrast, TOGAF, the Open Group Architecture Framework specifies guidelines for designing, planning, implementing, and governing an enterprise information technology architecture [14]. When the implementation of ArchiMate is discussed, it is often done within the TOGAF approach to provide the context of an enterprise architecture project [20].

Any conceptual modeling methods such as ArchiMate facilitates the management of complexity by applying abstraction. According to [21], modeling methods are composed of *modeling language, modeling procedure*, and *mechanisms & algorithms*. A modeling language can be further decomposed into: *syntax*, the available language elements; *notation*, the graphical representation of syntactic elements; and *semantics*, the meaning of the syntactic elements. The modeling procedure describes steps and results of utilizing a modeling method in order to create valid models. Lastly, mechanisms & algorithms define the model processing functionality that is provided by the modeling method (e.g., simulations and queries).

Conceptual modeling methods are used to create abstract representations of some part of the real world for *"human users, for purposes of understanding and communication"* [22]. This traditional view is still valid, however, nowadays conceptual models are also viewed as a formalized knowledge base that enables machine processing and intersubjective understanding [23]. Conceptual modeling methods therefore not only target the best abstraction level for a specific domain by means of a metamodel, but also the enrichment of the modeling language with proper functionality to increase the value of the models. This approach to conceptual models is adopted by OMiLAB, the platform used for the development of TEAM, which is discussed in the next section.

## 2.3  The Open Models Laboratory (OMiLAB)

The Open Models Laboratory (OMiLAB, www.omilab.org) is an open platform for the conceptualization of modeling methods, combining open source and open communities with the goal of fostering conceptual modeling. OMiLAB constitutes a high number of international contributors [24]. Almost 50 different modeling methods have already been successfully conceptualized within OMiLAB [25], such as Multi-Perspective Enterprise Modeling (MEMO) [26] and SOM [27]. A more comprehensive view on successful conceptualizations within OMiLAB is given in [25][2]. The TEAM tool was implemented as a project within OMiLAB.

## 3  Research Design: Focus Group Evaluation

As stated, we report on the evaluation of the first prototype version of the TEAM modeling tool. In order to obtain the in depth feedback required, we adopted a *focus group* (FG) as research method. A FG is a qualitative research method that is effective when collecting data about the opinions of people or how they think, feel, or act regarding a specific topic [28]. The method is particularly useful for collecting data in complex scenarios where specialized knowledge is required. Using a FG for data collection in our evaluation of TEAM was therefore applicable because EAM has an extensive scope and we were particularly interested in the opinions of the participants (EA experts and practitioners) regarding EAM requirements when using TEAM. As a prerequisite, the FG needs to be designed in such a way that participants are able to provide high-quality, in-depth feedback. We therefore designed the FG as a workshop specifically aimed at EA experts and practitioners with several years of experience, and we included carefully developed feedback mechanisms that triangulate in order to collect data. Because the experience of the participants varied, we created a baseline by introducing the necessary background in the workshop. The workshop was structured as follows:

1. **Session 1: Enterprise Architecture Management:** During this session the theory, history and focus of EAM were introduced, followed by the focus areas of EAM namely (1) managing the EA of an enterprise; and (2) managing the enterprise using the EA.

---

[2] Full method repository is available at http://austria.omilab.org/psm/tools, last visit: 08.05.2018.

2. **Session 2: ArchiMate and TEAM:** This session consisted of two parts namely: (1) an overview of Archimate (most participants were familiar with ArchiMate and TOGAF); and (2) an introduction to the TEAM tool.
3. **Session 3: Focus Group Case Study:** In this session a detailed case study was introduced where participants were guided to use the TEAM tool. For more details of the case study, see Sect. 3.1.
4. **Session 4: Focus Group Feedback:** In this session the participants were asked to give high-level feedback on the TEAM tool, EAM and further development, especially given their experience, see Sect. 4.

The data was collected from eight workshop participants, of which seven were established EA specialists either working full-time as enterprise architects within organizations or as EA consultants responsible for projects initiating EA at various levels within organizations. The group included: (a) professional consultants and trainers who specialized in EA and ArchiMate; (b) professional users who employ EAM frameworks and tools in their respective enterprise or public administration and who are in charge of the EAM management; as well as (c) academics who research and teach EAM at graduate and post-graduate level but with previous experience in EA implementation. The next section presents the case study which was used to evaluate the TEAM tool.

### 3.1 Focus Group Case Study

The *Charlie's Auto Repair Shop* case study was employed to evaluate prototype one of TEAM. After an introduction to TEAM the experts were asked to model each of the three parts of the case. 45 min was allocated for each modeling task and 15 min were used for discussion. A final one hour long session was dedicated to discussing: (a) the quality and eventual shortcomings of the case itself given EAM; (b) the completeness and accuracy of the mapping between the ArchiMate standard and the tool; (c) usability of the current, and requirements for future versions of the TEAM tool; and (d) usefulnesses of the TEAM tool functionality for EAM.

**Case Description.** In line with the idea that EA and its management play a pivotal role in enterprise transformations, the case study's focus is on the transformation of a traditional car repair SME into a car repair-as-a-service business - strongly reliant on IT and the business opportunities enabled by it. *Charlie's Car Repair Shop's* original business model focused on providing parts and specialized repair for old-timers. Information technology played a marginal role in the back office of the business for administrative and bookkeeping activities. A management change triggered the modification of the business model. The assets of the old business - repair facility and machinery, spare parts, and mechanical expertise - will now be leveraged with the support of IT to realize a car repair-as-a-service business model where old-timer owners can book the assets to work on their cars. The customers will be charged usage-based fees for the different service components.

The underlying motivation is to monetize the old-timer owner's love and knowledge about cars. These persons are known to the repair shop as having two characteristics important for the repair-as-a-service business model. They tend to be financially well off and are able to invest in the costly maintenance and repairs. Moreover, they care about a particular car and also have a lot of knowledge about its mechanics.

Following a general introduction to the case, the first part of the case study detailed the new strategy defining *goals*, the *expected outcomes* as well as the *necessary capabilities*. The second part then derived exemplary *business services* to be offered to the clients, *technology services* as well as *business processes* necessary for the provisioning of the new services. The identified services were also linked to their *technology assets* like software and hardware. Lastly, the third part described the *physical elements* which establish the "execution environment" for the services, like repair spaces, repair machinery etc. These physical elements were linked to the previously defined technology assets.

In alignment with the ArchiMate 3.0.1 standard and following the TOGAF framework, the case includes also Internet of Things and physical assets - thus expanding the EAM space considered in previous versions of the standard.

**Exemplary Case Solutions.** TEAM provides the full spectrum of the Archi-Mate 3.0.1 modeling language. The language concepts are grouped into the ArchiMate 3.0.1 layers - called *model types*: *strategy layer, business layer, application layer, technology layer, physical layer, implementation/migration layer, motivation layer*, and *analysis model*. While each of the model types contains only the concepts specific to it, e.g. a *business service class* is included in the business layer, the analysis model is a container of all ArchiMate 3.0.1 classes thus allowing a top to bottom model for the whole EA. For purposes of this case study participants were encouraged to use the analysis model type. Increasing readability within the model is achieved by using the *grouping class* to graphically compose objects which also belong semantically together (seen in Fig. 4 by the dotted boxes).

In the first part, *"The Strategy"*, the participants needed to cognitively differentiate between a *goal* and an *outcome* as well as between a *capability* and a *resource*. To ease the identification of the correct ArchiMate concepts, cues are provided in the case description, for example *"...the need to build up the auto shop's IT Operations and Management capabilities"*, which points the participant to the concept to use, i.e., *capability* and its name *IT Operations and Management*. One solution to the first part of the case study is represented in Fig. 3.

Business services need to support the goals defined for the new strategy. On their part they must be aided by appropriate business processes as well as technology services. For example, the newly instituted *Repair space rental* service triggers a newly defined business process which in itself employs the *Billing* technology service. In addition, not shown in the case, one could include a *Rental space booking* application running on a web-based client-server hardware

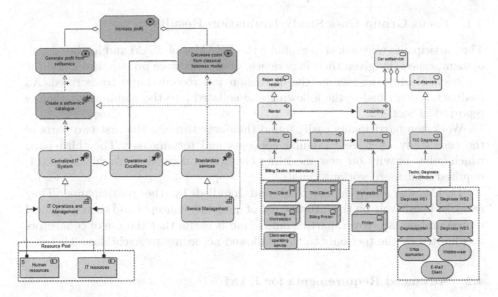

**Fig. 3.** Strategy model in TEAM.

**Fig. 4.** Services and processes model in TEAM.

which allows customers to book their repair slots on-line. For practicing purposes and due to limited time, only an excerpt of the services and processes involved was discussed in the case study. One possible solution of the second part is presented in Fig. 4.

The new business model also triggered changes on equipment level (see Fig. 5). While previously the machinery necessary for mechanical repairs did not need any ICT, now, with the time-dependent billing of usage, each machine must be able to "identify" at least the client to be billed as well as the start and end time of the rental. To this end, car repair machines must be equipped with card reading devices and enabled to transmit the necessary information to the *Billing application* and ultimately to the *Billing technical service*.

The new language concepts available in ArchiMate 3.0.1 on the strategy - and on the physical layer enable the enterprise architects to create a comprehensive model stack on which different analytics can be applied, both at design but also at "run" time, thus enabling the enterprise architect's management capabilities.

## 4    Evaluation and Advanced Requirements for EAM

The evaluation feedback was obtained during the focus group case study and feedback sessions. During the case study session where the tool was used by the participants, feedback was obtained through interaction and discussion with the participants, as well as through documented observations by the research team when supporting the participants.

## 4.1   Focus Group Case Study Evaluation Results

The participants were asked to evaluate the TEAM tool, EAM and further development, especially given their experience. Questions were prepared to guide the feedback. During the session, the discussion was recorded and transcribed. All feedback is described in the following and collated into the requirement themes reported in Sect. 4.2.

Workshop participants easily found their way through the first two parts of the case study as it used familiar concepts and terminology. The third part, which relies heavily on new modeling constructs defined in ArchiMate 3.0.1, required a bit more working time.

TEAM was easily understood and handled by the participants. They remarked positively on the intuitive use of modeling concepts and their graphical representation. Moreover, participants found it useful that the use of connectors was limited by the tool only to those allowed according to ArchiMate 3.0.1.

## 4.2   Advanced Requirements for EAM

For eliciting the requirements, we analyzed the focus group feedback from the workshop participants from both the case study and the feedback sessions and condensed the feedback into four advanced EAM requirement themes. Each requirement theme is described using the aspects: *Rationale*, detailing the ratio behind it; *Metamodel Requirements*, describing the requirements on metamodel level; *Implementation*, indicating how the requirement theme should be implemented in a modeling tool; and *Execution*, exemplifying the execution by the modeler. Finally, we indicate in Sects. 4.3 and 4.4 how these requirements could be incorporated conceptually into the next versions of the TEAM tool.

### Theme 1 - Information Management

Rationale: It is reasonable to have the possibility of attaching comments and descriptions to the ArchiMate concepts. The generic nature of these attributes enables the modeler to document further properties - besides solely the name - for each concept. Moreover, such meta data can be used for analysis as well as possible future developments. For example, the descriptions can reveal, which additional attributes might be required.

Metamodel Requirements: Two new attributes, termed *Description* and *Notes* of datatype *string*, should be introduced into the TEAM metamodel. They should be provided for each ArchiMate concept.

Implementation: The two attributes shall be adding to the metamodel and their values should be stored with the models. Visualization and editing of these attributes shall be enabled.

Execution: The modeler shall be able to see and edit description and notes in the properties of each modeled concept.

**Theme 2 - Lifecycle Management**

Rationale: When dealing with ICT, lifecycle management plays a vital role. Questions like "until when are software systems supported with updates?", or "when becomes a certain component invalid?" are crucial for EAM. There should be different kinds of dates in the various layers. For example, the application layer components should have attributes for licenses, which can be outdated or invalid. Time elements in the model should offer possibilities regarding queries and a kind of lifecycle management in the model.

Metamodel Requirements: In general, there should be one time attribute for nearly all ArchiMate concepts. In addition, the attributes purpose and name should vary from layer to layer, as there are specific requirements and types of dates. A valid until date should be used for application layer concepts.

Implementation: The new attributes should be visualized to the modeler for editing. Additionally, two *queries* should be realized that enable the modeler to efficiently list in-/valid application components of the current model.

Execution: The modeler should define a date at the beginning of the query execution. The tool then lists all instances that fulfill the query criteria. It should be possible to click on the elements in the list to navigate directly to the corresponding instance in the model.

**Theme 3 - Responsibility Management**

Rationale: The assignment of responsibilities should enforce a higher level of engagement and ease EAM. Thus, technology layer components should be assigned to actors/roles in the business layer. To its end, a visualization functionality shall be realized that displays the connections between the components on the different layers.

Metamodel Requirements: To combine business and technology layer, semantic links between concepts of those two layers should be added. Such semantic links might be realized as references or pointers that are specified at the corresponding metamodel classes.

Implementation: Reference attributes between technology and business layer should be added for selected elements of the two layers. Furthermore, a functionality shall be provided that generates, starting from a technology layer model, the list of corresponding actors/roles of the business layer.

Execution: The modeler shall be enabled to edit the specific reference attributes in order to semantically link concepts of the two layers. Moreover, the modeler shall be enabled to generate the list of responsibilities. All list items shall enable direct navigation to the corresponding instances in the models.

**Theme 4 - Business Continuity Management**

Rationale: In today's fast changing business models, built on top of complex ecosystems, failure and service unavailability is inevitable. Enterprises therefore aim to establish a business continuity management (BCM) strategy. Conceptual modeling and modeling tools can play a vital role in BCM [29,30]. A prerequisite for managing crisis events is to be aware of the mutual effects different EA instances have on each other. A semantic link between business and technology models should be established. The goal is to identify the impact of a technology element (e.g., function, process, interface, event, service) on a business layer element of the same type.

Metamodel Requirements: Especially concerned are function, process, interface, collaboration, interaction, event and service of the technology and the business layer. A reference attribute, which relates the elements of these two layers shall be added.

Implementation: 'Influence on' reference attributes shall be used to define relationships between elements of the technology layer and the business layer.

Execution: The reference attributes shall be editable by the modeler, thereby enabling the efficient specification of relationships. Moreover, a functionality shall be realized that queries the models for these attribute values and lists all relationships. This functionality shall be parameterizable by the type of concepts interested in. The modeler may e.g., parameterize a certain business function to be out of order and receive a list of technology components related to this function.

### 4.3   Conceptualization of Modeling Tools with ADOxx

Meta modeling platforms are used for the development of modeling tools. They raise the abstraction level of modeling tool development to a more elaborate level that is adequate for method engineers. The goal is to enable also non-programmers to realize their modeling tools. This is achieved by providing a rich set of pre-configured functionality the user then only needs to adapt to his/her domain. Moreover, users can benefit from existing tool developments on a certain platform.

ADOxx [31] is a meta modeling platform that has been successfully used in research and industry. The aim of the platform is to raise the abstraction level of modeling tool development to a less implementation-specific level [32]. ADOxx takes care of all domain-independent and non-functional requirements like model management, user management, storage, and user interaction. What is left to be done by the tool engineer is according to [33]: (1) configure the specific modeling language by referring it's concepts to the meta concepts of the platform; (2) provide a proper visualization for the concepts and combine concepts into logical clusters, i.e., model types; and (3) realize additional functionality like model transformations, model queries, or simulations.

### 4.4   The TEAM Tool

Figure 6 visualizes a screenshot of the TEAM modeling tool realized with the ADOxx metamodeling platform. TEAM realizes all layers of ArchiMate 3.0.1 following the TOGAF framework, as well as the requirement themes described in Sect. 4. This enables TEAM to do basic ArchiMate modeling and TOGAF support as well as acting as a facilitator for EAM. Besides the modeling palette,

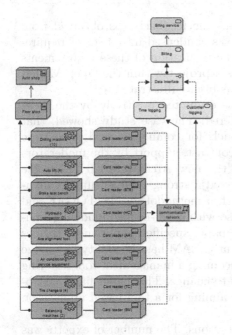

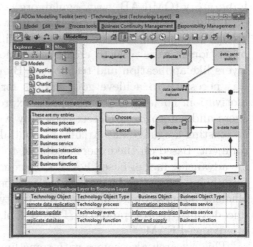

**Fig. 5.** Equipment model in the TEAM tool.

**Fig. 6.** Executing model queries in the TEAM tool.

listing the available ArchiMate language concepts of the currently opened model on the left side, the tool also comes with an intuitive context menu that features the model queries - e.g., for the lifecycle management - and the additional functionality - e.g., for the business continuity management.

At the top of Fig. 6, indicated by the letter 'a' is the menu bar implemented for the business continuity management and responsibility management. When clicking on 'a', the modeler is presented a multi-select box (see Fig. 6 'b') where he/she can de-/select the ArchiMate concepts he/she is interested in, thereby parameterizing the query. After confirming the selection, TEAM executes the query and visualizes the query result window (see Fig. 6 'c') on the bottom). The results window lists the relationships between the selected business object type instances and the technology objects of the currently opened models (in Fig. 6 *Business service* and *Business function* were selected).

## 5    Conclusions and Future Research

This paper reported on an action design science research project that targeted the identification and conceptualization of requirements for an advanced enterprise architecture management approach that integrated the TOGAF framework with the ArchiMate 3.0.1 modeling language. The data was collected using a workshop focus group design where in-depth feedback was obtained during tool use in a case study and a feedback session. The feedback was obtained from eight EAM experts and practitioners and was condensed into a set of requirement themes for advanced EAM. Finally, the realization of these requirements with the ADOxx metamodeling platform as a project within the Open Models Laboratory (OMiLAB, www.omilab.org) was briefly illustrated.

Intuitive usage of the modeling tool was evaluated positively by the focus group. Results for the modeling tasks differed. The case study showed, that practitioners were able to create good models for commonly used ArchiMate layers like application and technology. By contrast, support by the moderators was necessary to achieve good results for the new ArchiMate 3.0 layers like motivation. Focus group participants expressed a strong need to support managers and enterprise architects not only with a methodology like TOGAF and an existing language like ArchiMate, but also with a full-fledged modeling environment. Based on the expert feedback, the paper specified requirement themes for advancing model-based EAM. Consequently, EAM has the ability to emerge from being limited to IT experts towards becoming a management tool fostering efficient business operations and the ability to change. This paper finally introduced a first prototype of the TEAM tool, aiming for a tool-based application of advanced EAM.

This research also comes with some limitations. The number of experts was quite low, however we ensured a homogeneous set of participants in the workshop and the discussion. Moreover, some feedback might be biased by the tool that has been used. It is important to differentiate in future design cycles more clearly between the conceptual approach and the tool support.

In future research we will extend the case study with tasks, that utilize some of the advanced features. This extended case study shall then be used to evaluate the second TEAM prototype - eventually leading to a mature modeling environment for advanced EAM. Moreover, we will consider to extend the functionality, e.g., with semantic technologies as proposed in [34,35] and mechanisms for ensuring consistency between the multiple ArchiMate layers [36–38].

**Acknowledgment.** Part of this research has been funded through the South Africa/Austria Joint Scientific and Technological Cooperation program with the project number ZA 11/2017.

# References

1. Zimmermann, A., Jugel, D., Sandkuhl, K., Schmidt, R., Schweda, C., Moehring, M.: Architectural decision management for digital transformation of products and services. CSIMQ (6), 31–53 (2016)
2. Tiwana, A., Konsynski, B., Bush, A.A.: Research commentary - platform evolution: coevolution of platform architecture, governance, and environmental dynamics. Inf. Syst. Res. **21**(4), 675–687 (2010)
3. Prahalad, C.K., Ramaswamy, V.: Co-creation experiences: the next practice in value creation. J. Interact. Mark. **18**(3), 5–14 (2004)
4. Mont, O.K.: Clarifying the concept of product-service system. J. Clean. Prod. **10**(3), 237–245 (2002)

5. Matt, C., Hess, T., Benlian, A.: Digital transformation strategies. Bus. Inf. Syst. Eng. **57**(5), 339–343 (2015)
6. Ahlemann, F., Stettiner, E., Messerschmidt, M., Legner, C. (eds.): Strategic Enterprise Architecture Management. Springer, Heidelberg (2012). https://doi.org/10.1007/978-3-642-24223-6
7. The Open Group: The open group: ArchiMate 3.0.1 specification (2017). 07 Nov 2017
8. Pittl, B., Bork, D.: Modeling digital enterprise ecosystems with ArchiMate: a mobility provision case study. Serviceology for Services. LNCS, vol. 10371, pp. 178–189. Springer, Cham (2017). https://doi.org/10.1007/978-3-319-61240-9_17
9. Sein, M.K., Henfridsson, O., Purao, S., Rossi, M., Lindgren, R.: Action design research. MIS Q. **35**(1), 37–56 (2011)
10. Zachman, J.: A framework for information systems architecture. IBM Syst. J. **26**, 276–292 (1987)
11. Zachman, J.A.: The Concise Definition of The Zachman Framework by: John A. Zachman (2008)
12. IFIP-IFAC Task Force: GERAM: Generalised Enterprise Reference Architecture and Methodology, Version 1.6.3. Technical report March, Integration, IFIPIFAC Task Force on Architectures for Enterprise (1999)
13. Simon, D., Fischbach, K., Schoder, D.: An exploration of enterprise architecture research. Commun. Assoc. Inf. Syst. **32** (2013). Article 1
14. The Open Group: TOGAF, an Open Group standard (2017)
15. de Vries, M., van der Merwe, A., Gerber, A.: Towards an enterprise evolution contextualisation model. In: Proceedings of the First International Conference on Enterprise Systems, Cape Town, South Africa, pp. 1–12. IEEE (2013)
16. Lapalme, J.: Three schools of thought on enterprise architecture. IT Prof. **14**(6), 37–43 (2012)
17. Ross, J.W., Weill, P., Robertson, D.: Enterprise Architecture as Strategy: Creating a Foundation for Business Execution. Harvard Business Press, Brighton (2006)
18. OMG: ArchiMate 3.0.1 Specification. The Open Group, June 2016. http://pubs.opengroup.org/architecture/archimate3-doc/
19. Lankhorst, M. (ed.): Enterprise Architecture at Work: Modelling, Communication, and Analysis. Springer, Berlin/ New York (2005). https://doi.org/10.1007/3-540-27505-3
20. Vicente, M., Gama, N., da Silva, M.M.: Using ArchiMate and TOGAF to understand the enterprise architecture and ITIL relationship. In: Franch, X., Soffer, P. (eds.) CAiSE 2013. LNBIP, vol. 148, pp. 134–145. Springer, Heidelberg (2013). https://doi.org/10.1007/978-3-642-38490-5_11
21. Karagiannis, D., Kühn, H.: Metamodelling platforms. In: Bauknecht, K., Tjoa, A.M., Quirchmayr, G. (eds.) EC-Web 2002. LNCS, vol. 2455, p. 182. Springer, Heidelberg (2002). https://doi.org/10.1007/3-540-45705-4_19
22. Mylopoulos, J.: Conceptual modelling and Telos. In: Loucopoulos, P., Zicari, R. (eds.) Conceptual Modelling, Databases, and CASE: an Integrated View of Information System Development, pp. 49–68. Wiley, New York (1992)
23. Bork, D., Fill, H.G.: Formal aspects of enterprise modeling methods: a comparison framework. In: 2014 47th Hawaii International Conference on System Sciences (HICSS), pp. 3400–3409. IEEE (2014)
24. Bork, D., Miron, E.T.: OMiLAB - an open innovation community for modeling method engineering. In: Niculescu, A., Negoita, O.D., Tiganoaia, B. (eds.) 8th International Conference of Management and Industrial Engineering (ICMIE 2017), pp. 64–77 (2017)

25. Karagiannis, D., Mayr, H.C., Mylopoulos, J.: Domain-Specific Conceptual Modeling. Springer, Cham (2016). https://doi.org/10.1007/978-3-319-39417-6
26. Bock, A., Frank, U.: Multi-perspective enterprise modeling—conceptual foundation and implementation with ADO*xx*. In: Karagiannis, D., Mayr, H., Mylopoulos, J. (eds.) Domain-Specific Conceptual Modeling, pp. 241–267. Springer, Cham (2016). https://doi.org/10.1007/978-3-319-39417-6_11
27. Ferstl, O.K., Sinz, E.J., Bork, D.: Tool support for the semantic object model. In: Karagiannis, D., Mayr, H., Mylopoulos, J. (eds.) Domain-Specific Conceptual Modeling, pp. 291–310. Springer, Cham (2016). https://doi.org/10.1007/978-3-319-39417-6_13
28. Freitas, H., Oliveira, M., Jenkins, M., Popjoy, O.: The focus group, a qualitative research method. J. Educ. **1**(1), 1–22 (1998)
29. Benaben, F., et al.: A conceptual framework and a suite of tools to support crisis management. In: Proceedings of the 50th Hawaii International Conference on System Sciences (2017)
30. Rejeb, O., Bastide, R., Lamine, E., Marmier, F., Pingaud, H.: A model driven engineering approach for business continuity management in e-health systems. In: 2012 6th IEEE International Conference on Digital Ecosystems Technologies (DEST), pp. 1–7. IEEE (2012)
31. ADOxx.org: ADOxx Metamodelling Platform (2018) https://www.adoxx.org/live/home, Accessed 11 Mar 2018
32. Efendioglu, N., Woitsch, R., Utz, W.: A toolbox supporting agile modelling method engineering: ADOxx.org modelling method conceptualization environment. In: Horkoff, J., Jeusfeld, M.A., Persson, A. (eds.) PoEM 2016. LNBIP, vol. 267, pp. 317–325. Springer, Cham (2016). https://doi.org/10.1007/978-3-319-48393-1_23
33. Bork, D., Sinz, E.J.: Design of a SOM business process modelling tool based on the ADOxx meta-modelling platform. In: Pre-proceedings of the 4th International Workshop on Graph-Based Tools. University of Twente, Enschede, pp. 90–101 (2010)
34. Gerber, A., der Merwe, A.V., Kotze, P.: Towards the formalisation of the TOGAF contenet metamodel using ontlogies. In: The 12th International Conference on Enterprise Information Systems (2010)
35. Buchmann, R.A., Karagiannis, D.: Enriching linked data with semantics from domain-specific diagrammatic models. Bus. Inf. Syst. Eng. **58**(5), 341–353 (2016)
36. Awadid, A., Bork, D., Karagiannis, D., Nurcan, S.: Toward generic consistency patterns in multi-view enterprise modelling. In: Twenty-Sixth European Conference on Information Systems (2018, in press)
37. Bork, D., Buchmann, R., Karagiannis, D.: Preserving multi-view consistency in diagrammatic knowledge representation. In: Zhang, S., Wirsing, M., Zhang, Z. (eds.) KSEM 2015. LNCS (LNAI), vol. 9403, pp. 177–182. Springer, Cham (2015). https://doi.org/10.1007/978-3-319-25159-2_16
38. Karagiannis, D., Buchmann, R.A., Bork, D.: Managing consistency in multi-view enterprise models: an approach based on semantic queries. In: Twenty-Fourth European Conference on Information Systems (ECIS) (2016). Research Paper 53

# Towards OntoUML for Software Engineering: Optimizing Kinds and Subkinds Transformed into Relational Databases

Zdeněk Rybola[✉] and Robert Pergl

Faculty of Information Technology, Czech Technical University in Prague,
Prague, Czech Republic
{zdenek.rybola,robert.pergl}@fit.cvut.cz
http://ccmi.fit.cvut.cz

**Abstract.** Model-driven development approach to software engineering requires precise models defining as much of the system as possible. OntoUML is a conceptual modelling language based on UFO, which provides constructs to create ontologically well-founded and precise conceptual models. In the approach we utilize, OntoUML is used for making conceptual models of software application data. Such a model is then transformed into its proper realization in a relational database, preserving all the implicit constraints defined by various types of universals and relations in the original OntoUML model. In this paper, we discuss possible optimizations of the transformation of Kinds and Subkinds – rigid sortal universal types, a backbone of OntoUML models.

**Keywords:** MDD · OntoUML · Optimization · Relational database
Transformation

## 1 Introduction

Software engineering is a demanding discipline that deals with complex systems [8]. The goal of software engineering is to ensure high-quality software implementation of these complex systems. To achieve this, various software development approaches have been formulated. One of these approaches is the Model-Driven Development (MDD), which is based on elaborating models and transformations between them [14]. The most common use case of MDD is the creation of a conceptual (platform-independent) model of the application data and its transformation into source codes or database scripts.

To ensure high quality of a software system, high-quality expressive conceptual models are necessary to define all requirements and constraints for the system [8]. Moreover, it should hold that more specific models preserve the constraints defined in the more abstract models [9].

© Springer Nature Switzerland AG 2018
R. Pergl et al. (Eds.): EOMAS 2018, LNBIP 332, pp. 31–45, 2018.
https://doi.org/10.1007/978-3-030-00787-4_3

This paper is a part of a series, where we investigate the usage of OntoUML for Software Engineering (see, e.g., [19–21]). As OntoUML is based on Unified Foundational Ontology (UFO), it is domain-agnostic and it provides mechanisms to create ontologically well-founded conceptual models [9], it qualifies for creating such precise conceptual models of application data. However, it is necessary to transform such model into its realization properly, without losing the implicit constraints OntoUML introduces. Furthermore, as relational database management systems (RDBMSs) are still the most popular type of data storage[1], we focus on a proper realization of the OntoUML conceptual models in relational databases.

In the approach introduced in [19], the transformation of an OntoUML conceptual model into its realization in a relational database is divided into three consecutive steps: (1) transformation of an OntoUML conceptual model into a UML platform-independent model, (2) transformation of the resulting UML PIM into a relational platform-specific model, (3) and finally the transformation of the resulting RDB PSM into an implementation-specific model of SQL scripts.

In this paper, we discuss the transformation of Kinds and Subkinds from the initial OntoUML model and possible optimizations of the resulting models of these types after each of the steps, in order to simplify the model, decrease its complexity and redundancy and improve efficiency.

## 2   Background

In this section, we outline the background of our paper. We introduce OntoUML and UFO, our approach to the transformation of OntoUML conceptual models into their proper realization in a relational database and the work related to our approach.

### 2.1   OntoUML

OntoUML is a conceptual modelling language focused on building ontologically well-founded models. It was formulated in Guizzardi's PhD Thesis [9] as a lightweight extension of UML based on UML profiles.

The language is based on *Unified Foundational Ontology* (UFO) [12], which is based on the cognitive science and modal logic and related mathematical foundations, such as sets and relations. Thanks to this fact, it provides expressive and precise constructs for modellers to capture the domain of interest. Unlike other extensions of UML, OntoUML does not build on the UML's ontologically vague "class" notion, but builds on the notion of *universals* and *individuals*. It uses the basic notation of UML Class Diagram like classes, associations and generalization/specialization together with stereotypes and meta-attributes to define the nature of individual elements more specifically. On the other hand, it omits

---

[1] According to the ranking published on https://db-engines.com/en/ranking in February 2018, 7 of 10 most popular DBMSs are relational.

a set of other problematic concepts (for instance aggregation and composition) and replaces them with its own ontologically sound concepts.

UFO and OntoUML address many problems in conceptual modelling, such as the distinction between universals and individuals, the identity principle and the rigidity of properties [9], the concept of roles [10] or part-whole relations [11]. The language has been already successfully applied in many different domains such as Logistics [3] or University Campus Management [5].

## 2.2   Our Approach

As OntoUML is based on UFO and it supports creation of ontologically well-founded models, it is well-suited for creating precise conceptual models. Such model can be also used for modelling conceptual data models of the developed application, defining various constraints and restrictions for the domain objects, simply by specifying the appropriate universal and relation type (Kinds, Sub-kinds, Roles, Phases, etc.). In order to use such conceptual models in the Model-Driven Development, these models must be transformed into their realizations in such a way, that the constraints defined by the individual universal and relation types in the OntoUML model are not lost.

In [19], our approach to the transformation of such conceptual data models in OntoUML into their proper realization in a relational database was introduced. In this approach, the transformation is divided into three consecutive steps (Fig. 1):

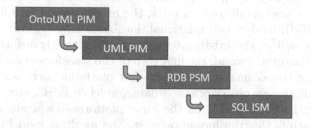

**Fig. 1.** Overview of the transformation process

1. transformation of an OntoUML conceptual model (OntoUML PIM) into a UML platform-independent model (UML PIM),
2. transformation of the resulting UML PIM into a relational platform-specific model (RDB PSM),
3. and finally the transformation of the resulting RDB PSM into an implementation-specific model of SQL scripts (SQL ISM).

In the first step, the initial OntoUML PIM model is transformed into a pure UML PIM model. Since OntoUML applies certain constraints to the types based on the kind of universal represented by a particular type, these constraints should be carried over to the other consecutive models. In our approach, these constraints are realized by a combination of the generalization, specific multi-plicities of the associations and additional OCL constraints for such constraints, which cannot be expressed directly in the diagrams. The resulting UML PIM presents the very same semantics as the original OntoUML PIM, however, it is defined by means of a standard well-known notation.

In the second step, the resulting UML PIM with the constraints derived from the initial OntoUML PIM is transformed into a RDB PSM. In this transforma-tion, the UML classes with attributes are transformed into database tables with columns and the relations are transformed into references. Furthermore, we also transform the OCL constraints from the UML PIM into OCL constraints defined on the database model. Moreover, to preserve the same restrictions in the result-ing RDB PSM, we also address the meta-properties of the generalization sets and the multiplicity constraints of the associations. In certain cases, this leads to defining additional OCL constraints restricting the correct data in the tables.

In the final step, the resulting RDB PSM with the OCL constraints from the previous step is transformed into an SQL ISM. This model consists of SQL DDL scripts for creating the database schema – the tables, columns and standard SQL constraints (PRIMARY KEY, FOREIGN KEY, UNIQUE, etc.). Addition-ally, we deal with the proper realization of the OCL constraints derived from the initial OntoUML PIM during the transformations to preserve the database consistency.

Although the transformation could be done in a single step consisting, i.e., of generating the SQL DDL scripts directly from the OntoUML model, our approach brings several advantages. First, the existing know-how for the trans-formation of UML models into relational databases may be utilized (see, e.g., [13,18,22]), as well as the existing tools supporting this transformation (e.g., Enterprise Architect[2]). Second, the first step of the transformation may be used as a part of the transformation into any other platform, such as a pure object model of Smalltalk, an object-oriented data model of EJB[3], etc., since it is a transformation between models on the same platform-independent level. And, finally, after each of the transformation steps, the resulting model may be anal-ysed and refactored, in order to optimize the model, simplify it and remove redundancies and duplicities. However, such refactoring and optimizations are only possible manually and after careful consideration of the modeller, as they can have great impact on the quality of the model and its evolution.

This paper deals with selected optimizations of models during the trans-formations of an OntoUML conceptual model into its proper realization in a relational database. In particular, we focus on the possible optimizations of the

---

[2] Enterprise Architect is a popular commercial CASE tool used for creating models, http://www.sparxsystems.com.au/products/ea/index.html.

[3] Enterprise Java Beans, http://www.oracle.com/technetwork/java/javaee/ejb/index.html.

resulting models created by transformation of Kinds and Subkinds from the
initial OntoUML PIM.

## 2.3    Related Work

The idea of using OntoUML as the conceptual modelling language in context
with the software development and the MDD approach was introduced in [6].
In the master thesis, the author discusses the conceptual modelling in two levels – ontological and informational. He also proposes a transformation of an
OntoUML conceptual model into an object-oriented implementation model in
UML. The author limits himself only to a subset of OntoUML and UFO concepts
and they does not discuss any variants or optimizations of the resulting model.
Also, the author's approach to certain parts of the transformation vary from our
approach; for instance, the transformation of Roles and their representation in
the UML model. Finally, the author discusses only the transformation into the
implementation UML model, while we propose a complete transformation of the
OntoUML conceptual model into its proper realization in a relational database.
There are also other works dealing with the transformation of OntoUML into
other languages, such as OWL [24] and Alloy [4], or into an object-oriented
implementation model in UML [17].

Regarding the transformation of the UML PIM into a relational database, it is
a well-known process documented for instance in [13] or [18]. However, in order to
realize the original OntoUML PIM properly, it is necessary to properly transform
and realize also the OCL constraints derived from the universal and relation
types used in the OntoUML conceptual model, as well as other constraints such
as multiplicities of associations or meta-properties *isDisjoint* and *isCovering* of
the generalization sets.

In [22], an approach for the realization of special multiplicity constraints in
a relational database was proposed. The approach was inspired by DresdenOCL
Toolkit[4], where OCL constraints are transformed into database views querying
data violating the constraints. It was also inspired by the realization of inverse
referential integrity constraints used in IIS*Case [1,2].

There are also several other approaches for the realization of OCL constraints
in a relational database. In [16], the authors present their approach to checking
constraints by incremental SQL queries that select the violating data. In [23], the
author describes an extension plugin for Enterprise Architect that generates the
SQL code realizing OCL constraints. His approach is based on translating OCL
expressions into SQL queries and realizing the constraints by database functions
used to detect the constraint violation. Another related work can be found in [7],
where the authors transform OCL constraints into stored procedures.

## 3    Transformation of Kinds and Subkinds

As discussed in [9], the *Kind* universals form the backbone of the whole
OntoUML model, defining the types of individuals with unique identity prin-

---

[4] https://github.com/dresden-ocl/dresdenocl.

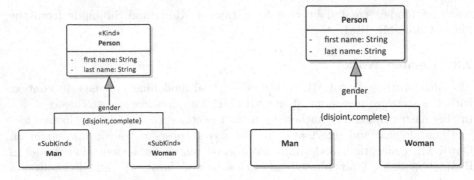

**Fig. 2.** OntoUML PIM of persons      **Fig. 3.** Resulting UML PIM of persons

ciples. This identity principle is provided to the instances of the *Kind* type, determining their unique identities.

The *Subkind* universals, on the other hand, define subtypes of these types, distinguishing different variants or cases of the individuals with the same basic identity principle [9]. Therefore, the *Subkinds* form generalization sets specializing other *Kinds* or *Subkinds*. Unlike *Kinds*, *Subkinds* do not provide their own identity principles to their instances, but they inherit the given identity principle from their ancestor and extend it, providing this extended identity principle to their instances. Therefore, being an instance of a *Subkind* type automatically means the individual is also an instance of the supertype.

As both *Kinds* and *Subkinds* universals are rigid, the individuals, which are instances of a *Kind* or *Subkind* type cannot cease to be their instances [9]. This is exactly the interpretation of classes and their instances in a UML model [15]. Therefore, when transforming an OntoUML PIM into a UML PIM, each *Kind* and *Subkind* type can be simply transformed into a class with appropriate attributes and relations. Thanks to the rigidity of *Kind* and *Subkind* universals, also the generalization sets of the *Subkind* types can be realized in the UML PIM as standard UML generalization sets with the same meta-properties *isDisjoint* and *isCovering* [21].

Let's suppose we want to model the fact that we need to persist people with their first and last names and the information about their genders, distinguishing men and women. In Fig. 2, the OntoUML PIM for this situation is shown. As the fact of *being a man* or *being a woman* applies only to some instances of persons, the types Man and Woman are modelled as subtypes of the type Person. As both these facts apply to their respective instances necessarily (in the modal sense of worlds [9]) and extend their identity, they are classified as *Subkinds*. Moreover, as each person can only be exclusively a man or a woman, the generalization set of the *Subkinds* is defined as {disjoint,complete}. This is an appropriate model according to the specification of OntoUML and the principles of UFO, as it distinguishes different identity principles of different kinds of entities and it respects their rigidity.

---

**Constraint 1.** OCL invariant for the enumeration attribute `gender` of class `Person`

---

```
context Person inv EN_Person_Gender:
self.gender = 'Man' OR self.gender = 'Woman'
```

---

When transforming this OntoUML PIM into a UML PIM following the transformation rules defined in [21], we come to the UML PIM shown in Fig. 3 – the individual types are transformed into classes and the rigid generalization set is preserved. However, the transformation results in two empty subclasses `Man` and `Woman` of the class `Person`. In the OntoUML PIM, these subtypes carried the ontological sense of distinct identities. However, this information is not so important in the UML model. Moreover, when transforming such a UML PIM into a RDB PSM, it is necessary to properly realize the generalization set and its meta-properties [21]. Therefore, a discussion arises if such a model can be optimized to prevent unnecessary model constructs and complicated realization in other models and the database itself.

## 3.1   Reduction of the Generalization Set in the UML PIM

One possible improvement of the situation described in the previous section is a reduction of the specializing generalization set in the resulting UML PIM. In the case when the individual subclasses do not contain any properties (attributes or relations) and they serve only for distinguishing various subtypes of their supertype (like in the case of Fig. 3), the whole generalization set may be reduced into a single *enumeration attribute* of the superclass (see Fig. 4).

This *enumeration attribute* serves for identifying the subtype of the instance of the superclass of the original generalization set. For such identification, the title of the former subclasses may be used. Additionally, a special *enumeration constraint* should be defined to restrict the possible values of such *enumeration attribute* only to the titles of the appropriate subclasses. Such constraint may be defined as an OCL invariant shown in Constraint 1. Moreover, the *enumeration attribute* should be defined *immutable*[5], as the reduced generalization set is rigid and an instance of the superclass cannot change the enumeration value, thus changing its subtype.

Then, when transforming this optimized UML PIM into an RDB PSM as proposed in [21], no generalization needs to be realized. The class is simply transformed into a table with a column for the *enumeration attribute* (see Fig. 5 for the resulting RDB PSM). However, to prevent loosing the *enumeration constraint* and the immutability of the attribute during the transformation, also these two constraints must be transformed properly.

While the *enumeration constraint* can be simply transformed into an OCL invariant defined for the table `PERSONS` as shown in Constraint 2, the immutabil-

---

[5] In Enterprise Architect, which we use for the modelling purposes, the immutability of attributes is depicted by the constraint {`readOnly`}.

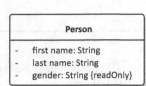

|  | PERSONS |
|---|---|
| | «column» |
| *PK | PERSON_ID: NUMBER(8) |
| * | FIRST_NAME: VARCHAR2(50) |
| * | LAST_NAME: VARCHAR2(50) |
| * | GENDER: VARCHAR2(50) |
| | «PK» |
| + | PK_PERSONS(PERSON_ID) |

**Fig. 4.** Optimized UML PIM with immutable enumeration attribute gender

**Fig. 5.** Resulting RDB PSM based on the optimized UML PIM with immutable enumeration attribute gender

---

**Constraint 2.** OCL invariant for the enumeration column GENDER of table PERSONS

```
context PERSONS inv EN_Person_Gender:
self.GENDER = 'Man' OR self.GENDER = 'Woman'
```

---

ity of the *enumeration attribute* must be handled specially. As a relational database does not provide any construct for immutability, the restriction must be defined as a special OCL constraint in the RDB PSM. Moreover, the restriction restricts the dynamic changes of the value, instead of the valid values themselves. Therefore, an OCL postcondition is used for defining the *immutability constraint* of values in a column in the RDB PSM. Furthermore, as inserting a new record in the table or deleting a record do not result in a change of the value of a persisted instance, only the UPDATE DML operation must be checked. Therefore, the OCL constraint can be defined as shown in Constraint 3.

Finally, when transforming the RDB PSM into the SQL ISM as proposed in [19], SQL statements are generated to create the individual tables' standard constraints like PRIMARY and FOREIGN KEYs. According to that approach, the additional OCL constraints can be realized by several possible constructs: (a) *database views* used for querying only valid data satisfying the constraints and hiding the invalid data; (b) *updatable database views with CHECK option* used for both querying and manipulating only the valid data in the tables; (c) *CHECK constraints* used for checking the inserted values into the restricted

---

**Constraint 3.** OCL postcondition for the UPDATE operation realizing the *immutable* meta-property of attribute gender

```
context PERSONS::UPDATE() post IM_PERSON_GENDER_UPD:
self.GENDER = self.GENDER@pre
```

**SQL 1.** CHECK constraint for *enumeration constraint* on the column GENDER in the table PERSONS

```
ALTER TABLE PERSONS ADD CONSTRAINT EN_Person_Gender CHECK (
   GENDER = 'Man' OR GENDER = 'Woman');
```

**SQL 2.** Trigger definition for the *immutability constraint* on the column GENDER in the table PERSONS

```
CREATE TRIGGER IM_PERSON_GENDER_UPD
BEFORE UPDATE ON PERSONS
FOR EACH ROW
BEGIN
   IF  : old.GENDER <> : new.GENDER THEN  raise_application_error
      (-20101, 'OCL_constraint_IM_PERSON_GENDER_UPD_violated!');
   END IF;
END;
```

columns for all DML operations; or (d) *triggers* used for checking the data for all necessary DML operations.

As the *enumeration constraint* shown in Constraint 2 restricts values in a single column of a single table, it can be realized by all the possible constructs. The most simple and effective of them is assumed to be the CHECK constraint, which restricts the possible values of a column and which is checked whenever the value changes. The example of the CHECK constraint realizing the *enumeration constraint* shown in Constraint 2 is shown in SQL 1.

In contrast to the *enumeration constraint*, the *immutability constraint* must prevent changes of the column value once the record is inserted. Therefore, it can only be realized by a trigger for the UPDATE operation, which compares the old and new values in the column and throws an exception, when the values is changed. An example of such a trigger for the *immutability constraint* shown in Constraint 3 is shown in SQL 2.

### 3.2  Problems of the Reduction of Generalization Sets in the UML PIM

Using the approach proposed in the previous section might seem beneficial. The reduction of the generalization sets into an *enumeration attribute* leads to less classes in the UML PIM and less tables in the RDB PSM and the database itself. Also, the rigidity of the generalization and the meta-properties of the generalization set can be realized very easily by a CHECK constraint for the *enumeration constraint* and a single trigger for the *immutability constraint*. However, there are several problems with such optimization.

The first problem is that this optimization can be applied only in the case that the original subtypes in the OntoUML PIM do not define any additional properties (attributes and relations) beside the extended identity principles. Take, for instance, the OntoUML PIM shown in Fig. 6, where the two distinct subtypes

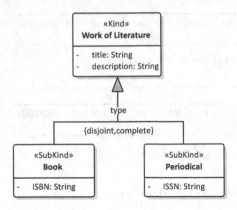

| Work of Literature |
| --- |
| - title: String |
| - description: String |
| - type: String {readOnly} |
| - ISBN: String [0..1] |
| - ISSN: String [0..1] |

**Fig. 6.** OntoUML PIM of works of literature

**Fig. 7.** Optimized UML PIM with immutable enumeration attribute `type` and optional attributes ISBN and ISSN

---

**Constraint 4.** OCL invariant for the exclusivity constraint for the attributes of the subtypes of type `Work of Literature`

```
context Work_of_Literature inv EX_Work_of_Literature_Type:
def Book: Boolean = self.type = "Book"
    AND self.ISBN <> OclVoid AND self.ISSN = OclVoid
def Periodical: Boolean = self.type = "Periodical"
    AND self.ISBN = OclVoid AND self.ISSN <> OclVoid
Book XOR Periodical
```

---

specializing the *Kind* `Work of Literature`, namely the *Subkinds* `Book` and `Periodical`, are defined. For each of the subtypes, a different special attribute is important – the ISBN value for the books and the ISSN value for the periodicals.

When applying the approach suggested in Subsect. 3.1, the two subtypes might be expressed by an *enumeration attribute* `type`. However, the additional attributes defined by the subtypes would need to be realized as additional attributes of the supertype `Work of Literature`, as well. In Fig. 7, the optimized UML PIM is shown. Moreover, the values of these attributes should be restricted in such a way, that for each `Book` instance, the value of attribute ISBN is set, while the value of attribute ISSN is not set, and vice versa for each `Periodical` instance. Thus, instead of the simple *enumeration constraint* for the `type` attribute, an *exclusivity constraint* must be defined to restrict the values of the attributes of the original subtypes, as well as possible values of the *enumeration attribute*. An example of such an *exclusivity constraint* is shown in Constraint 4.

Obviously, such an *exclusivity constraint* would also need to be realized in the RDB PSM as an OCL invariant defined in context of the table realizing the class `Work_of_Literature` and restricting the values in the appropriate columns. Then, when transforming the RDB PSM into an actual SQL ISM, even this

**SQL 3.** CHECK constraint for the *exclusivity constraint* on the columns ISBN and ISSN in the table WORK_OF_LITERATURE

```
ALTER TABLE WORK_OF_LITERATURE
  ADD CONSTRAINT EX_Work_of_Literature_Type CHECK (
(TYPE = 'Book' AND ISBN IS NOT NULL AND ISSN IS NULL)
  OR (TYPE = 'Periodical' AND ISBN IS NULL AND ISSN IS NOT NULL));
```

*exclusivity constraint* must be realized. Fortunately, as the constraint restricts only values in a single table and each of the records individually, it can be simply realized by a CHECK constraint (or any other type of realization discussed in [19]). An example of the CHECK constraint realizing the *exclusivity constraint* is shown in SQL 3.

As can be seen from the example constraints and their realization, the more properties there are in the subtypes, the more complicated the OCL constraints and their realizations become. Also, the more subtypes there are in the reduced generalization set, the more complicated the constraints are. Therefore, it is not recommended to use this type of optimization in cases when there are properties present in the subtypes.

Even when the subtypes do not have any properties, the optimization discussed in Subsect. 3.1 has another potential disadvantage – losing the concept of the subtypes. After the reduction, there are no subtypes any more. There is only a single class with an attribute distinguishing the subtype. This can bring problems when the system evolves.

It can happen easily in the course of time that a new property (an attribute or a relation) should be introduced for a subtype initially defined in the OntoUML PIM. However, in the UML PIM and the other consecutive models, there is no concept representing the subtype. The new property would need to be added to the class representing the supertype in the UML PIM. However, as the values of such a property are valid only for one of the represented subtypes, the *exclusivity constraint* for the attribute would need to be defined in the UML PIM and realized in the SQL ISM just as discussed above.

Another option for introducing a new property for any of the subtypes is reverting the reduction of the generalization set. However, that would mean complicated refactoring of the model and separation of the individual subtypes as distinct subclasses. With existing data in the tables realizing the model, such refactoring becomes considerably complicated and risky.

Because of the problems discussed in the previous paragraphs, the proposed reduction is recommended only in the situations, when there are no actual properties defined by the subtypes and the risk of losing the concept of the subtypes is acceptable.

### 3.3  Realization of the Generalization Set in the RDB PSM

When preserving the concept of the generalization set in the UML PIM just as discussed in [21], the generalization set and its meta-properties *isDisjoint*

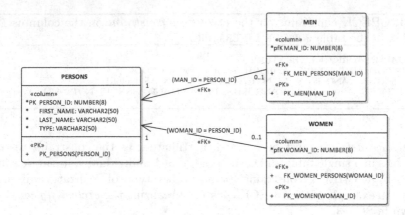

**Fig. 8.** RDB PSM of the generalization set realized by referencing tables

and *isCovering* must be properly realized in the relational database. In [21], three well-known possible realizations of the generalization sets in the RDB PSM are suggested: (a) related (or also referencing) tables, (b) individual (or also separate) tables and (c) a single table.

In the case of referencing tables, the realization of the generalization set with empty subclasses such as shown in Fig. 3 would lead to tables MEN and WOMEN containing each only a single column restricted by a PRIMARY KEY constraint and a FOREIGN KEY constraint referencing the table PERSONS. The resulting RDB PSM of the UML PIM shown in Fig. 3 realized by referencing tables is shown in Fig. 8. Additionally, following the approach presented in [21], the meta-properties of the generalization set should be realized properly, checking the existence of a referencing record in the appropriate subclass table according to the type of the actual instance stored in the tables. Also, the immutability of the generalization relation should be realized in the RDB PSM by defining an *immutability constraint* for the reference values in the subclass tables and then realizing it by a trigger in the SQL ISM in a similar way as the *immutability constraint* for the *enumeration attribute* shown in SQL 2.

Obviously, such solution does not make much sense in a case such as this, when the subclasses do not have any properties. It would require inserting simple records into the subclass tables, but still checking their existence in the constraints.

The second possible realization, using the separate tables for the generalization set, means creating a table for any possible type of instances from the generalization set with all its properties. However, as the subclasses Man and Woman define no additional properties, it would lead to having two tables with the very same columns and constraints, with just a different name. Additionally, any uniqueness of a column of the original superclass Person would need to be realized by a *distributed unique constraint* [21]. Obviously, this solution is also not very good.

Finally, the last suggested realization of the generalization set is using a single table combining all the classes of the generalization set. All attributes of the individual subclasses are realized by columns added to the table representing the original superclass. These columns are not restricted by a NOT NULL constraint, as the values are valid only for some of the records. On the other hand, the values of these columns are restricted by a *generalization set constraint*, enforcing the non-empty and empty values in the columns based on the actual type of the stored instance identified by a value in a special column [21].

However, if you apply this approach to the model shown in Fig. 3, you will come out with exactly the same model as shown in Fig. 5. As there are no properties in the subclasses, only the column distinguishing the actual type of instances must be added. Instead of the *generalization set constraint*, the appropriate version of the *enumeration constraint* can be defined, restricting the possible values in the type column.

Nevertheless, this realization has the same drawbacks as in the case of the reduction of the generalization set discussed in Subsect. 3.2. The more attributes are defined in the subclasses and the more subclasses there are, the more complicated the *generalization set constraint* becomes. Also, the concept of separate subclasses is lost, which may bring problems when evolving the model and identifying new properties of the subclasses, just as discussed in Subsect. 3.2.

Therefore, the realization of the generalization set using the approach of a single table is recommended only in the cases of a generalization set without any additional properties defined in the subtypes and when there is a minimal risk of the evolution of the generalization set in the future. In the other cases, the realization of the generalization set by separate or referencing tables is recommended.

# 4   Conclusions

In the recent years, OntoUML has become an interesting option for conceptual modelling of structural conceptual models. In our recent research, we focused on the usage of OntoUML in software engineering, in particular, for conceptual modelling of application data and a transformation of such model using the MDD approach.

In this paper, we discussed the complications of the approach to the transformation of *Kinds* and *Subkinds* – two of the universal types used in OntoUML – and their generalization sets into their proper realization in a relational database originally presented in [21]. In particular, we discussed the situation of applying the approach to a generalization set of *Subkinds* without any additional properties but the extended identity principles. In such a case, the standard transformation results in empty subclasses in the UML PIM and unnecessarily complicated realization in the relational database.

For such cases, we suggested a possible optimization of the resulting UML PIM that is based on the reduction of the whole generalization set into an immutable *enumeration attribute* used for identifying the subtype of the actual instance. Such *enumeration attribute* must be restricted by a special *enumeration constraint* to restrict the possible values of the attribute only to the values representing the original subtypes. We also suggested a transformation of such an optimized model into an RDB PSM and an actual relational database, suggesting the possible realizations of the *enumeration constraint* and the *immutability* of the *enumeration attribute*.

We also discussed the problems of the suggested optimization method – the complications of using this approach for generalization sets with subtypes with additional properties, as well as the problems of losing the concept of subtypes and evolution of the model.

Additionally, we also discussed the consequences of realizing the unoptimized generalization set of empty subclasses in the RDB PSM and the actual relational database, analysing the constraints of the individual realizations presented in [21] – the referencing-tables realization, the separate-tables realization and the single-table realization.

In these discussions, we came to the conclusion, that the proposed optimization by reducing the generalization set in the UML PIM into an immutable *enumeration attribute* with an *enumeration constraint* and its realization in the database is beneficial, but it can be applied only in the cases of generalization sets consisting of subtypes without additional properties and in cases where there is minimal risk of losing the concept of the subtypes in the actual database from the evolution point of view.

# References

1. Aleksić, S., Ristić, S., Luković, I.: An approach to generating server implementation of the inverse referential integrity constraints. In: Proceedings of the 5th International Conference on Information Technologies, ICIT, May 2011
2. Aleksić, S., Ristić, S., Luković, I., Čeliković, M.: A design specification and a server implementation of the inverse referential integrity constraints. Comput. Sci. Inf. Syst. **10**(1) (2013)
3. Andreeva, E., Poletaeva, T., Abdulrab, H., Babkin, E.: One solution for semantic data integration in logistics. In: Barjis, J., Pergl, R., Babkin, E. (eds.) EOMAS 2015. LNBIP, vol. 231, pp. 75–86. Springer, Cham (2015). https://doi.org/10.1007/978-3-319-24626-0_6
4. Benevides, A.B., Guizzardi, G., Braga, B.F.B., Almeida, J.P.A.: Assessing modal aspects of OntoUML conceptual models in alloy. In: Heuser, C.A., Pernul, G. (eds.) ER 2009. LNCS, vol. 5833, pp. 55–64. Springer, Heidelberg (2009). https://doi.org/10.1007/978-3-642-04947-7_8
5. Carolla, M., Spitta, T.: Methodological aspects of a data reference model for campus management systems. Working Paper (2014)
6. Carraretto, R.: Separating ontological and informational concerns: a model-driven approach for conceptual modeling. Master thesis, Federal University of Espirito Santo (2012)
7. Egea, M., Dania, C.: SQL-PL4OCL: an automatic code generator from OCL to SQL procedural language. Softw. Syst. Model., 1–23 (2017)
8. Ghezzi, C., Jazayeri, M., Mandrioli, D.: Fundamentals of Software Engineering, 2nd edn. Prentice Hall, Upper Saddle River (2002)

9. Guizzardi, G.: Ontological Foundations for Structural Conceptual Models, vol. 015. University of Twente, Enschede (2005)
10. Guizzardi, G.: Agent roles, qua individuals and *the Counting Problem*. In: Garcia, A., Choren, R., Lucena, C., Giorgini, P., Holvoet, T., Romanovsky, A. (eds.) SELMAS 2005. LNCS, vol. 3914, pp. 143–160. Springer, Heidelberg (2006). https://doi.org/10.1007/11738817_9
11. Guizzardi, G.: The problem of transitivity of part-whole relations in conceptual modeling revisited. In: van Eck, P., Gordijn, J., Wieringa, R. (eds.) CAiSE 2009. LNCS, vol. 5565, pp. 94–109. Springer, Heidelberg (2009). https://doi.org/10.1007/978-3-642-02144-2_12
12. Guizzardi, G., Wagner, G.: A unified foundational ontology and some applications of it in business modeling. In: CAiSE Workshops, pp. 129–143 (2004)
13. Kuskorn, W., Lekcharoen, S.: An adaptive translation of class diagram to relational database. In: International Conference on Information and Multimedia Technology, ICIMT 2009, pp. 144–148, December 2009
14. Mellor, S.J., Clark, A.N., Futagami, T.: Model-driven development. IEEE Softw. **20**(5), 14 (2003)
15. OMG: UML 2.5, March 2015. Accessed 12 Mar 2018
16. Oriol, X., Teniente, E.: Incremental checking of OCL constraints through SQL queries. In: Proceedings of the 14th International Workshop on OCL and Textual Modelling, pp. 23–32 (2014)
17. Pergl, R., Sales, T.P., Rybola, Z.: Towards OntoUML for software engineering: from domain ontology to implementation model. In: Cuzzocrea, A., Maabout, S. (eds.) MEDI 2013. LNCS, vol. 8216, pp. 249–263. Springer, Heidelberg (2013). https://doi.org/10.1007/978-3-642-41366-7_21
18. Ramakrishnan, R., Gehrke, J.: Database Management Systems, 3rd edn. McGraw-Hill, Boston (2002)
19. Rybola, Z., Pergl, R.: Towards OntoUML for software engineering: introduction to the transformation of OntoUML into relational databases. In: Pergl, R., Molhanec, M., Babkin, E., Fosso Wamba, S. (eds.) EOMAS 2016. LNBIP, vol. 272, pp. 67–83. Springer, Cham (2016). https://doi.org/10.1007/978-3-319-49454-8_5
20. Rybola, Z., Pergl, R.: Towards OntoUML for software engineering: transformation of anti-rigid sortal types into relational databases. In: Bellatreche, L., Pastor, Ó., Almendros Jiménez, J.M., Aït-Ameur, Y. (eds.) MEDI 2016. LNCS, vol. 9893, pp. 1–15. Springer, Cham (2016). https://doi.org/10.1007/978-3-319-45547-1_1
21. Rybola, Z., Pergl, R.: Towards OntoUML for software engineering: transformation of kinds and subkinds into relational databases. Comput. Sci. Inf. Syst. **14**(3), 913–937 (2017)
22. Rybola, Z., Richta, K.: Possible realizations of multiplicity constraints. Comput. Sci. Inf. Syst. **10**(4), 1621–1646 (2013)
23. Sobotka, P.: Transformation from OCL into SQL. Master thesis, Charles University, Prague, Czech Republic, May 2012
24. Zamborlini, V., Guizzardi, G.: On the representation of temporally changing information in OWL. In: 2010 14th IEEE International Enterprise Distributed Object Computing Conference Workshops (EDOCW), pp. 283–292. IEEE (2010)

# Enterprise Engineering

# An Improved Way for Measuring Simplicity During Process Discovery

Jonas Lieben[1,2]([✉]), Toon Jouck[1], Benoît Depaire[1], and Mieke Jans[1]

[1] Hasselt University, Martelarenlaan 42, 3500 Hasselt, Belgium
jonas.lieben@uhasselt.be
[2] FWO, Egmontstraat 5, 1000 Brussel, Belgium

**Abstract.** In the domain of process discovery, there are four quality dimensions for evaluating process models of which simplicity is one. Simplicity is often measured using the size of a process model, the structuredness and the entropy. It is closely related to the process model understandability. Researchers from the domain of business process management (BPM) proposed several metrics for measuring the process model understandability. A part of these understandability metrics focus on the control-flow perspective, which is important for evaluating models from process discovery algorithms. It is remarkable that there are more of these metrics defined in the BPM literature compared to the number of proposed simplicity metrics. To research whether the understandability metrics capture more understandability dimensions than the simplicity metrics, an exploratory factor analysis was conducted on 18 understandability metrics. A sample of 4450 BPMN models, both manually modelled and artificially generated, is used. Four dimensions are discovered: token behaviour complexity, node IO complexity, path complexity and degree of connectedness. The conclusion of this analysis is that process analysts should be aware that the measurement of simplicity does not capture all dimensions of the understandability of process models.

**Keywords:** Understandability metrics · Simplicity · Process models
Exploratory factor analysis · BPMN

## 1 Introduction

Many organisations are aware of the importance of becoming process-oriented. A first step is modelling the current processes [1]. This can be done by conducting stakeholder interviews or discovering the model from event logs [1,2]. A graphical notation is used for expressing the process models. Examples of these notations are BPMN (Business Process Model and Notation) and Petri nets. The usefulness of the process models depends among other things on how understandable they are [3]. To this end, many researchers of the business process management (BPM) domain have proposed metrics for measuring different aspects of process model understandability. These metrics belong to different perspectives such as

© Springer Nature Switzerland AG 2018
R. Pergl et al. (Eds.): EOMAS 2018, LNBIP 332, pp. 49–62, 2018.
https://doi.org/10.1007/978-3-030-00787-4_4

the organisational perspective and the control-flow perspective. The control-flow perspective takes into account everything that is related to the execution order of activities [4].

In the domain of process discovery, models discovered using an algorithm are evaluated based on four quality dimensions including the simplicity [4]. Simplicity is related to Occam's Razor's principle, which implies that the simplest process model should be chosen for explaining the behaviour observed in the event log [4]. It is most of the times measured using the process model size, the structuredness and entropy [4,5]. Also metrics such as the control-flow complexity have been proposed to measure simplicity [5]. Simplicity is strongly associated with the understandability metrics belonging to the control-flow perspective.

It is remarkable that there are many more understandability metrics proposed in the BPM literature compared to the number of simplicity metrics. It is possible that these simplicity metrics capture not all dimensions measured by the understandability understandability metrics from the BPM field. Therefore, we define the following research question: "To what extent do the simplicity measures used in process discovery cover the whole spectrum of control flow related understandability metrics in BPM?"

There are three contributions delivered by this paper:

- the identification of existing understandability metrics belonging to the control flow perspective. For this research article, we identified 18 existing metrics for measuring aspects of the understandability using a structured literature review. The metrics were implemented using the programming language R [6] and are publicly made available as an R package on CRAN[1]. This implementation was needed, because a software implementation for a part of the metrics was not publicly available. All metrics can be found in Sect. 2.
- the discovery of the understandability metrics' underlying dimensions by the means of an exploratory factor analysis. We performed the analysis using BPMN models, which are both manually modelled and artificially generated. The BPMN notation is chosen, because it is one of the most popular ones used in the industry. The reason is that the notation is easier to comprehend than for example Petri nets [7,8]. Section 4 contains all results of the factor analysis. The methodology is explained in Sect. 3.
- An analysis of which dimensions are not measured by the current simplicity metrics. Based on this analysis, we propose an alternative way for measuring the simplicity in order that all dimensions are represented. This is explained in Sect. 5.

## 2   Related Work

Many metrics exist for the measurement of the understandability of process models. Both the field of business process management and the field of process discovery proposed several metrics in the literature. In the field of process discovery, simplicity is one of the four proposed quality dimensions and is strongly

---

[1] https://cran.r-project.org/web/packages/understandBPMN/index.html.

associated with process model understandability. The other three are fitness, precision and generalisation [4]. The process model that is the easiest to comprehend while explaining all the observed behaviour should be chosen, if one wants to optimize for simplicity [4]. Simplicity is most of the times calculated using process model size, structuredness and entropy [4]. The process model size is equal to the number of nodes in a model [9–11]. The structuredness is related to the mismatches in gateways. If a model has a parallel split gateway combined with an exclusive join gateway, it scores worse in terms of structuredness than a model with matching gateways such as a parallel split gateway combined with a parallel join gateway [5]. The entropy refers to the distribution and use of different components of a process model. An example of this entropy is the connector heterogeneity [3,11–13]. In addition to these metrics, the control flow complexity and the cyclomatic metric of McCabe are proposed for measuring simplicity [5]. The control flow complexity is a measure which takes into account the complexity of the behaviour of a process model stemming from the use of different gateways and the number of outgoing sequence flows of these gateways [3,5,11,14,15]. The cyclomatic metric takes into account the number of activities and the complexity of the behaviour resulting from exclusive gateways [5].

In the field of BPM, understandabillity is defined as the extent to which the reader can make correct conclusions about the process model [13]. Many more metrics are proposed for measuring the understandability of process models in the field of BPM in comparison with the field of process discovery. Not all metrics are related to the control-flow perspective. Examples are the connectivity level between pools and the number of swimlanes and pools [12,16,17], which belong to the organisational perspective. In our study, we identified 18 understandability metrics related to the control-flow perspective. These metrics (column 1) together with their references (column 2) can be found in Table 1.

## 3 Research Methodology

In order to reach the results of our research paper, we performed several steps. The first step was the identification of existing understandability metrics belonging to the control-flow perspective (Sect. 3.1). The second step was gathering the data, which consisted of BPMN models (Sect. 3.2). The third and last step was conducting the factor analysis (Sect. 3.3).

### 3.1 Metrics Identification

We conducted a literature review of academic journals and conference papers for identifying existing understandability metrics of the BPM domain. To search for the scientific articles, Google Scholar was used with the keywords "understandability", "complexity", "BPMN", "process models", "metrics" and "influence". This resulted in 68 articles from journals and conference proceedings and one doctoral thesis. All found articles were read and the proposed understandability metrics were listed. Only the understandability metrics belonging to the control

**Table 1.** Understandability metrics and references with definition

| Metric | Reference |
| --- | --- |
| Process model size | [9–11,18] |
| Number of empty sequence flows | [19] |
| Number of duplicate tasks | [20] |
| Density | [3,11] |
| Coefficient of network connectivity | [3,11,12] |
| Average connector degree | [3,11] |
| Maximum connector degree | [3,11] |
| Sequentiality | [3,11,12,15] |
| Cyclicity | [11,13] |
| Diameter | [3,11–13] |
| Depth | [9,11,15,21] |
| Token split | [3,11,13] |
| Control flow complexity | [3,11,14,15] |
| Connector mismatch | [3,11,15,21] |
| Connector heterogeneity | [3,11–13] |
| Separability | [3,11,13] |
| Structuredness | [3,11,13] |
| Cross-connectivity | [22] |

flow perspective were selected. The journals and conference proceedings which had a relevant metric can be found in Table 2. Since a software implementation of some metrics lacked, we implemented all metrics as an R package [6].

**Table 2.** Journals and conference proceedings with relevant metrics

| Journals |
| --- |
| Business & Information Systems Engineering |
| Decision Support Systems |
| IEEE Transactions on Systems, Man, and Cybernetics-Part A: Systems and Humans |
| IEEE Transactions on Industrial Informatics |
| International Journal of Computer Science and Network Security |
| Conference Proceedings |
| Advanced information systems engineering |
| Proceedings of IEEE International Conference on Cognitive Informatics |
| Proceedings of International Conference on Business Information Systems |

## 3.2 Data

The sample of observations used for the factor analysis consisted of two types of models. Models of the first type were made by people. The source is BPM AI (Business Process Management Academic Initiative). This repository contains a large number of models created by students and staff of academic institutions [23]. We selected the models which were made in BPMN 2.0 and which had a connectedness of at least 50%. Afterwards, the models were filtered on the occurrence of boundary events and on modelling mistakes such as unconnected activities. These models are not within the scope of this analysis, because we are focussing on the understandability of models within the context of a process discovery algorithm. The current process discovery algorithms cannot yet discover processes with boundary events or processes with many unconnected activities. The number of resulting models after filtering is 4150.

Models of the second type were created using the PTandLogGenerator [24]. One sample of 300 models was generated. The maximum number of activities was set to 20. The minimum and mode were respectively 2 and 10 activities. This resulted in process trees which were converted to BPMN models. As process trees have a different notation for representing process models than BPMN, the translated BPMN models can have a representational bias [25]. Mismatches in gateways can for example not be represented in process trees. The bias will not pose a problem, because the first type of models is directly made in BPMN.

We chose to use two types of models, in order to increase the generalisation of our analysis. As we want to get an insight into the underlying dimensions of the understandability of models discovered using a process discovery algorithm, it is not a good approach to only use models made by people. However, not all possible constructs can be generated using the PTandLogGenerator such as mismatches in gateways. Hence, we chose to combine BPMN models created by process modellers with automatically generated models.

After having gathered all the models, the metrics were calculated for each model and some descriptive statistics such as the mean and standard deviation were calculated. These statistics were useful for getting a first overview of the data. The descriptive statistics can be found in Table 3. We included the mean, median, standard deviation, minimum and maximum.

A couple of interesting patterns can be discovered from the descriptive statistics. There are some models which can be considered an outlier in terms of size, because the average is bigger than the median. Not many models have empty sequence flows or duplicate tasks. The models from the PTandLogGenerator have even no empty sequence flows, but some of them have duplicate tasks.

The density is rather small, because the density ranges from zero to one with one representing a dense model. This metric represents the percentage of sequence flows compared with the theoretical maximum number of sequence flows [3,11]. The density is correlated with the sequentiality which determines how sequential the process is. As the density is rather small for most models, the processes are to some extent sequential.

**Table 3.** Descriptive statistics for each metric of all process models included in the sample

| Metric | Mean | Median | Std | Min | Max |
|---|---|---|---|---|---|
| Size | 21.624 | 18 | 15.378 | 1 | 134 |
| # empty sequence flows | 0.021 | 0 | 0.223 | 0 | 7 |
| # duplicate tasks | 0.531 | 0 | 1.861 | 0 | 41 |
| Density | 0.09 | 0.062 | 0.112 | 0.001 | 1 |
| Coefficient of network connectivity | 0.976 | 1 | 0.213 | 0.037 | 2.95 |
| Average connector degree | 2.727 | 3 | 1.062 | 0 | 8 |
| Maximum connector degree | 3.112 | 3 | 1.454 | 0 | 12 |
| Sequentiality | 0.336 | 0.286 | 0.26 | 0 | 1 |
| Token split | 1.208 | 0 | 1.984 | 0 | 42 |
| Control flow complexity | 6.26 | 4 | 7.178 | 0 | 129 |
| Connector mismatch | 1.369 | 1 | 1.819 | 0 | 34 |
| Connector heterogeneity | 0.387 | 0 | 0.444 | 0 | 1 |
| Cyclicity | 0.069 | 0 | 0.151 | 0 | 0.897 |
| Diameter metric | 10.929 | 8 | 9.507 | 0 | 85 |
| Depth metric | 1.392 | 1 | 1.352 | 0 | 13 |
| Separability metric | 0.183 | 0.077 | 0.246 | 0 | 1 |
| Cross-connectivity | 0.104 | 0.077 | 0.103 | 0 | 0.75 |
| Structuredness | 0.847 | 0.966 | 0.286 | 0 | 1 |

Processes do have non-sequential parts which are gateways or activities with more than three connected sequence flows. On average, a gateway or activity with multiple incoming or outgoing sequence flows has three connected sequence flows. In addition, the models have sometimes a mismatch in gateways, even though this number is also quite small. The number of activities being part of an explicit loop is limited. Even more than 50% of the processes do not have any explicit loops. Some parts of the processes are also separable, because the separability metric is on average 0.183. The combination of this metric, with the results from the depth and sequentiality indicate that there are several gateways used in the process models. Even though there are several gateways used, they are most of the times modelled in the right way. This conclusion is derived from the structuredness, which is on average 0.847. This means that the gateways most of the time match and that most explicit loops are modelled using exclusive gateways.

### 3.3  Factor Analysis

A first step when performing a factor analysis is choosing the type of factor analysis. Several types of factor analyses exist and are used for different purposes. We chose an R-type common factor analysis, because the main goal is the discovery of the underlying dimensions of the metrics. This type only considers the shared variance, which defines the structure of the variables [26].

The sample size of 4450 observations is sufficient to perform an exploratory analysis. It is recommended to have at least 50 observations and at least 20 observations per variable to perform a factor analysis [26]. Therefore, this requirement is fulfilled.

An important assumption when performing a factor analysis is that there is enough intercorrelation between the variables [26]. We performed two tests to validate this assumption: the Bartlett's Test of Sphericity and the Measure of Sampling Adequacy (MSA) values [26]. When the Bartlett's Test of Sphericity is statistically significant, it indicates that there is enough overall correlation between the variable to perform a factor analysis. The overall and individual MSA values indicate also whether there is enough intercorrelation. As MSA values increase, when the sample size increases [26], we used a cut-off of 0.6. Variables which had a lower MSA value were discarded, because they do not exhibit enough intercorrelation with the other variables. This is unacceptable in the context of a factor analysis and reduces the quality of the factor solution.

The number of factors is determined using the scree test. After having determined the number of factors, the factor analysis was performed iteratively. During each iteration, the communalities of the variables were assessed. The communality determines the amount of variance which is included in the factor solution [26]. Some variables were again left out, because their communalities were smaller than 0.3 and this can decrease the reliability of the analysis [27].

To make the interpretation easier, a factor rotation was performed. The chosen rotation was the varimax rotation. As this is an orthogonal rotation, the factors are not correlated anymore, which is in contrast with the oblique factor rotation methods [26]. We chose an orthogonal factor rotation, because this allows the development of new uncorrelated scales for measuring the understandability of process models with regards to the control-flow perspective [26].

The removal of the variables due to low communalities and low MSA values does not pose a problem in the context of this factor analysis, because we are interested in the underlying dimensions of the understandability metrics. The metrics which are not included into the factor analysis can still be regarded as separate dimensions for each omitted variable.

## 4   Results

The standard deviations of the variables in Table 3 indicate that we can perform a useful factor analysis, because a necessary condition for a factor analysis is a sufficient amount of variance in the data [26]. In addition, there is enough intercorrelation between the variables, because the Bartlett's Test of Sphericity is statistically significant at 0.01. The overall MSA value is 0.77 and the individual MSA values range from 0.61 to 0.87. We discarded no variable due to a low MSA value.

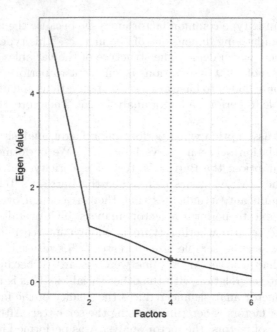

**Fig. 1.** Scree plot for determining number of factors

We determined the number of factors using the scree test by making a plot. The eigenvalues are assigned to the Y-axis, while the factor number is plotted on the X-axis. The point where the curve starts to straighten out indicates the number of factors [26]. The scree test criterion implies that four factors should be chosen (Fig. 1). Note that the latent root criterion, which states that the number of factors should equal to the number of factors with eigenvalues bigger than one [26], implies that two factors should be chosen. However, this number of factors is deemed too low to make a useful interpretation.

Not all variables are used for the factor analysis, because some variables had communalities which were too low. However, the factor analysis was again executed using the 15 variables which had communalities bigger than 0.3. These variables with their corresponding communalities can be found in Table 4. The variables with a communality lower than 0.3 are the number of empty sequence flows, the number of duplicate tasks and the structuredness.

In Table 5, the factor loadings can be found. The factor loadings determine how the metrics correlate with a given factor [26]. The higher the absolute value of the loading, the bigger the correlation. We removed the loadings which had an absolute value lower than 0.35. These loadings are considered insignificant, given our big sample size [26].

Table 4. Factor communalities

| Metrics | Communalities |
|---|---|
| Size | 0.706 |
| Density | 0.613 |
| Coefficient of network connectivity | 0.756 |
| Average connector degree | 0.995 |
| Maximum connector degree | 0.859 |
| Sequentiality | 0.527 |
| Token split | 0.483 |
| Control flow complexity | 0.676 |
| Connector mismatch | 0.355 |
| Connector heterogeneity | 0.331 |
| Cyclicity | 0.460 |
| Diameter | 0.995 |
| Depth | 0.558 |
| Separability | 0.352 |
| Cross-connectivity | 0.337 |

Table 5. Factor loadings

| | Factor 1 | Factor 2 | Factor 3 | Factor 4 |
|---|---|---|---|---|
| Size | 0.810 | | | |
| Density | | | | 0.745 |
| Coef. of network conn. | | 0.531 | | 0.450 |
| Avg. connector degree | | 1.174 | | |
| Max. connector degree | | 0.888 | | |
| Sequentiality | | −0.621 | | |
| Token split | 0.705 | | | |
| CFC | 0.846 | | | |
| Connector mismatch | 0.613 | | | |
| Connector heterogeneity | 0.493 | | | |
| Cyclicity | | | 0.693 | |
| Diameter | | | 0.982 | |
| Depth | | | 0.489 | |
| Separability | −0.389 | | | |
| Cross-connectivity | −0.440 | | | |

## 5    Discussion

Four main dimensions are discovered as a result of the factor analysis. It should be emphasized that some metrics were not included in the factor analysis, because they measure different things than what is captured by the main dimensions. These metrics are the number of empty sequence flows, the number of duplicate tasks and the structuredness. Each metric can be considered a different dimension for the purpose of this factor analysis.

We give each main dimension a label and explain why the metrics belong to the factors. Also an intuitive interpretation of what the dimension captures is given. Afterwards, the dimensions are related to the current simplicity metrics.

### 5.1    Dimension 1: Token Behaviour Complexity

The size, token split, control flow complexity, connector mismatch, connector heterogeneity, seperability and cross-connectivity all belong to dimension one. We label it token behaviour complexity. The token behaviour complexity includes the number of tokens which are consumed by activities. A token consumption happens when an activity of the model is executed. The bigger the size of a model, the more token consumptions can occur, because there are more activities. The token split measure indicates in which activities and gateways the tokens are split [3,11,13]. If tokens are split, more token consumptions can occur. The control flow complexity is closely related to the token split but assigns different weights to the type of gateways [14]. When a mismatch occurs, the token behaviour can become more complex as well. If for example a parallel split gateway is matched with an exclusive join gateway, multiple tokens will continue flowing through the model and many activities will be repeated and executed in parallel. The connector heterogeneity also belongs to this dimension, because if there are several types of connectors, the complexity of the token behaviour increases [3,11–13]. The higher the heterogeneity, the higher the probability that there are inclusive and parallel gateways present in the model. The separability measures how easy it is to split the model into several independent parts [3,11,13]. If it is easier to split the model, the token behaviour is less complex, and therefore this metric is negatively related to the token behaviour complexity. Also the cross-connectivity is negatively related, because the token behaviour becomes more complex when the value of this metric decreases. In that case, there is a higher probability of several types of gateways.

The token behaviour complexity captures **the number of token consumptions** for one process execution. In addition, it takes into account **the complexity of the routing of the tokens**. When exclusive gateways are used, the routing becomes more complex, which reduces for example the separability and cross-connectivity. The token behaviour complexity is high, when the process model contains many gateways and activities.

## 5.2   Dimension 2: Node IO Complexity

The coefficient of network connectivity, the average and maximum connector degree and the sequentiality belong to dimension two. We give this dimension the label node incoming outgoing complexity or node IO complexity. The node IO complexity takes into account the number of incoming and outgoing sequence flows for a given node. If there are more incoming and outgoing sequence flows on average for activities and gateways, the overall number of sequence flows increases and hence the coefficient of network connectivity increases. The same reasoning can be applied for the average and maximum connector degree. The sequentiality negatively loads on dimension two, because if a process is sequential, it consists only of activities with exactly one incoming and outgoing sequence flow [3,11,12,15]. This means that there are less outgoing and incoming flows of nodes.

The node IO complexity captures the **number of connected sequence flows with activities and gateways**.

## 5.3   Dimension 3: Path Complexity

Dimension three is labelled the path complexity. This dimension includes three metrics: cyclicity, diameter and depth. We define a path in a similar way as a path in graph theory [28] and not as a trace. This means that if there is a parallel or inclusive split gateway, only one of the outgoing sequence flows is chosen and becomes part of the path. In addition, each path starts with a start event and ends with an end event. The diameter is the length of a path [3,11–13] and the bigger the length, the larger a path. When there are loops, the path becomes longer and more complex [11,13]. The complexity of the paths also increases when the depth increases. If the depth increases, there are more gateways, which make the path longer.

We define the path complexity as **the length of a path in the process model allowing one repetition of a loop**. This definition gives the most weight to the diameter, while taking into account cyclicity and depth just as the factor loadings do. When the path complexity is high, there is a long path present in the model, or a path with many and long loops.

## 5.4   Dimension 4: Degree of Connectedness

Dimension four gets the label degree of connectedness. This dimension includes the density and the coefficient of network connectivity. A process model diagram is more connected, when it has more sequence flows cet. par. the process model size. The density of a model captures this, because it is calculated by dividing the number of sequence flows with the process model size [3,11]. Also the coefficient of network connectivity is linked with the dimension. This metric is calculated in a similar way, but the denominator is replaced with the theoretical maximum number of sequence flows. The theoretical maximum is calculated by multiplying the process model size with the process model size minus one [3,11,12].

We define the degree of connectedness in the same way as the **density**. When there are many **flows given the process models size**, the degree of connectedness is high.

### 5.5   Relation of Understandability Dimensions with Simplicity Metrics

The simplicity of a process model is often measured using the size of the process model, the structuredness and the entropy [4]. Both the size and the entropy, which is named the connector heterogeneity in Table 5 belong to dimension one, token behaviour complexity. The structuredness of the process model is not included in the factor analysis, because the communality is too low. The structuredness can be regarded as a separate dimension.

In addition to the three most used simplicity metrics, the control flow complexity and the cyclomatic metric of McCabe are proposed [5]. The control-flow complexity is part of dimension one as well. The cyclomatic metric of McCabe takes into account the number of activities and the complexity in behaviour resulting from exclusive gateways. These concepts are mainly related to the token behaviour complexity.

We can conclude from the previous paragraphs that most simplicity metrics are associated with the token behaviour complexity. The current simplicity metrics all omit the node IO complexity, the path complexity and the degree of connectedness. Also empty sequence flows and the number of duplicate tasks are omitted. As empty sequence flows are not part of a process model resulting from a discovery algorithm, this metric can be considered irrelevant in this context.

To calculate the simplicity, we propose that at least 6 metrics are used: one for each dimension and two for the metrics which are not part of the factor analysis. We recommend to use the metrics with the highest loadings until further research is conducted. These metrics are control-flow complexity for token behaviour complexity, average connector degree for node IO complexity, diameter for path complexity and density for the degree of connectedness. In addition, the number of duplicate tasks and structuredness should be used.

## 6   Conclusion

When someone has discovered a process model using a process discovery algorithm, the model should be evaluated using several quality dimensions. The quality dimension simplicity is often measured with the size of a process model, the structuredness and the entropy. In addition, metrics such as the control-flow complexity and the cyclomatic metric of McCabe are proposed to measure simplicity. The current metrics do not take all dimensions of the process model understandability into account even though simplicity is closely related to the process model understandability. This conclusion can be made based on the results of an exploratory factor analysis of 18 understandability metrics, which all belong to the control-flow perspective.

Four dimensions were discovered: token behaviour complexity, node IO complexity, path complexity and degree of connectedness. Three of the 18 metrics were not included in the analysis, because these variables had too low communalities. These metrics were the number of empty sequence flows, the number of duplicate tasks and the structuredness. As they measure different things than the discovered dimensions, they can each be considered a separate dimension.

Most simplicity metrics only load on the token behaviour complexity dimension. This is the case for the process model size, the entropy, the control flow complexity. The cyclomatic metric of McCabe is also related to the token behaviour complexity. Structuredness was not part of the factor analysis. A better approach for calculating the simplicity is using six metrics, of which four belong to the discovered dimensions.

There is still room for further research. The discovered dimensions can be validated using a confirmatory factor analysis. This analysis can be done with models resulting from several discovery algorithms. It is also not yet clear how big the correlation is between the dimensions and the simplicity metrics. Moreover, this paper is a starting point for the development of a single understandability metric which captures all dimensions belonging to the control-flow perspective.

# References

1. van der Aalst, W.M.P.: Business process management: a comprehensive survey. ISRN Softw. Eng. **2013**, 1–37 (2013)
2. van der Aalst, W., et al.: Business process mining: an industrial application. Inf. Syst. **32**(5), 713–732 (2007)
3. Reijers, H.A., Mendling, J.: A study into the factors that influence the understandability of business process models. IEEE Trans. Syst. Man, Cybern.-Part A: Syst. Hum. **41**(3), 449–462 (2011)
4. van der Aalst, W.M.P.: Process Mining: Discovery Conformance and Enhancement of Business Processes. Springer, Heidelberg (2011). https://doi.org/10.1007/978-3-642-19345-3
5. Lassen, K.B., van der Aalst, W.M.: Complexity metrics for workflow nets. Inf. Softw. Technol. **51**(3), 610–626 (2009)
6. Ihaka, R., Gentleman, R.: R: a language for data analysis and graphics. J. Comput. Graph. Stat. **5**(3), 299–314 (1996)
7. Sarshar, K., Loos, P.: Comparing the control-flow of EPC and petri net from the end-user perspective. In: van der Aalst, W.M.P., Benatallah, B., Casati, F., Curbera, F. (eds.) BPM 2005. LNCS, vol. 3649, pp. 434–439. Springer, Heidelberg (2005). https://doi.org/10.1007/11538394_36
8. Recker, J.C., Dreiling, A.: Does it matter which process modelling language we teach or use? An experimental study on understanding process modelling languages without formal education, Toowoomba (2007)
9. Laue, R., Gruhn, V.: Complexity metrics for business process models. In: Business Information Systems, Klagenfurt, Austria, January 2006
10. Petrusel, R., Mendling, J., Reijers, H.A.: How visual cognition influences process model comprehension. Decis. Support Syst. **96**(Suppl. C), 1–16 (2017)
11. Mendling, J.: Detection and prediction of errors in EPC business process models. PhD thesis, Wirtschaftsuniversitt Wien Vienna (2007)

12. Fernndez-Ropero, M., Prez-Castillo, R., Caballero, I., Piattini, M.: Quality-driven business process refactoring. In: International Conference on Business Information Systems (ICBIS 2012), pp. 960–966 (2012)
13. Mendling, J., Strembeck, M.: Influence factors of understanding business process models. In: Abramowicz, W., Fensel, D. (eds.) BIS 2008. LNBIP, vol. 7, pp. 142–153. Springer, Heidelberg (2008). https://doi.org/10.1007/978-3-540-79396-0_13
14. Cardoso, J.: Control-flow complexity measurement of processes and Weyuker's properties. In: 6th International Enformatika Conference. vol. 8, pp. 213–218 (2005)
15. Figl, K.: Comprehension of procedural visual business process models: a literature review. Bus. Inf. Syst. Eng. **59**(1), 41–67 (2017)
16. Polani, G., Cegnar, B.: Complexity metrics for process models a systematic literature review. Comput. Stand. Interfaces **51**(Suppl. C), 104–117 (2017)
17. Gschwind, T., Koehler, J., Wong, J.: Applying patterns during business process modeling. In: Dumas, M., Reichert, M., Shan, M.-C. (eds.) BPM 2008. LNCS, vol. 5240, pp. 4–19. Springer, Heidelberg (2008). https://doi.org/10.1007/978-3-540-85758-7_4
18. Pavlicek, J., Hronza, R., Pavlickova, P., Jelinkova, K.: The business process model quality metrics. In: Pergl, R., Lock, R., Babkin, E., Molhanec, M. (eds.) EOMAS 2017. LNBIP, vol. 298, pp. 134–148. Springer, Cham (2017). https://doi.org/10.1007/978-3-319-68185-6_10
19. Gruhn, V., Laue, R.: Reducing the cognitive complexity of business process models, pp. 339–345, June 2009
20. La Rosa, M., Wohed, P., Mendling, J., Ter Hofstede, A.H., Reijers, H.A., van der Aalst, W.M.: Managing process model complexity via abstract syntax modifications. IEEE Trans. Ind. Inf. **7**(4), 614–629 (2011)
21. Muketha, G.: Complexity metrics for measuring the understandability and maintainability of business process models using goal-question-metric (GQM). Int. J. Comput. Sci. Netw. Secur. **8**(5), 219–225 (2008)
22. Vanderfeesten, I., Reijers, H.A., Mendling, J., van der Aalst, W.M.P., Cardoso, J.: On a quest for good process models: the cross-connectivity metric. In: Bellahsène, Z., Léonard, M. (eds.) CAiSE 2008. LNCS, vol. 5074, pp. 480–494. Springer, Heidelberg (2008). https://doi.org/10.1007/978-3-540-69534-9_36
23. Kunze, M., Berger, P., Weske, M., Lohmann, N., Moser, S.: BPM academic initiative-fostering empirical research. In: BPM, pp. 1–5 Demos (2012)
24. Jouck, T., Depaire, B.: Generating artificial data for empirical analysis of control-flow discovery algorithms: a process tree and log generator. Bus. Inf. Syst. Eng. **10**, 18 (2018)
25. van der Aalst, W.: On the representational bias in process mining, pp. 2–7. IEEE, June 2011
26. Hair, J., Black, W., Babin, B., Anderson, R.: Multivariate Data Analysis, Number Seventh edn. Pearson Education Limited, London (2013)
27. Child, D.: The Essentials of Factor Analysis. A&C Black, London (2006). GoogleBooks-ID: rQ2vdJgohH0C
28. Sim, K.A., Tan, T.S.: Wong, K.B.: On the shortest path in some k-connected graphs, p. 050010 (2016)

# IT-Business Alignment Problem Solution by Means of Zachman Model: Case of Woodworking Enterprise

Pavel Malyzhenkov[1(✉)], Tatiana Gordeeva[1], and Maurizio Masi[2]

[1] Department of Information Systems and Technologies,
National Research University Higher School of Economics, Bol. Pecherskaya 25,
603155 Nizhny Novgorod, Russia
pmalyzhenkov@hse.ru, tatyana.gordeeva.1997@mail.ru
[2] Department of Economy, Engineering, Society and Business,
University of Tuscia, Via del Paradiso, 47, 01100 Viterbo, Italy
maurizio.masi@unitus.it

**Abstract.** This research aims to use an architectural approach to create an alignment of IT and business in a chosen industrial enterprise, based on Zachman model. All development processes, existing within the enterprise, their relations and interactions, which are needed to fulfill the enterprise mission, are represented in a chosen Enterprise Architecture framework. The framework does not just perform the main attributes and components of the organization, but it also provides the company with an opportunity to understand and analyze crucial weaknesses and inconsistencies that needed to be identified and rectified. Nowadays enterprises use a wide range of established Enterprise Architecture frameworks, some of which were developed for specific fields, while others can be applied broadly. One of the frameworks with such functionality is the Zachman Enterprise Architecture Framework, a unique tool to create an architectural description and apply solutions for overcoming challenges that have been identified for a considered enterprise. So, the main *goal* of the study is to provide a practical guidance, which enables the alignment between business and IT, based on the Zachman Enterprise Architecture Framework.

**Keywords:** IT-business alignment · Enterprise Architecture
Zachman Framework

## 1 Introduction

Structures of most industries, which have been considered stable for a number of decades, have begun to change dramatically. This has led to the necessity of certain enterprise changes. To function in conditions of continuous changes, enterprises must be able to manage the development of organization processes. Most approaches, offered by classical management are ineffective. The main reason is the lack of both systemic and coherent enterprise management. Designing complexity changes requires interdisciplinary qualification. One of such approaches to the analysis of enterprise functioning is presented by Zachman model, which enables to analyze it systematically [1, 6, 8].

© Springer Nature Switzerland AG 2018
R. Pergl et al. (Eds.): EOMAS 2018, LNBIP 332, pp. 63–75, 2018.
https://doi.org/10.1007/978-3-030-00787-4_5

The impact of information technology on enterprises has improved significantly over the last few decades [2–4, 11]. IT is evolving toward a strategic role to shape new business strategies. In fact, the economic performance of an enterprise is based on the ability to create a strategic fit between external and internal domains, and functional integration between business and IT strategies.

Although the literature consists of a significant number of conceptual studies on IT-business alignment, there is a lack of research, aimed to apply the alignment concept practically [7, 12, 13, 15].

Zachman Enterprise Architecture Framework enables a company to solve such issues as the use of integrated conceptual models for experts from different areas; focusing on certain aspects with a holistic view of enterprise activities; compliance of cell descriptions, ensuring alignment of business and IT, and maintaining independence of specific software use. The importance of the Framework is that it describes each aspect of the system in coordination that enables it to outline its most significant relationships, rules, and conditions.

The rest of the paper is organized as follows. Section 2 summarizes the theoretical background relevant for the approach proposed. Section 3 both represents AS-IS Zachman model on the base of chosen woodworking enterprise and proposes TO-BE Zachman model to identify possible solutions for current IT-business misalignment. Finally, Sect. 4 outlines conclusions and identifies branches of future research directions of the topic.

## 2 Theoretical Background

Analyzing IT-business alignment, it can be noted that a large number of researchers are interested in the topic and are trying to develop and implement different models. IT-business alignment is ranked as one of the main management concepts. 30 years of studies have indicated that IT-business alignment on the level of an enterprise is an integral problem.

Saat et al. [16] proposed in their paper to consider the problem of IT-business alignment as qualities for IT governance, IT and business systems. Proposing meta-models of Enterprise Architecture for each situation enables an increase in IT-business alignment. The authors present the core meta-model as well as situation specific extensions.

Integration of such Enterprise Architecture framework as The Open Group Architecture Framework and conceptual alignment model is also considered as a method of EA development [10]. Strategic guidance is provided through the linkage between SAM and TOGAF framework components.

Although significant progress has been made to understand alignment, there are several problems in the field of the research. Luftman et al. [9], based on a capability-based lens, outline different kinds of weaknesses of the existing models. The research presents a formative construct, which is rooted in the theory of dynamic capabilities, and defines the scope and nature of activities, contributing to alignment.

Due to the range of EA frameworks, comparison of them is an essential step in choosing an appropriate tool for IT-business alignment [19]. Applying to a specific application, such as object oriented development and distributed systems, or being enterprise oriented and specific to IT system development, determines criteria, that enable to choose a framework, suitable for a certain enterprise. Views and abstraction, coverage of the Systems Development Life Cycle are one of the main features to provide comparison of the frameworks.

The case of woodworking company is specific, as we consider enterprise as a system with unstable definition of its levels, so it is important to provide comprehensive views in frame of the tool for IT-business alignment. Comparing five leading frameworks [19], including Zachman Framework for Enterprise Architecture, Department of Defense Architecture Framework (DoDAF), Federal Enterprise Architecture Framework (FEAF), Treasure Enterprise Architecture Framework (TEAF) and The Open Group Architectural Framework (TOGAF), Zachman Framework is the most comprehensive framework, while other EA Frameworks stakeholder perspectives can be presented via the Zachman technology. The use of alignment tool in our study is representative, that unable to determine existing enterprise's problems in AS-IS model and provide its TO-BE structure. Zachman model presents recommendations, but does not provide methods and procedures. Comparing to other tools, Zachman Framework represents timelines and justification, which are necessary features for motivation determination for every perspective, when AS-IS and TO-BE models are determined.

Comparison of frameworks with the Systems Development Life Cycle shows that Zachman model is weighted mostly towards planning and analysis, ensuring all views are addressed and determine necessary requirements [19]. It provides guidance that can be implemented in the SDLC.

In this way, with the emergence of such new enterprise models as technology-based enterprises, and a large quantity of them being generated through technological advances information, the Zachman Framework is represented as a modeling tool of utility and value to construct an Enterprise Architecture, integrating and aligning business goals and the IT infrastructure. Implementing an Enterprise Architecture requires an important effort within an enterprise [17, 18].

In 1987 Zachman developed the first version of the generalized model [20]. For a long period of time the model was considered as a standard in the field of enterprise architecture, which idea was to provide a consistent description of every aspect in coordination with others. The method provides the ability to split the Architecture description on the one hand, and to consider an Enterprise Architecture as a holistic unit on the other.

Perspectives in Zachman model differ in accordance with their concepts and limitations [21]. The description of artefacts, presented as cells in the model, do not only depict informative part, which is necessary for product development, but also must be understandable for the described perspectives. In a particular case, perspective correspond to the level of enterprise management.

Aspects in Zachman model are represented as independent variables, which reflect complexity and relationship with other objects. These dimensions of classification system correspond to specific categories of questions with different levels, depending on specification and abstraction of the relevant perspective. Zachman model considers the following aspects: "What?", "How?", "Where?", "Who?", "When?" and "Why?" [20].

The conceptual idea of the Framework is indicated by recursiveness of metamodels and models formation logic on the generalized scheme basis. It provides an ability to manage enterprise and architecture changes on the basis of a common repository and use it for work with different models and its states.

The Zachman Enterprise Framework enables to solve the following task:

- Use of one conceptual model for specialists from different fields;
- Focusing on certain aspects, while having a holistic view on enterprise activities and business processes;
- Adhering to the correspondence of cells description, to ensure IT-business alignment;
- Maintaining independence from specific software and products use.

## 3 Zachman Model: Practical Application

### 3.1 Description of the Chosen Business Case

CJSC N is the largest forest and woodworking industry enterprise in the region X. The company is on the list of socially significant enterprises. The number of employees is about 1000 people, while the main product is glued plywood, manufactured in strict accordance with international standards. The enterprise is located in a forest-rich region. This circumstance, as well as a thought-out marketing policy, enables the plant to systematically increase production volumes. Its capacity allows to produce more than 100'000 m$^3$ of plywood per year. More than 90% of products are exported to such countries as the USA, Egypt, Germany, Italy, the UK, Greece, Turkey, Slovenia, the Czech Republic. Products of the plant are also respond to market demand in Azerbaijan, Georgia and Kazakhstan.

Glued plywood, produced by the enterprise, is widely used in housing and civil construction, furniture production, shipbuilding, manufacture of different parts in radio and instrument making. Products are manufactured in accordance with classical technology with the use of low-toxic binders, which provide high strength characteristics and operational properties.

The glued plywood is a laminated material with outer layers of hardwood veneer, glued from three or more sheets of peeled veneer. Birch plywood is produced in accordance with established regulatory documentation.

Enterprise CJSC N has such strategic objectives as profit increase, continuous improvement of product quality, analysis of customer expectations and requirements, compliance with them and reduction in different types of losses and efficient use of enterprise resources. To achieve them CJSC N aims to improve and optimize enterprise's business processes through the use of up-to-date equipment and advanced information systems and technologies. The enterprise uses Galaktika ERP system and 1C (Russian enterprise level automation platform) to automate certain business processes. However, the lack of automation of such processes as warehousing, order and contact management, full integration of business processes and accounting systems unable the company to reduce different types of losses and use enterprise resources effectively. As a result, the main company's issue is profit decrease and low improvement of product quality, based on customer requirements.

## 3.2 Zachman Model: "AS-IS" State

Every artefact of the Framework reflects a view of an appropriate perspective for a certain aspect of described processes. In its traditional view, Zachman framework is used for classification of models on different abstraction level of technology development. Our case provides an opportunity to consider enterprise as a system with certain perspectives. The following model enables to depict current functioning of CJSC N and its level of business support by IT.

*Perspective "Planner"*
Scope Contents depicts the size, shape, relationships and purpose of the final structure. In this way, the first aspect of the perspective in frame of the case determines known entities of the enterprise, data, that is used in production chain. To answer the question "What" for the perspective Planner, the main administration objects of the enterprise are described. Product is presented by glued plywood (100'000 $m^3$ per year), while Client is on the market of the USA, Egypt, Germany, Italy, the UK, Greece, Turkey, Slovenia, the Czech Republic for housing and civil construction, furniture production, shipbuilding, manufacture of different parts in radio and instrument making. Resources include trained personnel, financial resources and infrastructure. Products are manufactured in accordance with classical technology with the use of low-toxic binders, which provide high strength characteristics and operational properties. The number of employees is about 1000 people with relevant competence and meeting necessary job requirements. Finance include funds, provided for purchase of row materials and other components, payroll of employees. The perspective identifies the scope of the enterprise, relationships with the general environment, in which it operates, behavior and functionality through business processes, subsequently detailed by next perspectives.

Production facilities of the enterprise are located in Region K, which determines its geographical aspect and answer the question "Where?" of the next aspect. The answer to the question "Who?" is a list of organizational units, executors of business processes, including subcontractors, suppliers, etc. Business plan specifies time aspects of enterprise functioning for the question "When?". Aspect "Why?" for Planner perspective is performed as a behavior aspect, which determines strategic objectives of the enterprise.

*Perspective "Owner"*
The second level of the constructed model defines basic and auxiliary business processes in term of business structure of CJSC N. Conceptual model determines enterprise semantic structure, presented by the Product with limitations and conditions to use, depending on the type and sort of plywood produced, Employees within processes in accordance with their roles and departments and Business-processes with identification of managers, owners, inputs and outputs of every process. Interrelated concepts, their properties, characteristics and classifications define enterprise structure causal relationship between objects under modelling. For the next column *How?* tree of business processes represents structured description of chosen for Planner perspective

business processes. Information exchange scheme in DFD standard specifies entities and their relationships (aspect *Where?*). The scheme enables to display dataflow from ordering row materials process to the process of taking payment for sold products from the customers. In order to describe time aspect.

The workflow model, built with IDEF0 business processes methodology, exists as an artefact, which answers the question *Who?* within the Model. Identification of inputs and outputs, execution and control mechanism is performed for each of the described organizational unit. The workflow model consists of the following units: to manage enterprise with the input "market information"; to manufacture, store and supply row materials; to store and recycle semifinished, to store and deliver products to customers with the output "contract for product supply" and "paid products are delivered to the customer". In order to describe time aspect of the perspective it is reasonable to consider a plan with integration parameters, as it depicts time period of processes within relationships between main units. Motivation is expressed through realization of business plan, which depicts the process of business operation implementation in accordance with product information, appropriate sales market and effectiveness of operations.

*Perspective "Designer"*
The third level of the Model for CJSC N is represented by the department of information technologies, which aim is to automate enterprise business processes. Here the solution at the level of functional requirements and information systems is considered and their rules and limitations are identified. Aspect *What?* for Architecture perspective is described by Information model of enterprise management. Artefact for the Function column is represented by Application Architecture, used in enterprise management process. For CJSC Application Architecture is presented by Galaktika ERP System, which has a modular structure.

Galaktika ERP supports open standards (XML, COM, ArchiveX, ODBC), that enables to integrate with specialized software and office application. Service-oriented Architecture and web-service technologies in the system provides additional opportunities for system integration with third-party producers and development of global distributed system. Galaktika ERP includes a means to configure system parameters centrally, update and implement necessary applications. Every module is designed for automation of certain narrow task. Modules are combined into contours that enables to automate the entire spectrum of tasks in one domain. Basic version of Galaktika, partly realized by CJSC N, includes such contours as Logistic, Accounting, Manufacturing Planning and Management, Staff Management and specialized solutions. Each of the modules belongs to the relevant cells within Builder and Developer perspectives to prove that Galaktika ERP provides improvement and optimization of enterprise's business processes and, subsequently, be a means of implementing enterprise business strategies. Business process participants and roles and time period within structured business processes answer the questions *Who?* and *When?* consequently. Motivation for the perspective is expressed by rules and limitations of business process limitations, efficient realization of strategic objectives.

*Perspective "Builder"*
In the traditional view of Zachman model technology plan provides sufficient details to understand tools, materials and technology constraints. Within this perspective row

materials purchasing and sales plan corresponds to *What?* Aspect as they describe in more details movement of the materials through the production chain, outlining constrains along the process, while Process Flow is drafting of the documents for purchasing row materials and sales. Treaties, contracts within relevant processes are presented by normative documents. Moreover, an integral part of enterprise economic activity is financial and accounting, that reflect distribution of fix assets in business process implementation. Participants of purchasing row materials and sales processes, time period within the processes depict Responsibility Assignments and Timing Cycles in the Model. Motivation component of the perspective is business logic implementation, consisting in the sale of an ordered quantity of products to a certain customer.

*Perspective "Developer"*
The fifth level of the model aims to use certain technologies for manufacturing and sales and their internal components. Production plan, outlining the main normative and technological documentation, is related with *What?* aspect. It corresponds to a traditional view of the perspective, as provides specification of the production processes with detailed requirements for its organization in workshops and quality control. Technological processes of product manufacturing depict functions. Standards of manufactured products, requirements, established by normative documentation are characterized for the artefact. The type of the product also answers the question *How?*. Production workshops in CJSC N determine Location column. Technological and quality control of raw materials, manufacturing, packaging, storage and sales of manufactured products. Participants of control processes are employees of the Technological department, Supply of raw materials department, Technical control department, factory laboratory center, metrological service, Maintenance and repair of equipment department, Accounting and product shipment department.

Production plan, consisting of shift coordination, information technologies capabilities and established terms of sales, is determined within *When?* column. Motivation aspect, which provides answer to the question *Why?*, is manufacturing of the product in accordance with standards, that enables to sell the product within Russia and abroad.

Fulfilling the model by artefacts (Table 1) enables to determine current enterprise position, the level of process automation at production stages, IT application for interaction with clients and other stakeholders of the company specifically. These components reveal how information technologies support business processes and lead to the achievement of business strategies.

Final level of the model, representing functioning enterprise, depicts actual data, which include exact information about manufacturing products to customers. Processes are reflected in the supply chain network, functioning through the whole enterprise. It allows to trace movement of a product from components and resources order to shipment of produced goods to a customer. For aspects *Who?* and *When?* processes participants and scheduled lead time are determined. Achieving business strategies is considered as motivation for production.

AS-IS Zachman Model determines that the number of implemented ERP modules is significantly smaller that it is supposed to be to provide a support of business strategies by IT. One of the main incompatibilities between the models is that Galaktika ERP does not currently include modules for manufacturing planning,

**Table 1.** Zachman model AS-IS

| | What? | How? | Where? | Who? | When? | Why? |
|---|---|---|---|---|---|---|
| Planner | Administration objects of enterprise: 1. Business system 2. Product 3. Customer 4. Production cycle 5. Resource 6. Technology 7. Staff 8. Finance | Business processes of CJSC N: 1. The Process of purchasing raw materials 2. The process of plywood production 3. The process of plywood sale 4. The process of recycling | Region K | Processes' participants | Business plan | Strategic enterprise objectives: 1. Profit increase 2. Continuous improvement of product quality, analysis of customer expectations and requirements, compliance with them 3. Reduction in different types of losses and efficient use of enterprise resources |
| Owner | Conceptual data model | Tree of enterprise management business processes | Information exchange scheme | Workflow model (within enterprise management) | Time period within Plan with integration parameters | Business plan |
| Designer | Information model of enterprise management | Application architecture- Galaktika ERP • Administration ERP module | Information workspace model (Galaktika ERP modules) | Business processes' participants and their roles | Time period within structured business processes | Rules for limitation of business process implementation |
| Builder | Purchasing row materials and sales plan | Drafting of documents for purchasing row materials and sales • Manufacturing logistics management ERP module • Target warehouse management ERP module • 1C (Russian enterprise level automation platform) | Regulations and purchasing row materials and sales documents • Maintenance and repair of equipment ERP module | Participants of purchasing row materials and sales processes • Staff management ERP module | Time period within purchasing row materials and sales plan • Staff management ERP module | Business logic implementation |
| Developer | Production plan • Quality management ERP Module | Technological processes of production • Manufacturing logistics management ERP module • 1C (Russian enterprise level automation platform) | Production workshops • Maintenance and repair of equipment ERP module | Participants of production and quality control processes • Staff management ERP module | Time period within production plan (shifts) • Staff management ERP module | Product manufacturing |
| Functioning enterprise | Actual data on manufactured products | Functioning processes | Network of supply chain | Participants of functioning processes | Actual data, partly obtained from the functioning chain | Achieved business strategies |

settlements for vendors and recipients and sales management. The lack of the modules deprives planning of long-term production and customer management. Currently, the system does not take into account material values accounting, received by customers, formation of a plan, representing order forecast. There is a function of setting price-list with discounts, however, it is weakly connected to a certain customer.

Besides, a finance component of Galaktika ERP is not implemented, while finance, accounting and tax accounting is managed through 1C (Russian enterprise level automation platform) and Data Import-Export ERP Module. The process is not fully-automated, it prevents creation of finance long-term planning in one integrated system and as a result the aspect does not support strategic objective of profit increase. Semi-automated system, modules of which do not fulfill every cell of the Model for Builder and Developer perspectives, does not support each of the strategic objectives, related to Planner Perspective, that create conditions for IT-business misalignment.

## 3.3   Zachman Model: "TO BE" State

In order to improve the current role of IT and achieve the alignment between IT and business, enterprise must have structured methods of IT management for business plan implementation (Table 2).

The model presented above outlines how strategic objectives can be supported by information technologies, currently used by the enterprise. Changes from AS-IS model are in bold. It is clear that business strategies are achieved by certain modules of Galaktika ERP system. Each of the modules, characterized for every cell, satisfy the following objectives, identified by CJSC N:

(1)  continuous improvement of product quality, analysis of customer expectations and requirements, compliance with them;
(2)  reduction in different types of losses and efficient use of enterprise resources.

The main goal of CJSC N, implying profit increase, will be achieved in case of execution of two other strategic objectives. In this way, improvement of product quality, analysis of customer expectations and requirements, compliance with them is supported by Order management ERP Module, Vendors and recipients settlements ERP Module, Manufacturing planning ERP Module, Sales management ERP Module, Target warehouse management ERP Module, Automated finance management ERP Module, Automated accounting and tax accounting ERF Module, Warehouse man-agement ERP Module, Contract management ERP Module, Staff management ERP Module. The second objective, expressed as the reduction in different types of losses and efficient use of enterprise resources, can be achieved through Supply management ERP Module; Product specification ERP Module; Quality management ERP Module; Product specification ERP Module; Logistical support management ERP Module; Maintenance and repair of equipment ERP Module. Galaktika ERP provides improvement and optimization of enterprise's business processes.

Economic factors of proposed TO-BE model indicate changes of enterprise pro-duction profit. Currently CJSC N integrates Galaktika ERP and 1C, paying for maintenance of both systems. Service package of 1C, used by the enterprise, includes remote work of specialists and updates of the platform. Average annual cost of the

**Table 2.** Zachman model TO-BE

| | What? | How? | Where? | Who? | When? | Why? |
|---|---|---|---|---|---|---|
| Planner | Administration objects of enterprise: 1. Business system 2. Product 3. Customer 4. Production cycle 5. Resource 6. Technology 7. Staff 8. Finance | Business processes of CJSC N: 1. The Process of purchasing raw materials 2. The process of plywood production 3. The process of plywood sale 4. The process of recycling | Region K | Process participants | Business plan | Strategic enterprise objectives: 1. Profit increase 2. Continuous improvement of product quality, analysis of customer expectations and requirements, compliance with them 3. Reduction in different types of losses and efficient use of enterprise resources |
| Owner | Conceptual data model | Tree of enterprise management business processes | Information exchange scheme | Workflow model (within enterprise management) | Time period within Plan with integration parameters | Business plan |
| Designer | Information model of enterprise management | Application architecture- Galaktika ERP • Administration ERP module | Information workspace model (Galaktika ERP modules) | Business processes' participants and their roles | Time period within structured business processes | Rules for limitation of business process implementation |
| Builder | Purchasing row materials and sales plan • **Order management ERP module** | Drafting of documents for purchasing row materials and sales • Manufacturing logistics management ERP module • **Vendors and recipients settlements ERP module** • **Sales management ERP module** • **Supply management ERP module** • Target warehouse management ERP module • **Toll ERP module** • **Automated finance management ERP module** • **Automated accounting and tax accounting ERF module** | Regulations and purchasing row materials and sales documents • Maintenance and repair of equipment ERP module • **Warehouse management ERP module** | Participants of purchasing row materials and sales processes • **Contract management ERP module** • Staff management ERP module | Time period within purchasing row materials and sales plan • **Order management ERP module** • **Contract management ERP module** • Staff management ERP module | Business logic implementation |
| Developer | Production plan • **Product specification ERP Module** • Quality management ERP module | Technological processes of production • **Product specification ERP module** | Production workshops • Maintenance and repair of equipment ERP module | Participants of production and quality control processes | Time period within production plan (shifts) • **Manufacturing planning ERP module** | Product manufacturing |

*(continued)*

**Table 2.** (*continued*)

|  | What? | How? | Where? | Who? | When? | Why? |
|---|---|---|---|---|---|---|
|  |  | • **Logistical support management ERP module** <br> • **Automated finance management ERP module** <br> • **Automated accounting and tax accounting ERF module** | • **Warehouse management ERP module** | • **Staff** management ERP module | • **Logistical support management ERP module** <br> • Staff management ERP module |  |
| Functioning enterprise | Actual data on manufactured product | Functioning processes | Network of supply chain | Participants of functioning processes | Actual data, obtained from the functioning chain | Achieved business strategies |

service for medium-size enterprise is $40'000, while the coast of annual license is $2'000 [14]. Financial characteristic of Galaktika ERP is equal, being $40'000–$2'000 annual costs of service package and license [5].

Implementation of additional Galaktika ERP modules, which are included in the standard version, will require double service package for the first year for training users of the system and reconfiguration of Galaktika for enterprise supply chain processes.

Functional integration in a single ERP system, inclusion of additional modules prevents transactional costs. Use of Galaktika provides automation of financial management, accounting and tax accounting, that is crucially important in condition of doing business in international finance market with different currencies and terms. Galaktika ERP is certified by ISO (international quality standard ISO-9001:2008), [5] that enables CJSC N function internationally. Quality management and product specification modules help to adapt to customers in specific regions. It will provide compliance with customer expectations and requirements.

According to the estimation, in this way the implementation of addition modules, including Finance and Accounting modules instead of 1C, enables to increase the volume of sold products by 1.8 and around 14% decrease of working capital, 35% increase of service and sale quality improvement. Product quality modules will provide decrease of production defect by 20–25%. As a result, changes in IT strategy will lead to reduction of different types of losses and efficient use of enterprise resources. Profit increase by 20% is supposed to be one year after modification of current ERP system. As a result, changes in IT strategy will lead to reduction of different types of losses and efficient use of enterprise resources.

## 4 Conclusion

The paper focuses on the issue of alignment between IT and business on the case of woodworking enterprise. Adhering to the practice of EA framework use for IT-business alignment it is indicated that Zachman model is a valuable modeling tool for Enterprise Architecture construction, integrating and aligning business goals and IT infrastructure.

Descriptive representation of Zachman model enables to perform current position of the enterprise with relationships between its stakeholders. AS-IS model determines IT-business misalignment, proved by the lack of business strategies support by IT. TO-BE model outlines how strategic objectives can be supported by information technologies, currently used by the enterprise. Efficiency assessment of the changes is evaluated economically, that proves that implementation of TO-BE model will cause the improvement of economic performance. Changes in IT strategy will lead to reduction of different types of losses and efficient use of enterprise resources, presented as business strategies.

The future of the topic follows such branches as:

- formalization of the model to assess IT-business alignment, based on the architecture evaluation;
- creation of formal criteria for IT-business alignment and application in practice to increase production efficiency of the enterprise, while considering organizational size and structure, chosen business and IT strategies;
- a more formal analysis of economic impact of IT-business alignment procedures realization, for example, by means of Activity-Based Costing mechanism.

# References

1. Asefzadeh, S., Mamikhani, J., Navvabi, E.: Determination of gap in accreditation standards establishment process using Zachman framework at a health-educational hospital. In: Biotechnology and Health Sciences (2016). ISSN 2383-028x
2. Barat, S., Kulkarni, V., Clark, T., Barn, B.: Enterprise modeling as a decision making aid: a systematic mapping study. In: Horkoff, J., Jeusfeld, M., Persson, A. (eds.) The Practice of Enterprise Modeling. LNBIP, vol. 267, pp. 289–298. Springer, Cham (2016). https://doi.org/10.1007/978-3-319-48393-1_20
3. Bondara, S., Hsub, J.C., Pfougaa, A., Stjepandića, J.: Agile digital transformation of system-of-systems architecture models using Zachman framework. J. Ind. Inf. Integr. **7**, 33–43 (2017). https://doi.org/10.1016/j.jii.2017.03.001
4. Chorafas, D.N.: Enterprise Architecture and New Generation Information Systems. CRC Press, Boca Raton (2016)
5. Galaktika ERP. https://www.galaktika.ru/erp/
6. Hinkelmanna, K., Gerber, A., Karagiannis, D., Thoenssen, B., van der Merwe, A., Woitsch, R.: A new paradigm for the continuous alignment of business and IT: combining enterprise architecture modelling and enterprise ontology. Comput. Ind. **79**, 77–86 (2016). https://doi.org/10.1016/j.compind.2015.07.009
7. Jonkers, H., et al.: A language for enterprise modelling. In: Lankhorst, M. (ed.) Enterprise Architecture at Work. TEES, pp. 73–121. Springer, Heidelberg (2017). https://doi.org/10.1007/978-3-662-53933-0_5
8. Lapalme, J., Gerber, A., Ven der Merwe, A., Zachman, J., De Vries, M., Hinkelmann, K.: Exploring the future of enterprise architecture: a Zachman perspective. Comput. Ind. **79**, 103–113 (2016). https://doi.org/10.1016/j.compind.2015.06.010
9. Luftman, J., Lyytinen, K., Ben Zvi, T.: Enhancing the measurement of information technology (IT) business alignment and its influence on company performance. J. Inf. Technol. **32**(1), 26–46 (2017)

10. This entry is known to the authors, but is omitted here for anonymization reasons. It will be re-added for the final submission of the paper
11. Niemi, E., Pekkola, S.: Using enterprise architecture artefacts in an organization. Enterprise Inf. Syst. **11**(3), 313–338 (2017). https://doi.org/10.1080/17517575.2015.1048831
12. Nogueira, J.M., Romero, D., Espadas, J., Molina, A.: Leveraging the Zachman framework implementation using action-research methodology - a case study: aligning the enterprise architecture and the business goals. Enterprise Inf. Syst. **7**(1), 100–132 (2013). https://doi.org/10.1080/17517575.2012.678387
13. Pereira, C.M., Sousa, P.: A method to define an Enterprise Architecture using the Zachman Framework. In: Proceedings of the 2004 ACM Symposium on Applied Computing, SAC 2004, pp. 1366–1371 (2004). https://doi.org/10.1145/967900.968175
14. Price list of 1C Enterprise. www.1c.ru
15. Ross, J.W., Weill, P., Robertson, D.C.: Enterprise Architecture as Strategy: Creating a Foundation for Business Execution. Harvard Business Review Press, Boston (2006)
16. Saat, J., Franke, U., Lagerstrom, R., Ekstedt, M.: Enterprise architecture meta models for IT/business alignment situations. In: 14th IEEE International Conference on Enterprise Distributed Object Computing (EDOC) (2010). https://doi.org/10.1109/edoc.2010.17
17. Sessions, R.: Comparison of the Top Four Enterprise Architecture Methodologies. ObjectWatch, Inc. (2007)
18. Simon, D., Fischbach, K., Schoder, D.: Enterprise architecture management and its role in corporate strategic management. Inf. Syst. e-Bus. Manag. **12**(1), 5–42 (2014)
19. Urbaczewski, L., Mrdalj, S.: A comparison of enterprise architecture framework. Issues Inf. Syst. **VII**(2), 18–23 (2006)
20. Zachman, J.: The Zachman framework for enterprise architecture. Zachman Framework Associates (2006)
21. Zachman, J.P.: The Zachman Framework™ Evolution (2009)

# The Simplified Enterprise Architecture Management Methodology for Teaching Purposes

Dmitry Kudryavtsev[1(✉)], Evgeny Zaramenskikh[2],
and Maxim Arzumanyan[1]

[1] Graduate School of Management St. Petersburg University,
Volkhovskiy Per., 3, 199004 St. Petersburg, Russia
d.v.kudryavtsev@gsom.pu.ru,
maxim.arzumanyan@gmail.com
[2] Financial University Under the Government of the Russian Federation,
Leningradsky Prospect, 49, 125993 Moscow, Russia
zep2050@yandex.ru

**Abstract.** Enterprise architecture allows one to describe, analyze and design a company from the point of view of its structure, functioning and goals. Both business and IT components of an organization are considered in it. Enterprise architecture management methods and technologies help companies to implement their digital strategy, establish enterprise coherence and coordinate business transformation. Teaching enterprise architecture in universities is a difficult task because of the interdisciplinary nature of the subject, its generalized character and close connection with practical experience. In addition, modern enterprise architecture management methodologies are difficult for students and contain many details that are relevant to specific situations. Although there are several methodologies and approaches for enterprise architecture teaching, they do not reflect a recent change in application scenarios for enterprise architecture – shift from business-IT alignment to enterprise coherence and business transformation coordination. The work offers a simplified methodology of enterprise architecture management, which on the one hand will be available for students' comprehension, and, on the other hand, will allow students to understand and apply in practice the main methods and technologies of enterprise architecture. Requirements for the methodology are also collected and presented in the paper. The proposed methodology is used in several universities and demonstration of its application within the business school of one university is provided.

**Keywords:** Enterprise architecture · Enterprise modeling · Teaching
Enterprise transformation

## 1 Introduction

Enterprise architecture is a relatively new discipline. The emergence of the discipline is often associated with the first publications of Zachman in 1987 [1], but only relatively recently did enterprise architecture receive large-scale application and discussion in

© Springer Nature Switzerland AG 2018
R. Pergl et al. (Eds.): EOMAS 2018, LNBIP 332, pp. 76–90, 2018.
https://doi.org/10.1007/978-3-030-00787-4_6

scientific circles. This tool was originally used in complex IT projects to clarify business requirements and to design information systems and technical infrastructure. However, since the beginning of the 2000s, enterprise architecture has been increasingly used to support organizational transformations and allows managers to link various development initiatives, translate strategy into actions and ensure the consistency of different elements of an enterprise. Methods and technologies of enterprise architecture (EA) allow one to work with knowledge about the organization of a company and are used for purposes of business transformation, increasing operational efficiency, alignment of business and IT at the strategic level, etc. [2–4]. According to TOGAF, enterprise architecture (EA) is the fundamental organization of an enterprise and the guiding principles of its design and development [5]. The design and transformation of EA is also examined within enterprise engineering/business engineering [6, 7].

The relevance and demand for EA are increasing throughout the world, which is confirmed by the increase in the number of publications, conferences and projects, the emergence of international standards and the activity of the world's leading consulting companies (IBM Global Business Services, Cap Gemini, Accenture, etc.). In many countries, the necessity of using EA is recognized at the level of government directives and is fixed at the level of standards. EA is often perceived as a comprehensive mean of business and IT alignment. Now EA has increasingly become a tool for business transformation [8, 9].

Currently, there are no standards or universally recognized teaching materials in the EA field. Apart from being dynamic, new and interdisciplinary, EA is a discipline that focuses on practice, which creates additional restrictions for its mastery in the traditional university environment. According to Gartner's 2013 survey, EA has become the profession with the lowest level of specialist training [10]. Although several papers deal with an issue of enterprise architecture teaching, they were written about ten years ago (see related work section). Since then EA discipline has been changed [2, 3]. The suggested enterprise architecture management (EAM) methodology and our teaching approach are especially associated with the changes in application scenarios for EA – shift from business-IT alignment to enterprise coherence and enterprise transformation [8, 9, 11]. The idea of "integration of the established practices of modeling with local practices of creating and using model-like artifacts of relevance for the overall organization" [12] is also supported by the suggested methodology.

This article summarizes the experience of the academic community, discussed for several years on the site of the inter-university academic center of competence on enterprise architecture EA Lab[1]. In particular, it offers a simplified methodology of EA management, which on the one hand will be available for students' comprehension, and, on the other hand, will allow students to understand and apply in practice the main methods and technologies of EA. In addition to the methodology a corresponding teaching approach is demonstrated within one case study.

---

[1] URL: http://ealab.org/ in Russian and presentation in English https://www.slideshare.net/dmitryku/interuniversity-academic-center-of-competence-on-enterprise-architecture-ea-lab.

## 2  Related Work

Within the paper both EA management methodology and teaching approach are covered, so these two topics are covered in related work.

### 2.1  EAM Methodologies

The idea of creating a simplified EA management methodology is borrowed from Belgian researchers, the authors of the CHOOSE methodology for small and medium businesses [13]. However, the CHOOSE methodology is primarily focused on the structure of the enterprise model (the composition of objects and their interrelations), and poorly elaborates created artifacts (views focused on certain stakeholders and their concerns). In addition, it does not describe the process of working with models – the process of transforming the enterprise on the basis of modeling. In addition, the structure of the CHOOSE enterprise model is focused on modeling business architecture and it still needs to be integrated with the languages of IT-architecture modeling.

Koning, Bos, and Brinkkemper from Utrecht [14] suggested a lightweight method for modeling enterprise architecture. The core concept from [14, p. 375] – "to concentrate on the bridge between enterprise functions and the IT support for these functions, and to stay at a high abstraction level" is also promoted in our approach and core artifacts are similar: the description of enterprise context together with its business partners and the exchange of products and services, top-level breakdown of the main functions of an enterprise, and a simple description of IT support for business functions. But Utrecht's method focus on modeling, transformation of enterprise using EA models is not covered; we provide a stronger link between enterprise architecture with strategic management (business model canvas, strategy map etc.); minor differences in artifacts (e.g. enterprise function diagram additionally includes flows in [14]).

MEMO, Multi-perspective Enterprise Modelling, was developed by Ulrich Frank [15]. MEMO includes a number of domain-specific modeling languages (DSML) to describe different parts of an enterprise. In order to organize the diagrams created with these various languages, Frank proposed a framework of three so-called perspectives - strategy, organization and information system - each of which is structured by four aspects: process, structure, resources and goals. Currently the core of language architecture includes a language for modeling organizational goal systems, GoalML [16]; a language for modeling organizations, both organizational structures and business processes, OrgML; a language for representing strategic aspects such as value chains, SML; and a language for modeling IT resources with various levels of detail, ITML. Additional languages focus on modeling of resources, the design of performance indicator systems, decision processes, etc. Social, managerial and economic aspects of the firm are well-represented in MEMO – this looks promising since our research is driven by the need for the methodology, which will support an enterprise transformation scenario. But, similar to other mature methodologies, MEMO can be used for solving different problems and provides a lot of modeling elements (including specialization and attributes for basic modeling objects/types), but only a subset should be selected for teaching purposes. MEMO also does not recommend a modeling method, but rather "supports method engineering. For this purpose, a metamodel of modeling methods can be instantiated into particular methods or projects respectively" [15, p. 950]. So in order to tailor MEMO for our purposes (see requirements below) it is necessary to instantiate it into the specific teaching method.

The Business Engineering group developed a framework for business architecture management. Although this framework is still in the process of evolution, it is partially reflected in [17]. This framework is entitled as "ORG-Master framework" in [17] and as "Architectural Business Engineering (ABE) framework" in industrial projects afterwards. This framework includes enterprise ontology as a metamodel, business architecture development method, and is supported by the corresponding modeling tool (ORG-Master). The high-level business architecture modeling method was mostly taken from this methodology, but detailed guidelines, artifacts and the metamodel were simplified for teaching purposes. For example, the ABE framework has a long list of concepts for modeling activities/operations: functional systems, business processes, functions, value chain, capability, services. Since it is hard for a student to conceive differences between all these concepts, this list for modeling activities/operations was reduced for teaching purposes. Also, the ABE framework provides reference models and patterns in addition to a metamodel, this reference content was not included in the suggested methodology, but is used in an adhoc manner as supporting material.

Archimate [4, 18] – is language only, and includes too many modeling objects and relationships; but it is supported by many tools, including Archi, a free piece of software.

TOGAF [5] – can be considered as "meta-methodology", and must be customized for the specific project; it is applicable for many scenarios, but includes a lot of redundant elements for a student.

## 2.2 EA Teaching Approaches

Some papers focus on teaching approaches within EA course. The team of Wegmann of the École Polytechnique Fédérale de Lausanne described their EA course and teaching approach [19], which is based on their enterprise architecture method, called "Systemic Enterprise Architecture Methodology" (SEAM) [20]. Authors present a course that introduces EA and SOA to undergraduate computer science students. Although many teaching approaches are similar to what we've done (problem-based learning and usage of a case study for students' projects, role-playing etc.), this course seems to be more IT-focused (business-IT alignment scenario): "The students first play the role of a management team of a company – the company of interest - (first 4 weeks) and then the IT development team (remaining 10 weeks)" [19]. EA teaching approach in [21] provides an interesting integration with industry via projects with partners, but it is also based on authors' existing EA methodology, which doesn't satisfy all the requirements provided below.

# 3   Research Methodology and Structure of Work

This paper fits the paradigm of design science research, in accordance with which the researcher solves relevant problems by creating innovative artefacts suitable for reuse and contributing to scientific knowledge [22]. Design science research should be based on four basic principles: generalization, originality, validity and utility [22]. In accordance with [23], design science research includes 6 steps, which are presented in the paper:

1. Identification and justification of the problem (relevance): implemented in the introduction;
2. Identification of goals, requirements and limitations – see Sect. 5;
3. Design and development of the artefact – EA management methodology for teaching purposes – see. Section 6;
4. Demonstration of the use (approbation) of the created artefact– see Sect. 7;
5. Evaluation of the created artefact in terms of its effectiveness, efficiency, etc., although qualitative evaluations of the result are reflected in feedback from the audience, more fundamental evaluation of the result is a subject for further studies;
6. Publication of obtained results is the subject of this article.

# 4   Basic Concepts in Enterprise Architecture

Some basic concepts need to be defined to further describe the simplified EA management methodology. The EA elements can be business processes and enterprise functions, used data, applied software, etc. Such elements of enterprise architecture are called objects. During the EA description such objects are reflected with help of different representations, views: in the form of linear or hierarchical lists (registers), matrices (compliance tables) or diagrams, intended for different stakeholders in accordance with their concerns and viewpoints. These representations are commonly called artefacts. Both artefacts and objects are EA elements. For example, business architecture can include a "Process" object and a "Processes Map" artefact based on the description of the actual business processes. IT architecture can also include an "Application" object and an "Application Landscape" artefact that reflects existing information systems, the interrelation of different components, and so on.

EA contains a large number of objects and artefacts, and they are commonly grouped. This is done by using layers and aspects, the selection and description of which are presented below for a simplified EA management methodology.

# 5   Requirements for Simplified Enterprise Architecture Management Methodology

Requirements for the methodology were identified and taken into account during its development. When using the methodology, these requirements allow an understanding of the goals that can be achieved with its help as well as accepted assumptions and existing limitations. These requirements are as follows:

1. Key application scenario – enterprise coherence and transformation

   – Using objects and artifacts that are needed in the "transforming business based on IT capabilities" scenario (balance of business and IT, strategy and tactics);
   – Business architecture design, not only description for IT requirements;

2. Multi-perspective nature and integrating role of EA

   – Illustration of the idea of multi-layer EA: the interrelation of business-related objects with IT-related objects of the company (enterprise as an economic, social and technical system);
   – Examining of a company from different aspects and answers to a range of system-wide questions: Why? What? Where? How? Who? When? [1, 24];
   – Illustration of integration via EA of various management disciplines, such as strategic management, organizational design, business processes management, marketing, information systems design, project management [25];

3. Clear role of modeling and technology support for EA management

   – A single enterprise model, which is formed through a system of views (artifacts) based on the commonly accepted modeling language; objects in the model are not duplicated and, appearing in one view (artifact), are used in others; it is possible to see relationships of any EA object with other ones in the tool.
   – Specification of created artifacts and transparency of their interrelation with the concerns of the stakeholders;

4. Problem-based and project-based learning support

   – Linking EA models (artifacts) to the stages of typical projects concerning transformation of the enterprise (possibility of using the project-based learning approach, the formation of competencies through practical activity);

5. Industry focus and reuse of existing EA and managerial methods, tools and standards

   – The methodology must be aligned with the existing industry standards, popular EA management methodologies and modeling languages (TOGAF [5], Archi-Mate [4, 18]), in order to be closer to workforce market demand;
   – The methodology must be based on the existing management tools [12], which are familiar to practitioners (e.g. business model canvas [26], strategy maps [27]);

6. Vendor-neutral nature

   – There must be many options for IT tool support of the methodology;

7. Easy customization and extension

   – Presence of the basic part (necessary minimum for familiarity with the discipline) and additional extensions for adaptation to specific educational programs – "Plugin Architecture".

8. Clear link to existing practices of managing enterprise transformations

- EA as a link between strategy and transformation projects – explicit description of how work packages (projects) eliminate gaps between "as is" and "to be" models.

## 6  Methodology of Enterprise Architecture Management for Teaching Purposes

### 6.1  Enterprise Layers, Aspects, and Objects

The following layers and aspects are proposed for EA structuring.

The elements of enterprise architecture can be grouped on the basis of the domain they describe. In this case, it is common to talk about enterprise architecture layers, each of which contains elements that belong to the same area. The following layers of enterprise architecture are distinguished:

- The business layer that describes the activity of the enterprise and its development.
- The information systems (IS) layer that describes applications, data, and their interrelation.
- The technology layer that describes the hardware tools and the system software.

This composition of layers is consistent with TOGAF [5] and the core of Archi-Mate [4, 18] (Fig. 1).

Aspects:

- The "Purpose" aspect covers elements that describe the intentional perspective and grounds for decision-making in the organization. Goals, values, drivers, etc. belong to this aspect.
- The "Structure (Actors)" aspect includes the objects that, within the framework of enterprise architecture, can perform various actions and the corresponding artifacts. Such elements can be employees of the organization, organizational units, the scheme of organizational structure, etc.
- The "Operations (Function)" aspect includes the objects that can be described as operations or behavior without being bound to a specific executor, as well as related artifacts. This aspect can include processes and a map of processes, etc.
- The "Object of Operations" aspect includes the objects that are used or created in the organization, as well as the corresponding artifacts. Products and services, resources, documents and data – all this and much more can be attributed to this aspect.

The aspects of the enterprise architecture can be called "cross-cutting". They go through all domains of the enterprise architecture. However, the Purpose aspect is traditionally discussed at the level of business architecture. Of course, goals, values, requirements and other objects are present in each architectural area. They are essentially derived from business objectives.

This composition of aspects is consistent with the structure of ArchiMate [4, 18], the CHOOSE methodology perspectives for small and medium businesses [16, 17], close to aspects in MEMO [19] and extends architecture "triangle" from [17] (Fig. 1).

The identified aspects go through all the EA layers. In this regard, the elements of the enterprise architecture can be conventionally divided into both aspects and layers. Accordingly, an object or an artifact of the enterprise architecture can belong, for example, to the layer of Information systems and the Structure (Actors) aspect.

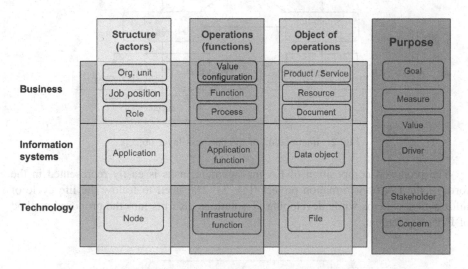

**Fig. 1.** Enterprise layers, aspects, and objects

In addition to the layers and aspects, the proposed methodology includes a meta-model, i.e., the modeled objects are defined (Figs. 1 and 2) and the interrelation between them is defined (Fig. 2).

The composition of objects and their interrelations are largely borrowed from the language of ArchiMate [4, 18], but in an abbreviated form, taking into account the requirements from Sect. 5.

## 6.2    Creation and Usage of EA Models

In real projects, the activities concerning creation and use of EA models will vary depending on the EA use scenarios (organizational development, digital transformation, etc.) and other restrictions (time, resources, maturity of an organization etc.). In teaching projects the scope of work and created models will also vary depending on the educational program (its level, specialization,…). However, the authors tried to identify the basic part, which will be suitable for the EA use scenario "business transformation based on the IT capabilities" and can be used in most educational programs, as well as extensions that will take into account a specific program.

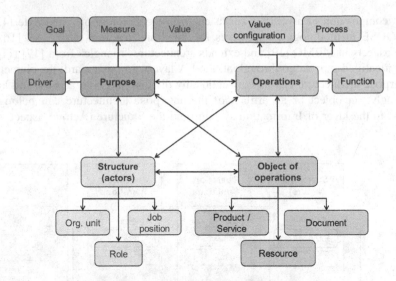

**Fig. 2.** Interrelation of the business layer objects

The proposed composition of EA management tasks is easily represented in the form of the EA transformation project (Fig. 3). The need to follow the life cycle of information systems while developing IT solutions also fits into the proposed method of EA management.

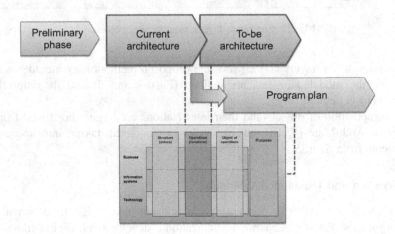

**Fig. 3.** Project scheme of EA management methodology for teaching purposes

### 6.2.1 Basic Part

The linking of artefacts (models) to the EA management tasks and to the corresponding stages of the EA transformation project allows the application of a project-based learning approach, where students, individually or in groups, take certain company and go through the stages presented in Table 1, create corresponding artifacts and defend their projects.

**Table 1.** EA management tasks and created artefacts, the basic part

| EA management tasks | Created artefacts |
|---|---|
| **1. Initial stage** | |
| Identification of stakeholders and their concerns | List of stakeholders |
| Identification of project motivation | Project goals and objectives |
| **2. Analysis of the existing enterprise architecture stage** | Current state models ("as is") |
| General view of the enterprise | Business model canvas "as is" |
| Identification of company goals, objectives and indicators for their measurement | Strategy map (or goal tree) Balanced scorecard |
| Identification of value proposition (VP) | Tree of products/services, value curve |
| Identification of the value configuration "as is" | Value creation model |
| Identification of the operations architecture "as is" | Function decomposition model or Processes landscape Business Process models (if necessary) |
| Organizational structure and responsibility matrix "as is" | Organization chart Responsibility matrix (or RACI-matrix) |
| IT architecture "as is" (existing information systems and technological infrastructure) | Model of application/IS usage Description of the application/IS landscape Infrastructure use model |
| General idea of EA "as is" | High-level (overview) EA model |
| **3. Design of the enterprise's target architecture stage** | Target state models ("to be") with visualization of changes |
| Development of target EA vision Development of target EA with detailing of representations by layers * Several alternative scenarios may be developed at this stage | Business model canvas "to be" High-level (overview) model "to be" Particular EA models, which will be affected by changes (composition of models as in the description of the current state), "to be" |
| **4. Implementation and transition stage** | |
| Planning of the transition between the EA states (current, target, transitional) | Transition planning model (linking EA changes/gaps with work packages) |
| Formation of development projects portfolio | Transformation and development program cards (proposed initiatives) |
| Planning for implementation and transition (see project management) | Schedule of transformation projects (for example, in MS Project) |
| **5. Evaluation of architecture implementation** | |

The proposed structure and composition of management tasks are consistent with the method of EA development in TOGAF methodology [5] and reuse a lot from [17] for business architecture part (this part includes more details). The authors consider the possibility of changing the composition of the tasks in the analysis of the current state of EA, the design of the target state and the construction of the transition between states depending on the need for detail.

#### 6.2.2    Extensions

Depending on the educational program and its level, the basic part can be supplemented by the following components:

- Elaboration of connection with the strategy: SWOT analysis to identify the drivers of transformations;
- Analysis of problems and their causes to identify the drivers of transformations;
- Knowledge tools (mind maps, conceptual maps, argument maps, etc.) to collect and systematize information in the course of project execution, to validate proposed solutions, etc.
- Detailed modeling of business processes for the implementation of initiatives/projects proposed as a result of the EA project;
- Identification of business requirements, stakeholder requirements, and solution requirements;
- IS analysis and design proposed for implementation of EA initiatives/projects;
- Data-oriented analysis (conceptual model can be created at business layer, data/information model – at IS layer etc.);
- Use of services as EA elements in case students study the service-oriented approach.

## 7    Demonstration and Approbation of the Proposed Methodology

### 7.1    Application Contexts for the Methodology

The proposed simplified EA management methodology has been tested and used by the authors while carrying out courses in leading universities of the Russian Federation:

- in Graduate School of Management of St. Petersburg University in the "Enterprise Architecture" course for undergraduate students since 2015;
- in the Peter the Great St. Petersburg Polytechnic University as a part of the course "Technologies of Business Engineering" for Masters students since 2015;
- in Financial University under the Government of the Russian Federation within "Enterprise Architecture" course for undergraduate students since 2016;
- in Higher School of Business Informatics of The National Research University Higher School of Economics for undergraduate students since 2015;
- In the Bonch-Bruevich Saint-Petersburg State University of Telecommunications within the framework of the "Enterprise Architecture" course for undergraduate students since 2015.

The students use the proposed simplified EA management methodology to do their term problem-oriented project. They choose an enterprise, and, perform the works presented in Sect. 6.2, find bottlenecks or unrealised opportunities in the current state of the enterprise, offer and validate their decision, as well as the technology of its implementation with the help of EA methods and tools.

## 7.2   Graduate School of Management Case Study

The course "Enterprise Architecture" has been provided in the Graduate School of Management (GSOM) of St. Petersburg University for bachelor-level students since 2015. The course duration is 45 h. The course is evolving from year to year. The last course version (Spring semester 2018) consisted of two major parts: the first was about solving managerial problems with implicit fragments of EA methodology ("without EA methods") and the second was about EA as a discipline & tool to solve the revealed problems.

Students played the roles of different specialists within one company. As we were working with business students, we suggested something quite familiar to them. Students were divided into groups of 4 persons with 4 "C-level" roles:

- Business development manager (responsible for business strategy),
- Product manager (responsible for creating new products & services),
- Operations manager (responsible for operations efficiency & effectiveness),
- IT manager (responsible for IT).

In such groups they were working on the same case. We prepared 4 challenge descriptions targeting each role. The sequence was: strategy, products, operations, IT. For each challenge we recommended models (artefacts) from the proposed EA management methodology (see Table 1), without telling students about the EA management methodology. These recommendations were in line with a selection approach suggested in [24], organized a "way of thinking" and were used to describe the "as-is" state, performing analysis and creating a "to-be" state. For example, for the strategy challenge we suggested thinking using business model canvas [26] and strategy maps [27].

The work on each assignment included the following steps:

- Group receives the challenge description,
- We present models, which can be used by students in order to describe the as-is & to-be state,
- Students work in groups, creating models in Power Point,
- Groups present their results. Presentation is held by a person whose role is associated with this challenge (4 roles, 4 challenges, 4 presentations, 4 persons).

Our aim was to illustrate to students through their experience and make them feel, how inconsistent and non-interoperable managers' decisions could be, even though they are made one by one in a small team [25]. And we succeeded. We gave them a task to gather their presentations into one and prepared a questionnaire about consistency. They found out that when planning new products, they forgot about strategy, when planning IT – about operations, when operations – about IT etc. That was the end of the first part.

The second part was about how to solve this problem with EA practice. Only at this point did we introduce the EAM methodology, described in this paper, to the students, including the metamodel concept, artefacts, tools for EA modelling, common repository, etc. They continued working in the same groups. At this point, we asked them to create a coherent model in a software tool (Archi) and to update a presentation.

At the end of the course we collected qualitative feedback. In general it was positive.

What students like in the course:

- Enterprise coherence and interrelations – "the main learning outcome for me is that it is important to always remember about the interconnectedness of different departments, fields etc. within the organization"; "I learned how activities within each company department are connected with activities in other departments → Learning that everything has an impact and we should always take a look in a more holistic way before changing something".
- Integrated group project – "working on our projects, so that we can experience theory also in practice"; "one project across the whole course – great"; "the group project every week was good at practicing acquired info from lectures"
- Simple modeling software with an integrated "repository" – "Understanding of EA modeling in Archi was great"

Areas for improvement (both from students' feedback and our own reflections):

- Avoidance of new EA-based silos (e.g. strategy, business operations, processes, functions etc.), additional structuring along the strategic themes seems to be a solution (e.g. from introduction of some service for customer to corresponding transformation of business operations and IT architecture);
- assessment of feasibility and economic efficiency of the proposed solutions – "the professors could be more critical in terms of solutions proposed by the teams – maybe some proposed solutions weren't financially viable or technically feasible";
- cooperation with industry partners in order to suggest topics and provide input data for students' projects;
- more then one example case is desired in order to demonstrate variations and avoid the same pattern in all students' work.

## 8  Conclusion

Enterprise architecture is a dynamically developing area in the design, management and transformation of modern companies as complex systems (business and IT). The methods and tools of enterprise architecture are used to analyze the existing state of the company and to design its future state, to present alternative scenarios for its development, as well as for system planning of company development projects.

We agree with [14] that "enterprise architecture modeling is a good means to express the essential functioning of an enterprise and it's IT support". We believe that EA can be an effective tool for coordinating enterprise transformations [9] and can help to move away from existing silos [25] in organizations and teaching curriculum. We also sure that enterprise modeling and EA should move from expert discipline to common practice [12].

In order to move from these beliefs to practice we offered a simplified methodology of EA management, created for teaching purposes. In particular, this material:

- Presents requirements for simplified enterprise architecture management methodology;
- Offers a structure of the created enterprise model (layers, aspects and objects of enterprise architecture are defined);
- Presents a generalized scheme of a project concerning development/transformation of the company using methods and tools of enterprise architecture, and describes the activity of creating and using models of enterprise architecture;
- Proposes artefacts (lists, matrices, diagrams) that emerge when creating and using enterprise architecture models;
- Identifies the basic part of the simplified methodology and the expansions which can be used for the formation of work programs of disciplines depending on the specialization and level of preparation.
- Presents application of the proposed methodology in the universities with a special focus on a case study, which describes teaching EA in the Graduate School of Management SpbU.

# References

1. Zachman, J.: A framework for information systems architecture. IBM Syst. J. **26**(3), 276–292 (1987)
2. Proper, H.A., Lankhorst, M.M.: Enterprise architecture-towards essential sensemaking. Enterp. Model. Inf. Syst. Arch. **9**(1), 5–21 (2014)
3. Lapalme, J., Gerber, A., Van der Merwe, A., Zachman, J., De Vries, M., Hinkelmann, K.: Exploring the future of enterprise architecture: a Zachman perspective. Comput. Ind. **79**, 103–113 (2016)
4. Lankhorst, M., et al.: Enterprise Architecture at Work, 4th edn. Springer, Heidelberg (2017). https://doi.org/10.1007/978-3-662-53933-0
5. TOGAF – The Open Group Architectural Framework (2011). http://www.opengroup.org/subjectareas/enterprise/togaf. Accessed 07 May 2016
6. Aier, S., Kurpjuweit, S., Saat, J., Winter, R.: Business Engineering Navigator-A "Business to IT" Approach to Enterprise Architecture Management (2009)
7. Dietz, J.L., et al.: The discipline of enterprise engineering. Int. J. Org. Des. Eng. **3**(1), 86–114 (2013)
8. Harmsen, F., Proper, H.A.E., Kok, N.: Informed governance of enterprise transformations. In: Proper, E., Harmsen, F., Dietz, J.L.G. (eds.) PRET 2009. LNBIP, vol. 28, pp. 155–180. Springer, Heidelberg (2009). https://doi.org/10.1007/978-3-642-01859-6_9
9. Proper, H., Winter, R., Aier, S., de Kinderen, S.: Architectural Coordination of Enterprise Transformation. Springer, Cham (2018). https://doi.org/10.1007/978-3-319-69584-6
10. Hunting and Harvesting in a Digital World: Insights From the 2013 Gartner CIO Agenda Report. Gartner research report (2013)
11. Wagter, R., Proper, H.A.E., Witte, D.: A practice-based framework for enterprise coherence. In: Proper, E., Gaaloul, K., Harmsen, F., Wrycza, S. (eds.) PRET 2012. LNBIP, vol. 120, pp. 77–95. Springer, Heidelberg (2012). https://doi.org/10.1007/978-3-642-31134-5_4
12. Sandkuhl, K., et al.: From expert discipline to common practice: a vision and research agenda for extending the reach of enterprise modeling. Bus. Inf. Syst. Eng. **60**(1), 69–80 (2018)

13. Bernaert, M., Poels, G., Snoeck, M., De Backer, M.: CHOOSE: towards a metamodel for enterprise architecture in small and medium-sized enterprises. Inf. Syst. Front. **18**(4), 781–818 (2016)

14. Koning, H., Bos, R., Brinkkemper, S.: A lightweight method for the modelling of enterprise architectures. In: Feuerlicht, G., Lamersdorf, W. (eds.) ICSOC 2008. LNCS, vol. 5472, pp. 375–387. Springer, Heidelberg (2009). https://doi.org/10.1007/978-3-642-01247-1_38

15. Frank, U.: Multi-perspective enterprise modeling: foundational concepts, prospects and future research challenges. Softw. Syst. Model. **13**(3), 941–962 (2014)

16. Bock, A., Frank, U.: MEMO GoalML: a context-enriched modeling language to support reflective organizational goal planning and decision processes. In: Comyn-Wattiau, I., Tanaka, K., Song, I.-Y., Yamamoto, S., Saeki, M. (eds.) ER 2016. LNCS, vol. 9974, pp. 515–529. Springer, Cham (2016). https://doi.org/10.1007/978-3-319-46397-1_40

17. Kudryavtsev, D., Grigoriev, L.: Ontology-based business architecture engineering technology. In: The 10th International Conference on Intelligent Software Methodologies, Tools and Techniques, pp. 233–252, 28–30 September 2011

18. Lankhorst, M.M., Proper, H.A., Jonkers, H.: The anatomy of the ArchiMate language. Int. J. Inf. Syst. Model. Des. **1**(1), 1–32 (2010)

19. Wegmann, A., Regev, G., de la Cruz, J.D., Lê, L.S., Rychkova, I.: Teaching enterprise architecture and service-oriented architecture in practice. In: 2nd Workshop on Trends in Enterprise Architecture Research (TEAR 2007). Via Nova Architectura, pp. 13–22 (2007)

20. Wegmann, A.: On the Systemic Enterprise Architecture Methodology (SEAM). In: Proceedings of 5th International Conference on Enterprise Information Systems Angers, France, pp. 483–493 (2003)

21. Buckl, S., Matthes, F., Schulz, C., Schweda, C.M.: Teaching enterprise architecture management–a practical experience. Technical report, Chair for Informatics 19 (sebis), Technische Universität München, Munich, Germany (2009)

22. Österle, H., et al.: Memorandum on design-oriented information systems research. Eur. J. Inf. Syst. **20**(1), 7–10 (2011)

23. Peffers, K., Tuunanen, T., Rothenberger, M.A., Chatterjee, S.: A design science research methodology for information systems research. J. Manag. Inf. Syst. **24**(3), 45–77 (2007)

24. Kudryavtsev, D., Gavrilova, T.: From anarchy to system: a novel classification of visual knowledge codification techniques. Knowl. Process Manag. **24**(1), 3–13 (2017)

25. Nisula, K., Pekkola, S.: How to move away from the silos of business management education? J. Educ. Bus. **93**(3), 97–111 (2018)

26. Osterwalder, A., Pigneur, Y.: Business Model Generation: A Handbook for Visionaries, Game Changers, and Challengers. Wiley, Hoboken (2010)

27. Kaplan, R.S., Norton, D.P.: Strategy Maps: Converting Intangible Assets into Tangible Outcomes. Harvard Business Press, Boston (2004)

# Toward Development Tools for Augmented Reality Applications – A Practitioner Perspective

Ethan Hadar[1,2]([✉])

[1] Accenture Labs, 2 Ha-Menofim Street, Herzelia, Israel
Ethan.hadar@accenture.com
[2] Zefat Academic College, Jerusalem St 11, Zefat, Israel

**Abstract.** Augmented Reality (AR) commoditized development kits by Apple and Google, software products from IBM and PTC, and eyewear from Microsoft, Epson and ODG are driving a new wave of AR-based business use cases. Yet, today's development tools for desktop or mobile applications do not natively contain aspects of natural interactions in such immersive environments. There is a gap between the need to understand and capture AR-related functional and non-functional requirements, and the state of modeling, testing, and simulation tools that AR developers have at their disposal. Specifically, how does one elicit and specify AR requirements, evaluate users' experience, simulate and validate business usefulness. In addition, AR developers should assure that interactions with digital overlay are safe for people, and refrain from violating information security and privacy requirements. The paper discusses concerns for the creation of development tools for AR-based application, driven by a Visual Operation Guidance use case, and analyzed according to AR development steps of Object Recognition, Contextual Enrichment and Guidance. Exemplifying non-functional aspects, the paper presents new Safety, Privacy and Information Security concerns, triggered by investigating the nature of AR applications. It is the goal of this paper to inspire research by the academia to formally analyze, design and propose mapping and capturing these concerns in usable tools, that fit developers' cognitive abilities, in order to expedite the creation of AR-based business processes and solutions.

**Keywords:** Augmented Reality · Business process innovation
Modeling tools · Security · Privacy · Safety

## 1 Introduction

Although not new, Augmented Reality (AR) utilization in enterprises has recently gained awareness for business use cases [6, 24] due to the commoditization of tracking technologies and development kits for AR by Apple's ARKit [3] and Google's ARCore [2]. Mobile AR tracking technologies [14, 30, 32] exists for a while, as well as novel AR smart glasses [8, 21, 31] and headsets [8] with embedded AR technology.

The emergence of AR started over forty years ago [28], yet the commoditization of development kits and wearable devices for practical AR business use cases emerged in

© Springer Nature Switzerland AG 2018
R. Pergl et al. (Eds.): EOMAS 2018, LNBIP 332, pp. 91–104, 2018.
https://doi.org/10.1007/978-3-030-00787-4_7

the recent decade. Initial proof-of-concepts for employing AR-based business use cases showed 15% to 33% savings in operational efficiency in the areas of manufacturing and logistics, and up to a staggering ratio of 1 over 20 return-on-investment in services [11, 12]. Although not widely investigated and proven over time, the business community predicts AR-based use cases will transform business processes due to the ubiquitous nature of interaction with the digital content overlay [11, 23].

AR technologies facilitate interactions with users involving enhanced 3D vision, spatial hearing, hands and arms gestures and vocal commands [5, 15], as well as controlling information flow related to Internet of Things (IoT) devices and controlling the physical surrounding environment [10, 19, 27]. AR user experience augments users' eyesight, and consequently challenges the ability of developers to understand the user's immersive experience [26]. Developers are required to create generic AR software solutions that abstract these cognitive interactions as well as encapsulate hardware complexity, such as the camera field-of-view and wearables' ergonomics. However, common methods and tools for developing desktop or mobile applications to date, do not formally and easily support aspects of natural interactions in immersive environments. Some of the eyewear hardware vendors do provide partial development studio designated for creating AR solutions on top of their own specific hardware configuration. Yet, there is still a gap between the need for understanding and capturing AR related requirements, and the state of modeling, testing, and simulation tools that AR developers have at their disposal.

Although business process owners reimagine existing processes and invent new ones with the support of immersive AR technologies, major challenges for scalable implementation of AR-based use cases remain. Some of these AR challenges are:

- Eliciting and capturing users' AR functional requirements.
- Evaluating users' AR experience in a digital and physical immersive setting.
- Simplifying the creation of AR content for AR-based business processes.
- Simulating and validating usefulness of AR-based business processes.
- Assuring interactions with digital overlay are safe for people.
- Ensuring a secure transaction of augmented information.
- Maintaining users' privacy while interacting with an AR system.

This paper discusses the functional and non-functional concerns that should affect the creation of generic development tools for AR-based application. Functional concerns are driven by the exemplary Visual Operation Guidance [11, 18] use case, and abstracted steps for AR development of Object Recognition, Contextual Enrichment and Guidance. Addressing non-functional aspects, this paper presents new Safety, Privacy and Information Security concerns triggered by investigating the nature of AR applications.

It is the goal of this paper to inspire research by the academia to formally analyze, design and propose mapping and capturing these concerns in usable tools, that fit developers' cognitive abilities, in order to expedite the creation of AR-based business process and solutions.

## 2 Background

Development methods for Augmented Reality (AR) are targeted towards constructing machine-readable instructions for presenting AR digital overlay and communicating with devices by AR content authoring and interpretation tools [28]. Yet, these methods do not include streamlining business process steps such as the case of visual guidance or ensuring users' safety and information security while interacting with the digital overlay and wearables. Even more so, when implementing enterprise use cases, stakeholders are interested in measuring and improving the performance of existing core business processes. Samini et al. [25] showed how measuring the efficiency of such core processes can be defined based on task completion time, learnability [23], user comfort, difficulty to operate [16] and accuracy such as the number of operational errors or misalignment [29] or the number of times a user skipped a task. These measurements are mandatory in order to create the foundation of business efficiency that drives growth. Setting functional and non-functional requirements for reimagined business processes to drive competitive growth is imperative, yet it requires a way to model, measure and evaluate the needs based on understanding the AR technology as well as user behavior.

To date, AR devices' manufacturers and AR software vendors are mainly focused on technically producing stable and reliable tracking technology, as well as tools for authoring AR content. The next challenge AR solution providers face is around AR wide acceptance such as proven business value and return on investment, ease of use for workers or consumers, and overall compliance with regulations [9]. Human factor elements of interactive business processes and new modalities of physical-digital interfaces affect perceptions and cognitive modes of activation. Initial works defining metrics for objectively comparing AR users' interaction techniques has started [25], yet these are mostly focusing on business performance and IT quality metrics. In their survey of quality evaluation techniques used in AR studies, Dünser et al. [7] showed that only 10% of the AR papers published in ACM and IEEE conducted real users' evaluation, and Lee et al. [17] showed that there are 22 usability principles for user-centered design and evaluation of AR applications on smartphones. Even more so, Sage [25] showed that there should be quality metrics for mental and physical effort, dizziness, nausea, smoothness and effort, ease of control, task completion time, accuracy, success rate, ease of use, perceived accuracy and perceived speed, intuitiveness, and comfort [4].

Business processes reimagined with AR require users' acceptance [7] in order to expedite the creation of AR-based enterprise solutions. As mobile developers and users had to cope with new usability modalities, the migration from mobile to immersive AR solutions introduces adjustments to requirements definition formalization and new quality metrics evaluation. It is not only a matter of migrating business processes from web or mobile apps to AR based applications. It is a matter of redefining peoples' interaction in 3D space with perceived digital entities [15, 16, 27], wearable eyewear or mobile devices sensorial elements, while ensuring that value is added to the new or refactored business processes.

## 3  Visual Operation Guidance for Enterprise Use Cases

Forrester [1] describes AR as the virtual overlay of contextual digital information that a computer generates on a physical-world object and a user sees in the display of a mobile device or smart glasses, which its camera captures in real time. To function, AR requires real-world object tracking via a camera, and computer-generated content such as sound, 2D or 3D digital information or animation. An AR solution involves human interactions with such digital overlay anchored on real-world objects. From an enterprise worker's perspective, the worker is augmented with abilities to interact with the physical world, leading to higher performance, quality, accuracy, and eventually, increased individual value to the enterprise.

This powerful human interface bridges the gap between the digital and physical worlds, and profoundly change training and people's skill development, allowing people to quickly perform complex tasks without prolonged conventional instruction.

According to HBR [12], in the area of maintenance and repair, Lee Services achieved twenty Dollars return on every single Dollar spent on AR for their field workers in facility management. KPN Services saved 11% in overall costs of their service teams and 17% decrease in work-error rates with a higher repair quality. Xerox Services increased their first-time fix rates by 67% while the average time it took to resolve problems dropped by two hours. In addition, Xerox Services increased by 76% their technical resolutions done by customers without any on-site help which manifested in their customer satisfaction rates of 95%. HBR [12] also reviewed the area of warehouse and logistics. DHL Logistics warehousing applied AR to the pick-and-pack business service resulting in 25% time-efficiency increase. Intel Logistics warehousing pick-and-pack time-efficiency was increased by 29% with zero mistakes.

The application for maintenance and repair, logistics pick-and-pack, assembly and more, are all based on the concepts of Visual Operation Guidance (VOG) [11]. AR digital overlay is formed to step-by-step guide user actions, in a procedural operation or tutorial for training purposes. The AR instructions can be provided as peer-guidance (PG) mode for remote support and collaboration, in which the instruction's walk-through is done by a person in real-time. Pre-curating AR instructions ahead of time by an expert or technical writer, is defined as self-guidance (SG) mode since the instructions can be consumed according to the worker need and be used off-line.

The usage of on-the-fly or ahead-of-time curated AR content in PG or SG modes, enables workers and technicians to do more activities, reduces business process duration time and eliminates business steps. Additional business values are reduction in experts' travel costs to remote sites and managing a large distributed workforce. In addition, capturing tacit and tribal knowledge of the aging workforce can be achieved by onboarding the ad-hoc created AR content in PG mode to reusable knowledge in SG mode. Employing VOG, workers can be rapidly trained and guided on-the-job and follow the company best practices, while a visual compliance or certification report is generated.

### 3.1  Abstraction of Use Cases Commonality

Abstraction of the above use cases into common functionalities is needed due to their generic impact on process modeling, users' interactions and technology adaptability. These common functionalities should serve as the base for creating development tools for AR applications.

Selecting a specific domain of guidance while following VOG, one can examine these high-level steps in order to understand the implications on tools requirements. The requirements should drive business improved efficiency and performance, with minimal quality issues. The steps of VOG are:

- **3D Object Recognition (OR)** – visual and sensorial fusion of the environment should occur in order to construct the context of a situational physical scene, such as recognition of 3D object, machine parts, people, signs, etc. For example, in an industrial context, the recognition can be limited to the maintained machine or factory line. This OR step indicates which object categories and class types can be recognized by the Deep Learning (DL) system and what type of information is displayed to the user. A typical example of a requirement is defining the amount of information and form of interaction to be displayed within the field-of-view (FoV). Should all the detected parts and object types be displayed? Should only those in the center of the FoV be presented as detected even though all FoV contained objects were detected? Should only specific types of objects be detected and highlighted? Should the position and angle of the camera relative to the objects be indicated? The more visual information on the recognized environment is presented, the more confused the user may become. As a user, maintaining focus while been visually guided is critical to the success of the business process, as such information overload control is highly important.
- **Contextual Enrichment (CE)** – once objects and items are detected and recognized during the OR step, additional layers of information can be presented. An example can be a connection to the digital twin of the machine under repair or operation, and retrieval of its sensorial data such as temperature, maintenance logs, and control settings. This CE step implies connectivity with other information systems that represent the historical and current status of the connected machine. The information overload discussion is relevant here as well, such as camera-object proximity relation. Should the size of the digital overlay graphical within the context of operation be proportional to the proximity to the IoT sensor? Should accordingly, the IoT digital overlay appearance be altered? Could information be removed from the FoV in order to reduce the danger of blocking the user sight in case of smart glasses? This CE step entails that in conjunction with decisions on what, where, when and how to present digital twin information, the decision should also correlate the IoT digital twin data with the visual situational context of the operation.
- **Guidance** – this step discusses implications of visual instructions displayed on the user's FoV in order to drive an operation such as fixing or assembling parts of a machine. The essence is a step-by-step in-context procedure, guiding the user similarly to a car navigation system, indicating the next operation to be performed.

This guidance is a combination of the above OR and CE steps in terms of constantly recognizing the part being operated upon, adjusted telemetry provided by the digital twin, and the needed operation. Specifically, there is a need to decide if and how the AR system will analyze the performed operation and alert in case there is discrepancy between the planed one and the actual operation performed. An example is a case in which the guiding system instructs the user to grab a monkey wrench, and the user grabs a hammer. The OR system can recognize the object as a hammer, correlate with the procedure that requires a monkey wrench, and indicate an error is occurring. Should the system intervene with the user operation? Should the system allow the user to indicate successful completion, or just allow the user to browse through the instructions for orientation purposes? Should the system interact with voice with the user during the guidance steps, and suggest to the digital twin proactive actions such as ordering a part or initiating a report? All suggested actions and recommendations must be performed in the context of the operation, the environment, the physical machine and the digital twin. It is a matter of smart guidance, not just visual instructions.

The above steps of Object Recognition, Contextual Enrichment, and Guidance, compose the modeling tools requirements and related concerns of the next sections.

## 4   Modeling, Testing and Simulation Tools Concerns

In addition to the business process element of the application, AR specific modeling, testing and simulation tools are needed for the creation of AR enriched experience. In particular, tools that capture and implement requirements that address the machine OR and CE steps or affected by the visual Guidance step. In AR systems, the visual comprehension modeling of the physical world and its connectivity to the digital twin is an inseparable part of training DL systems. Simulation and testing tools should document the required needs according to the steps as well as design new interaction and configuration of user experience.

Even more so, the tools should enable rapid creation of AR experience, connect to digital twin information, and support DL insights. Lengthily and time-consuming AR experience creation will diminish the assimilation success of a new AR system, as business owners need to employ an agile feedback tuning to these new interaction methods. Since the perceived success of an AR experience is extremely personalized, modeling tools should enable designers and engineers to quickly simulate the experience, iterate, and improve according to user experience feedback, minimizing disappointment.

Recalling that AR is an immersive experience, factoring the designers and engineers' cognitive aspects and perceptions of the potential usage versus real field implementation is a challenge as well. How can one simulate field conditions to the engineers that do not have access to the real physical environment or the objects in question?

The next sections examine specific needs and gaps in functionality, according to the above steps.

## 4.1 Object Recognition Tools Concerns

Modeling tools for OR are comprised of two separate building blocks. The first is training an artificial intelligence system on what it can recognize in terms of DL categories. The second is constructing a trackable 3D model for detection of the camera position and angle in real time, either based on marker-less SLAM methods [14] or using markers and pseudo-markers such as CAD information [30]. For DL training tools, supervised training, tagging, comparing the steps of batch learning and tuning the deep network parameters is a complex subject and is outside the scope of this paper. However, constructing a trackable 3D model is a pillar part of AR. As such, constant feedback on the quality of the constructed model is imperative by adjusting the density of camera positions defined by relative coordination system to the object and distance and view-point angle. In addition, significant landmarks that have distinguishable spatial contour, varied light conditions and reflection of surfaces, and other constraints should be captured and handled during the 3D model creation process of the object. As such, a modeling tool needs to simulate and test the quality of model alignment gradually while creating a 3D tracking model. The tool should enable constant feedback with reference to a test object, ensuring enough data is collected and modeled, in order to prevent discontinued tracking. The tool also needs to optimize the resulting 3D tracking model payload size avoiding the generation of redundant data load on the AR system. Such oversized load can impair the overall user experience due to network latency, particularly on field mobile devices that rely on a cellular grid. The main challenge in such modeling tools is to optimize the size of the 3D model without hampering tracking quality, as well its adaptation to different tracking devices. An example may be an indicator that instructs a modeler on how to rotate a capturing video device over the target object as the 3D tracking model is created. Another example can be setting the acceptable quality of an AR jittering fluctuations of the graphical overlay, according to a given device resolution, camera distance from the target object, and business usage. All affecting the resulting 3D tracking model size and are business process dependent.

## 4.2 Contextual Enrichment Tools Concerns

The goal of CE tools is to systematically capture the needed parameters of the digital twin and its IoT devices, and their bi-directional telemetry connectivity with the digital thread data streaming. The tools are used to map connectivity between the 3D tracking model and an abstract type of a digital twin machine, defining what type of information can be retrieved and in which business and visual context it should be presented. A simulated data model of the abstract digital twin should be tested to verify correctness of data types. As such, parameter setting for each IoT sensor and actuator type is needed such as transmitting or receiving frequency from the digital thread, measurement unit, graphical representation, visibility conditions, action-ability and associated drill-through. In addition, the real-time connectivity conditions defining how a specific instance of the abstract digital twin will be connected during operation with the AR system, needs to be set as well. Namely, instance recognition of the OR step should be linked to the abstract type of the digital twin in the CE step, with a specific object ID and instance and a specific digital thread during real-time guidance. In addition, the visual context and the instance IoT data need to be presented and aligned with the guidance procedure steps. Hence designing engineers needs to iterate between the CE modeling tools and the Guidance modeling tools, gradually configuring the requirements. In addition, initial graphical elements selection should be applied as a graphical symbol of the represented data, in case it is independent of a business process steps. An example may be selecting gauge indicator type for different data types such as those presented in [13, 22]: controlling layout, color coding, and faces such as circle, trend, analog clock, dial, speedometer and more, in which these 3D faces can be visible in certain perspective relative to the tracking camera, and non-visible in others. Positioning the graphical overlay on the 3D tracking model should be done on the OR tools as well, since graphical perspectives are best set visually and not on a data model textual representation. To conclude, OR the CE tools are partially coupled by the location of the IoT emitting and receiving devices. The decision on the appearance method of the information during the business process is defined in the AR business process phase defined in the Guidance modeling tools, hence the CE tools are also coupled with the next step.

### 4.3  Guidance Tools Concerns

Guidance tools are used to set step-by-step procedures associated with particular objects, such as repairing or restocking a machine, or assembling and disassembling its parts within a visual context. A single object may have different visual manifestations in terms of its static state such as a car with an open or closed engine cover. For each static manifestation, many different procedures can be applicable. An example may be adding oil versus adding rinsing water to a connected car engine. Both procedures require the same 3D tracking model in order to orient the user to the location of the liquid inlet, yet the instructions are different for each. Both will need to have the same 3D tracking models such as one to guide the user on how to open the engine cover, and another that operates on the open engine cover. The procedures will need to access different IoT sensors for the oil and water levels and be linked to the specific car instance under maintenance according to its digital twin. In essence, a VOG models' database can utilize the same collection of 3D tracking models, yet with different IoT telemetry and guided instructions relating to the same managed instance. The tools should curate the order of instructions, select IoT sensors telemetry and visual appearance and validate usability for the end-users.

Considering that a guidance experience is different for mobile devices and smart glasses in terms of information overload, designers and engineers should examine and relate to devices' type and specific vendors' products (see Sect. 5.1). Visual guidance also may employ animation elements to projected graphics. As such, the overall experience should be re-played and tested constantly within a simulation tool, without the need to test the AR system in situ. Varied perspectives and proximity to target objects should be correlated with shape and size of the projected digital overlay, as it impacts user experience. One example can be when one digital element is superimposed on the other. Another example is an occlusion synergy between physical and virtual objects controlling the visibly and layout of occluded content, such as if the virtual object will be hidden, partially or dimmed displayed. A third example can be the physical distance between the camera position and the tracked object, and how it should affect data abstraction and related graphical elements in order to prevent digital overlay cluttering. These requirements can be defined at the overall business process level, regardless of procedure steps, and can be applicable for a single static scene. This scene can be interlaced with additional scenes, forming a multi-scene procedure.

The goal of an innovative new business process is to improve its associated quality metrics. Such improvement can be by reducing the number of steps to be performed or reducing quality errors and increasing operation performance. Similar to user experience study employing a storyboard, an overall examination of how a new business process streamlines a former one should also be validated by tools.

Setting quality attributes at modeling time and measuring during simulation and testing time should be part of AR development tools. Hence, in addition to step-by-step visual instructions, Guidance tools should include the ability to define, measure, and report on quality attributes. Namely injecting measurement probes that can provide metrics throughout an AR-driven business process, can provide quality assessment relative to non-functional requirements. Such quality measurement and probe setting should be intrinsic to AR modeling, simulation and testing tools, similarly to any other business process key performance indicator.

## 5 Safety, Security and Privacy Concerns

Augmented Reality (AR) based guidance utilizes two main elements during a business process: a camera that captures the visual scene, and a digital overlay of information that is presented on a wearable smart glass or on a handheld mobile device. The elements and their combination generate challenges that should be addressed when conceiving an AR-based application, as well as during development lifecycle including requirements, design, and testing phases. In this section, we detail non-functional requirements of AR applications regarding workers safety, discuss vulnerability to information systems' data security, and the impact on employee's and bystanders' privacy.

### 5.1 Safety Concerns

AR introduces the ability to interact with real objects via displaying digital handles superimposed on target objects. These handles and additional information can obscure the real object or element in the surrounding. When using smart AR glasses, this digital overlay can block the operator eyesight in an unsafe manner. An extreme case may be a black screen such as one that appears in a device reboot, blocking the entire field of view. Considering the operator may handle sensitive or hazard equipment, the optimized business process for a hands-free operation may become worse than the original non-AR process. Wrongfully anchored digital overlay, misplaced and not up-to-date digital twin information, or misinterpreted operator gestures, can direct an operator to act on the data and activate a controller or make a misinformed decision. An example for an operator gesture misinterpretation can be opening instead of closing of a valve.

Another example is that lack of synchronized timely updates of the digital twin information can lead to a wrongful maintenance operation. As such, requirements setting should include AR specific safety measures adjusted to the level of usability of the system according to a potential risk. Such requirements may be a request for two phased approval for activation, a feedback and verification in a form of active monitoring of user actions, logging activation for audit and process improvement, adding training and conditional usage, etc.

Other safety requirements can be to correlate the visibility of digital overlay with the operator line-of-sight and business process steps. One example is to present the digital information in the peripherals of the smart glass in hazard steps, to ensure clear visibility. Another example will be to focus the digital overlay only in the center of the smart glasses, similar to a crosshair focus zone.

One should recall that similarly to swimming glasses or a diving mask, different smart glasses and eyewear vary in terms of the overall visibility area as well as area of the projected digital overlay. Variations also include different ergonomic characteristics such as weight consideration, gestures support and user input method. For example, as seen in Fig. 1, ODG-R9 glasses [21] provide a 50° field-of-view angle and weigh about 185 g, mounted on the operator nose and has air mouse. Epson's Moverio BT-350 Smart Glasses [8] provide a 23° field-of-view angle in diagonal and weigh 130 g. Vuzix Blade glasses [31], display a see-through card-like interface as the center of the screen and weigh 85 g and has touchpad. Microsoft Hololens visor [20] field-of-view angle is estimated as 30°, and weigh 579 g on one's forehead, with gestures support for interaction.

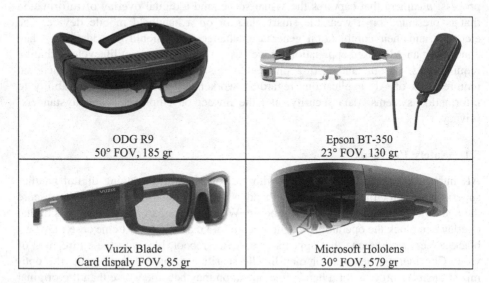

| ODG R9<br>50° FOV, 185 gr | Epson BT-350<br>23° FOV, 130 gr |
| Vuzix Blade<br>Card dispaly FOV, 85 gr | Microsoft Hololens<br>30° FOV, 579 gr |

**Fig. 1.** Smart Glasses from different vendors field of view (FOV) and weight. Extracted from products specification sheets of [8, 20, 21, 31].

As such, the designed AR user experience should either match a specific hardware and device brand, or be adaptive to the hardware view angles, interaction modes, and overall user ergonomic experience. In such cases, safety tests and simulations are needed for different devices. A typical test should be to examine the effect a field-of-view has on the digital content and the overall accomplishment of the business process. Similarly to mobile development in which different retina size and device types are simulated in the engineers' development environment, guidance tools should simulate smart glasses devices as well and test usability and safety aspects as per these devices.

## 5.2  Privacy Concerns

AR uses the camera primarily to capture the visual scene in order to compute the position and orientation of a device relative to the tracked environment, adjusting the perspectives and content of a digital overlay to a user's eyesight. However, in use cases that employ remote assistance by a peer, an expert or a cognitive artificial intelligence system, the camera sends captured scene images or videos, as well as audio and interacted augmentations. This data interchange of content, video and audio can be stored for further analysis such as recommendation system for safety alerts, audit trail on operations performed, tacit knowledge capturing, reports generation, and bi-directional guidance. This entails that a private data such as faces, passing bystanders identities, exposed documents and digital data surrounding the object under operation can be captured unintentionally. Recent privacy regulations such as GDPR (Global Data Protection Regulation) [9] require a separation between data processor and data storage in terms of liability. Consequently, clear measures should to be inserted in terms of data storage duration of an active session, segregation of the location of persisted data and rules for records retention and expiration. Additional requirements on data broadcasting outside the European Union borders or restrictions originating from HIPAA (Health Insurance Portability and Accountability Act) that sets the standard for protecting sensitive patient data, need to be considered. For example, in a case of PG usage in retail for fixing a cash register, a consumer's identity can be observed while interacting with the cashier. In healthcare, a case in which a heart monitor device is maintained, and on a nearby device, another patient's observed heart related data is captured and transmitted is prohibited. Will consumers approve having their identity captured via a camera that is positioned straight at them? Will the adjunct patient family approve this medical data privacy violation as part of the treatment?

In a consumer-oriented environment, users should be aware, approve and control what type of information can be stored, to what usage, and how they can request the deletion of this information. As such, the requirements should include control over recorded interactions by the operators, as well as the ability to handle recordings that may capture third party data, and prove compliance with GDPR, HIPAA or other regulations.

## 5.3  Information Security Concerns

Information security concerns are manifested by vulnerabilities introduced by the type of edge device, such a smart glasses and mobile device, which utilize either an

Android, iOS or proprietary operating system (OS). As an entry point to the organization, specific setting and management of these OS need to be enforced. However, in most smart glasses today, the OS cannot be upgraded or patched with security add-ons since these are specialized versions adjusted to the hardware. As such, when a discovered vulnerability is known, the device becomes the weakest element in the attack surface. In mobile devices, even ones that the employees bring from home (BYOD), an organization security management application is added, in which control over privacy, VPN, tracking and resetting of the device is introduced. With smart glasses such installation is limited due to the specialization of the OS. As such, access to the organization information needs to be provided via dedicated secured services. These constraints imply that dedicated application interfaces should be defined in addition to the application functionality.

Additional vulnerability is driven by physical security associated with information security such as password hijacking via visual sniffing, as the camera can record the operator keystrokes. Namely, AR smart glasses become a keylogger through visual comprehension.

Consequently, additional non-functional requirements concerning OS standards, device security enforcement policy, user registration and authorization hardening, and modes of operations should be added to the functional requirements.

## 6  Conclusion

Most of designers of Augmented Reality applications today are focusing on functional and graphical description of digital overlay, as well as new business process design. However, modeling AR application requirements should consider Object Recognition and Contextual Enrichment pre-processing steps that handle what objects and gestures to identify and what digital information should be linked from the digital twin or other sensorial information. Moreover, the usage of surveillance camera impacts the organization information security, its employees, and bystanders' privacy, in addition to employees' safety concerns introduced due to wearable devices. This paper presented some of these concerns that should be addressed in the next generation modeling, simulation and testing tools in order to analyze, design and implement AR solutions. There is also a need to create new safety, privacy and security practice awareness addressing new vulnerabilities triggered by augmented reality wearable devices. These concerns should be researched and investigated as part as non-functional requirements analysis, in addition to existing ones of an information system application. New tools should consider cross-relations between AR-based people's interaction and visual interpretation to artificial intelligence driven Object Recognition, and integration with digital twins within an enterprise environment use cases.

# References

1. Ask, J.A., Naparstek, L.: Augmented Reality: Emerging Tools To Explore. Forrester, 5 July 2016
2. ARCore. https://developers.google.com/ar/. Accessed 18 Feb 2018
3. ARKit. https://developer.apple.com/arkit/. Accessed 19 Feb 2018
4. Chang, G., Morreale, P., Medicherla, P.: Applications of augmented reality systems in education. In: Gibson, D., Dodge, B. (eds.) Proceedings of Society for Information Technology & Teacher Education International Conference, pp. 1380–1385. AACE, Chesapeake (2010)
5. Chang, Y.S., Nuernberger, B., Luan, B., Höllerer, T.: Evaluating gesture-based augmented reality annotation. In: 2017 IEEE Symposium on 3D User Interfaces (3DUI) 18 March 2017, pp. 182–185 (2017)
6. Druga, M.: Pokemon GO: where VR and AR have gone since its inception. IEEE Potentials **37**(1), 23–26 (2018)
7. Dünser, A., Grasset, R., Billinghurst, M.: A survey of evaluation techniques used in augmented reality studies. Human Interface Technology Laboratory New Zealand, 10 December 2008
8. Epson. https://epson.com/For-Home/Smart-Glasses/Smart-Glasses/c/h420. Accessed 18 Feb 2018
9. GDPR. https://www.eugdpr.org/. Accessed 18 Feb 2018
10. Hadar, E.: Cognitive augmented and mixed reality a new era of interaction. In: The 5th International Workshop on Cognitive Aspects of Information Systems Engineering (COGNISE), In Conjunction with the 29th International Conference on Advanced Information System Engineering CAiSE 2017, 13 June, Essen, Germany (2017)
11. Hadar, E., Shtok, J., Cohen, B., Tzur, Y., Karlinsky, L.: Hybrid remote expert - an emerging pattern of industrial remote support. In: CAiSE Forum, 29th International Conference on Advanced Information System Engineering, 12–16 June, Essen, Germany (2017)
12. HBR. https://hbr.org/2017/11/a-managers-guide-to-augmented-reality. Accessed 18 Feb 2018
13. Healthycities. https://healthycities.zendesk.com/hc/en-us/articles/219556348-Gauge-and-Icon-Overview. Accessed 18 Feb 2018
14. IBM AR Research. http://www.research.ibm.com/haifa/dept/imt/ist_dm.shtml. Accessed 18 Feb 2018
15. Kratz, S., Rohs, M., Guse, D., Müller, J., Bailly, G., Nischt, M.: PalmSpace: continuous around-device gestures vs. multitouch for 3D rotation tasks on mobile devices. In: ACM Proceedings of the International Working Conference on Advanced Visual Interfaces 21 May 2012, pp. 181–188 (2012)
16. Krichenbauer, M., Yamamoto, G., Taketomi, T., Sandor, C., Kato, H.: Augmented reality vs virtual reality for 3D object manipulation. J. IEEE Trans. Visual. Comput. Graph. (2017)
17. Lee, W.H., Lee, H.K.: The usability attributes and evaluation measurements of mobile media AR (augmented reality). Cogent Arts Hum. **3**(1), 1241171 (2016)
18. Lukosch, S., Billinghurst, M., Alem, L., et al.: Collaboration in augmented reality. Comput. Support. Coop. Work **24**, 515–525 (2015). https://doi.org/10.1007/s10606-015-9239-0
19. McKee, D.W., Clement, S.J., Almutairi, J., Xu, J.: Massive-scale automation in cyber-physical systems: vision & challenges. In: IEEE 13th International Symposium on Autonomous Decentralized System (ISADS), 22 March 2017, pp. 5–11 (2017)
20. Microsoft. https://www.microsoft.com/en-us/hololens. Accessed 18 Feb 2018
21. ODG. https://www.osterhoutgroup.com/r-9-smartglasses. Accessed 18 Feb 2018

22. Poly. https://poly.google.com/. Accessed 18 Feb 2018
23. Radu, I., Antle, A.: Embodied learning mechanics and their relationship to usability of handheld augmented reality. In: 2017 IEEE Virtual Reality Workshop on Embodied Learning through Virtual & Augmented Reality (KELVAR), 18 March 2017, pp. 1–5 (2017)
24. Sage, M.: Creating augmented reality experiences for enterprise: good practices, lessons learned, and technological insights. IEEE Consum. Electron. Mag. **6**(1), 42–44 (2017)
25. Samini, A., Lundin Palmerius, K.: Popular performance metrics for evaluation of interaction in virtual and augmented reality. In: 2017 International Conference on Cyberworlds (2017)
26. Swan, J.E., Gabbard, J.L.: Survey of user-based experimentation in augmented reality. In: Proceedings of 1st International Conference on Virtual Reality, 22 July, pp. 1–9 (2015)
27. Tanikawa, T., Uzuka, H., Narumi, T., Hirose, M.: Integrated view-input interaction method for mobile AR. In: 3D User Interfaces (3DUI) IEEE Symposium, 23 March, pp. 187–188 (2015)
28. Van Krevelen, D.W., Poelman, R.: A survey of augmented reality technologies, applications and limitations. Int. J. Virtual Real. **9**(2), 1 (2010)
29. Vlaminck, M., Luong, H., Philips, W.: A markerless 3D tracking approach for augmented reality applications. In: IEEE International Conference on 3D Immersion (IC3D) (2017)
30. Vuforia. https://www.vuforia.com/. Accessed 18 Feb 2018
31. Vuzix.    http://files.vuzix.com/Content/docs/north-american/web/Vuzix-Blade-Business-Smart-Glasses-01-18.pdf. Accessed 18 Feb 2018
32. Wikitude. https://www.wikitude.com/. Accessed 18 Feb 2018

# Formal Methods

# Enhanced Benchmark Datasets
# for a Comprehensive Evaluation of Process
# Model Matching Techniques

Muhammad Ali[1,2] and Khurram Shahzad[1,2(✉)]

[1] Software Development and Maintenance Center, University of Gujrat,
Gujrat, Pakistan
muhammad.ali@uog.edu.pk, khurram@pucit.edu.pk
[2] Punjab University College of Information Technology,
University of the Punjab, Lahore, Pakistan

**Abstract.** Process Model Matching (PMM) refers to the automatic identification of corresponding activities between a pair of process models. Recognizing the pivotal role of PMM in numerous application areas a plethora of matching techniques have been developed. To evaluate the effectiveness of these techniques, researchers typically use PMMC'15 datasets and three well-established performance measures, precision, recall and $F_1$ score. The performance scores of these measures are useful for a surface level evaluation of a matching technique. However, these overall scores do not provide essential insights about the capabilities of a matching technique. To that end, we enhance the PMMC'15 datasets by classifying corresponding pairs into three types and compute performance scores of each type, separately. We contend that the performance scores for each type of corresponding pairs, together with the surface level performance scores, provide valuable insights about the capabilities of a matching technique. As a second contribution, we use the enhanced datasets for a comprehensive evaluation of three prominent semantic similarity measures. Thirdly, we use the enhanced datasets for a comprehensive evaluation of the results of twelve matching systems from the PMM Contest 2015. From the results, we conclude that there is a need for developing the next generation of matching techniques that are equally effective for the three types of pairs.

**Keywords:** Business process management · Process Model Matching
PMMC'15 datasets · Enhanced datasets · Comprehensive evaluation

# 1 Introduction

Process Model Matching (PMM) refers to the automatic identification of activities between a pair of process models that exhibit the same or similar behavior [1, 2]. The participating activities are called corresponding activities and the pair is called corresponding pair [2, 3]. The identification of corresponding activities has a pivotal role in various applications domains, such as process querying, clone detection, and harmonization of process models [4–6]. Recognizing that, a plethora of PMM techniques have been developed [7].

© Springer Nature Switzerland AG 2018
R. Pergl et al. (Eds.): EOMAS 2018, LNBIP 332, pp. 107–122, 2018.
https://doi.org/10.1007/978-3-030-00787-4_8

To evaluate each of these matching technique, leading experts of the BPM domain have developed three benchmark datasets, formally called PMMC'15 datasets [8]. Since 2015, these datasets are widely used for the evaluation of PMM techniques [9], by using three well-established performance measures, precision, recall and $F_1$ score [7–9]. The performance scores of these measures are useful for a surface level evaluation of a matching technique. However, our synthesis of the PMMC'15 datasets and the evaluation results have revealed two interrelated issues regarding the evaluation of matching techniques. Prior to discussing the issues, in the remaining part of this section, we first highlight the diversity that can possibly exist in the corresponding pairs. Subsequently, in Sect. 1.2 we discuss the two issues that arise during the evaluation of a matching technique. Finally, in Sect. 1.3 we present the conceptual bases, from text process literature, that we have used for classifying the corresponding pairs.

## 1.1 Illustration of Diversity in Corresponding Pairs

Figure 1 illustrates the possible diversity between corresponding pairs using admission process models of two universities, University A and B. The diversity represents the varying levels of differences in the formulation of participating labels. In the figure, the corresponding pairs of the two process models are highlighted with grey shades. Note, we have used three different shades of gray color, light gray, ordinary gray and dark gray, to represent the diversity in corresponding pairs. The higher the difference in formulation of labels the higher is the darkness of the color.

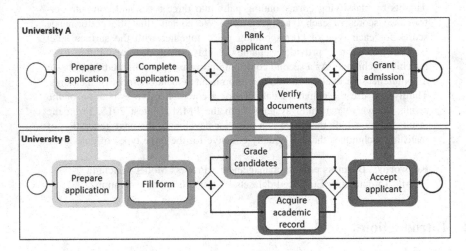

**Fig. 1.** Illustration of process model matching

In the example, there is no difference in the formulation of label 'prepare application' in the two process models. Due to the absence of this difference, this correspondence is highlighted with light gray color. Similarly, the two labels 'complete application' and 'fill form' are formulated quite differently, i.e. the words are replaced with their synonyms. Due to the slight difference in formulation of labels this correspondence is highlighted with ordinary gray color. Finally, the formulation of the two labels 'grant admission' and 'accept applicant' is completely different but their business semantics are the same. Due to this significant different in formulation of labels this correspondence is highlighted with dark gray.

The example illustrates the varying differences that may exist in corresponding pairs. In the presence of this diversity, an ideal matching technique should achieve a surface level performance scores as well as comparable performance scores for the corresponding pairs of all three shades.

## 1.2    Motivation for Enhancing the Benchmark Datasets

Leading experts from the BPM domain introduced three real-world datasets for the evaluation of process model matching techniques, formally called PMMC'15 datasets [1, 9]. The three datasets are named as, University Admissions (UA), Birth Registration (BR) and Asset Management (AM) datasets [1, 8]. Each dataset is composed of a collection of process models and gold standard correspondences between pairs of process models. The UA, BR and AM datasets are composed of 9, 9 and 72 real-world process models, respectively. Each dataset has 36 process model pairs and gold standard correspondences between activities of the 36 pairs. The detailed specification of the three datasets is presented in Table 1. We consider it important to clarify that these numbers are generated without any pre-processing on the datasets, and that our enhancements to the datasets will change these numbers. From the table it can be observed that UA dataset has 1575 pairs, BR dataset has 633 pairs and AM dataset has 799 pairs.

Table 1. Specification of the PMMC'15 datasets

|  | UA | BR | AM |
|---|---|---|---|
| Total no of pairs in the dataset | 1575 | 633 | 799 |
| Number of corresponding pairs | 202 | 183 | 151 |
| Number of trivial corresponding pairs | 136 | 70 | 102 |
| Number of non-trivial corresponding pairs | 66 | 113 | 49 |

The PMMC'15 datasets have been used in numerous studies for the evaluation and comparison of process model matching techniques [1–3, 8, 10]. All these studies rely on a single Precision, Recall and $F_1$ score to represent the effectiveness of a technique. Consequently, a matching technique with higher $F_1$ score is declared as more effective than the one with lower $F_1$ score. However, there are two interrelated issues with this combination of datasets and performance measures. In the presence of these issues a more thorough evaluation of the matching techniques is desired, before pronouncing a matching technique more effective than the other one. These issues are as follows:

- *Inflated $F_1$ score:* Our syntheses of the PMMC'15 datasets have revealed that a significant percentage of corresponding pairs in all the three datasets are either identical or similar. We formally refer to these pairs are *'trivial'* corresponding pairs. It is because, in these pairs, either there is no difference in the formulation of the participating labels or the change is as small as changing the form of a word and/or adding a stop word. From the table it can be observed that out of the 202 corresponding pairs in the UA dataset, 136 are *trivial* corresponding pairs. Similarly, in BR dataset 70 out of 183 pairs, and in AM dataset 102 out of 151 pairs are *trivial* corresponding pairs. Therefore, the inclusion of such a large percentage of *trivial* corresponding pairs artificially inflate the $F_1$ score achieved by a matching technique.

- *Surface level Evaluation:* As illustrated in the preceding subsection, the PMMC'15 datasets contain diverse corresponding pairs. In the presence of this diversity, the use of a single value of each performance measure, for the complete dataset, provides a valuable surface level evaluation of a technique. However, a single score does not provide important insights about the behavior of a matching technique, which essentially requires answers questions like, how effective is the technique for the diverse corresponding pairs, Light Gray, Ordinary Gray and Dark Gray pairs.

Based on the above discussion we conclude that there is a dire need to enhance the PMMC'15 datasets by classifying corresponding pairs based on the diversity of the pairs. Furthermore, in addition to the surface level performance scores, due attention should be paid to the performance scores of the diverse corresponding pairs.

### 1.3    Conceptual Bases for Classifying Corresponding Pairs

Several studies in the natural language processing domain have identified three language independent relationships between a text pair, depending upon the level of similarity between the two texts in the pair [11–13]. These relationships have been widely used for several text processing tasks, such as, plagiarism detection [12], text reuse in journalism [11, 13] and duplicate document identification [14]. The relationships are Near Copy, Light Revision, and Heavy Revision. A brief overview of each type of relationship is as follows:

- *Near Copy:* The two texts are called Near Copy of each other if one text can be generated by slightly rephrasing the other text. That is, by adding stop words or changing the form of the word. A possible near copy of 'best student' is 'the best student'.
- *Light Revision:* The two texts are called Light Revision of each other if one text can be generated by substantially paraphrasing the other text. That is, by replacing words with synonyms, or adding additional words, etc. A possible Light Revision of 'best student' is 'outstanding undergrad student'.
- *Heavy Revision:* The two texts are called Heavy Revision of each other if one text can be generated by significantly paraphrasing the other text. That is, by replacing words with alternate words, reordering the words or making any other change in which the semantic meanings of the text are not changed. A possible Heavy Revision of 'best student' is 'topper of the class'.

The rest of the paper is organized as follows: in Sect. 2 we present the details of the changes we have made to enhance the PMMC'15 datasets. In Sect. 3 we present the enhanced dataset for the evaluation of three semantic matching measures. In Sect. 4 we present the use of the enhanced dataset for the evaluation of 12 matching systems from the PMM Contest 2015. Finally, Sect. 5 concludes the paper.

## 2    Enhancing the PMMC'15 Datasets

This section presents the first contribution of our work, enhancing the PMMC'15 dataset for a comprehensive evaluation of PMM techniques. To that end, in this section, we first introduce the three types of pairs that are used to represent the diversity in corresponding pairs. Secondly, we discuss the preprocessing that we have performed on the datasets. Finally, we present the procedure that we have used for enhancing the datasets.

### 2.1    Representing Diversity in Corresponding Pairs

We propose three types of pairs to represent diversity in corresponding pairs. These types stem from the three types of relationships between text pairs, presented in Sect. 1.3, and the synthesis of the PMMC'15 datasets. The three types that we have used for classifying corresponding pairs are, Verbatim, Modified Copy and Heavy Revision. A brief overview of each type is as follows:

– *Verbatim (VB):* A corresponding pair is classified as Verbatim if the two labels in the pair are similar or almost the same. Based on the definition of Near Copy relation in a text pair as well as the synthesis of the PMMC'15 datasets, we have identified three criteria to declare a pair Verbatim. The three criteria and their examples from the PMMC'15 are presented in Table 2.

Table 2. Criteria and examples of declaring a pair Verbatim

| Criteria | Examples |
| --- | --- |
| Identical label | Creation birth certificate - create birth certificate |
| Identical label without stop words | Receive notification birth - receive notification of birth |
| Reordered words Identical, but | Check nationality of parents - check parent's nationality |

– *Modified Copy (MC):* A corresponding pair is classified as Modified Copy if the two labels in the pair have the same semantic meanings but the formulation of the labels is substantially different. Based on the definition of Light Revision relation in a text pair as well as the synthesis of the PMMC'15 datasets, we have identified three criteria for declaring a pair Modified Copy. The three criteria and their examples from the PMMC'15 are presented in Table 3.

Table 3. Criteria and examples of declaring a pair Modified Copy

| Criteria | Examples |
| --- | --- |
| Adding/deleting a few words | Register child - register baby as German 1 |
| Replacing synonyms | Confirm identity - check identity |
| Switching labeling style | Register child - child registration |

- *Heavy Revision (HR):* A corresponding is classified as Heavy Revision if the formulation of the two labels is significantly different, or one label subsumes the other label. We have identified two criteria for declaring a pair Heavy Revision. The criteria and their examples from the PMMC'15 are presented in Table 4.

**Table 4.** Criteria and examples of declaring a pair Heavy Revision

| Criteria | Examples |
|---|---|
| Substantially revised labels | Receive documents - receive the citizen decision |
| Subsume the other label | Register child - child registration |

## 2.2   Pre-processing the PMMC'15 Datasets

Prior to annotating a type to a corresponding pair, we also synthesized the publicly available[1] results of 12 matching systems as well as the gold standard[2] included in the results. The synthesis revealed two types of discrepancies in the gold standard that must be omitted before annotating a type to each corresponding pair. These discrepancies are as follows:

- There are 188 corresponding pairs in the gold standard of the UA dataset that do not have a meaningful label. For example, 'IntermediateCatchEvent' – 'IntermediateCatchEvent', and 'ExclusiveGateway' – 'ExclusiveGateway'.
- In each of the three datasets, there are several corresponding pairs that have the same business impact, but they are declared as unequivalent in the gold standard. Examples of these pairs are as follows: 'wait for results' – 'wait for results' and 'clearing is posted' – 'clearing is posted'. The amount of these pairs in the UA, BR and AM datasets are 13, 42 and 213, respectively.

In the first step of the pre-processing, the unlabeled pairs in the UA dataset were removed. In the second step of the pre-processing, discrepancies among the equivalent pairs were rectified in the three datasets. That is, 13 activity pairs for UA dataset, 42 activity pairs for BR dataset and 213 activity pairs for AM dataset were corrected. Accordingly, the UA, BR and AM datasets that we used for annotation was composed of 360, 423 and 456 corresponding pairs, respectively.

## 2.3   Annotating Types to Corresponding Pairs

We have annotated a type to each corresponding pair in the pre-processed dataset. The three types that we have used for the annotations are, VB, MC and HR. For the annotations we rely on the classification criteria presented in Tables 2, 3 and 4.

As a first step, each corresponding pair was independently annotated by two researchers using the classification criteria. Secondly, the annotations were compared and conflicts were identified. Subsequently, all the conflicts were resolved by a

---

[1] The results can be downloaded from https://ai.wu.ac.at/emisa2015/contest.php.

[2] Gold standard refers to the benchmark correspondences generated by BPM experts.

consensus approach, that is, by individually discussing each conflicting pair. As an outcome of this activity, all the corresponding pairs were annotated with a mutually agreed pair type, VB, MC or HR. Table 5 shows the distribution of pairs according to types. From the table it can be observed that a significant number of pairs are annotated as VB or HR. However, there are fewer pairs that are annotated as MC. This imbalance in the number of pairs in the three types, reinforces that a single Precision, Recall or $F_1$ score is not sufficient for a fair evaluation of the PMM technique. Hence, in the rest of the paper, we separately compute the performance scores for individual pair types, in addition to the overall performance scores.

**Table 5.** Distribution of corresponding pairs according to types

| Datasets | VB pairs | MC Pairs | HR pairs | Total |
|----------|----------|----------|----------|-------|
| UA | 106 | 53 | 201 | 360 |
| BR | 125 | 79 | 219 | 423 |
| AM | 322 | 25 | 109 | 456 |
| Total | 553 | 157 | 529 | 1,239 |

## 3   Evaluation of Semantic Similarity Measures

This section presents our second contribution, a comprehensive evaluation of three prominent the semantic similarity measures, using the enhanced PMMC'15 dataset. Below, we first introduce the three semantic similarity measures. Subsequently, we present an overview of the experimental setup and analysis of the results.

### 3.1   Semantic Similarity Measures

WordNet is a well-established lexical database for English language that is widely used to computing semantic similarity between two concepts [15]. The database consists of over 150,000 nouns, verbs, adverbs and adjectives. The concepts are organized into related synonyms, also called synsets [16, 17]. In addition to the synsets, the concepts in WordNet are linked with each other via a variety of relationships, such as is-a and part-of relationships, to form a network of concepts.

For this study, we have selected three prominent semantic similarity measures that are previously in PMM literature. These measures are, Lin [18], similarity [19] and Path similarity [20]. A brief overview of each similarity measure is as follows:

*Lin Similarity.* This similarity measure computes similarity between concepts based on the Information Content (IC) of Least Common Subsumer (LCS) in the WordNet database [17]. Subsequently, the similarity of a label pair is calculated by averaging of all optimal words pairs. Formally, word level Lin score is computed by using Eq. 1.

$$Lin(c1, c2) = \frac{2 * IC(LCS(c1, c2))}{IC(c1) + IC(c2)} \quad [16] \tag{1}$$

*Lesk Similarity.* This similarity measures computes the degree of similarity between two words by calculating the overlap in the dictionary definition of the two words [19, 21]. Subsequently, the similarity of a label pair is calculated by averaging of all optimal words pairs' Lesk value.

*Path Similarity.* This similarity measure uses the shortest path between two words in the WordNet database to compute similarity between two labels, by using Eq. 2 [20].

$$Sim(L1, L2) = \frac{\sum_{w1 \in L1 \backslash L2} \max(\partial(w1, w2) | w2 \in L2 \backslash L1)}{|L1 \backslash L2|} \tag{2}$$

Where $\partial(w1, w2)$ is path similarity value of words pair w1 and w2 from WordNet.

## 3.2    Experimentation and Analysis of Results

We implemented the three semantic similarity measures in Python and used them for the experimentation. Each implemented similarity measure takes input a set of activity pairs and returns similarity scores of each input pair. Experiments are performed using the complete dataset (including all pairs in the dataset), as well as using the three types of pairs, separately. The results of the complete datasets provide a surface level evaluation of the matching technique whereas, the results of each type of pair provide valuable insights about the capabilities of the matching techniques. Similarly, separate experiments are performed for each dataset, UA, BR and AM dataset.

The semantic measures return a similarity score between 0 and 1, whereas the performance measures, precision, recall and $F_1$ score, requires binary decisions, 'Yes' and 'No'. For a technique $\beta$, the decision 'Yes' represents that the technique $\beta$ has declared the pair as corresponding pair (equivalent pair), whereas the decision 'No' represents that the technique has declared the pair as unequivalent pair. To convert the similarity scores between 0 and 1 to Yes and No, we have used a cut-off threshold 0.75. The choice of cut-off threshold stems from the fact that multiple matching systems participated in latest episode Process Model Matching Contest 2015 have shown promising results at this threshold or a similar threshold [8]. The overall performance scores and the performance of each individual types of pairs are presented in Table 6.

Note, for the complete dataset, we have presented all the performance scores in the table. In contrast, for the three types of pairs, we have only presented the Recall scores because the precision scores of all techniques for all types of pairs are 1, due to the absence of unequivalent pairs. A further analysis of the results are as follows:

*Overall Results of the Techniques.* From the overall results presented in Table 6, it can be observed that there is no significant difference between the performance of techniques for the UA dataset. That is, the $F_1$ score achieved by the three techniques for UA dataset are comparable. The similarity trend can be observed for the other two datasets. However, the performance scores achieved by all the techniques for AM dataset are higher than BR dataset. Furthermore, the performance scores achieved by all the techniques for BR dataset are higher than UA dataset, indicating that BR dataset contains harder-to-detect pairs than UA dataset. From the table it can also be observed that the cause of below-par $F_1$ scores is the lower Recall scores. These lower Recall

**Table 6.** Results of the semantic similarity measures.

| Datasets | Measures | Overall | | | VB | MC | HR |
|---|---|---|---|---|---|---|---|
| | | P | R | $F_1$ | R | R | R |
| UA dataset | Lin | 0.86 | 0.55 | 0.67 | 1 | 0.66 | 0.28 |
| | Lesk | 0.85 | 0.55 | 0.66 | 1 | 0.66 | 0.28 |
| | Path | 0.90 | 0.49 | 0.63 | 0.99 | 0.17 | 0.30 |
| BR dataset | Lin | 1 | 0.35 | 0.52 | 0.96 | 0.33 | 0.01 |
| | Lesk | 1 | 0.34 | 0.50 | 0.96 | 0.27 | 0.01 |
| | Path | 0.98 | 0.30 | 0.47 | 0.88 | 0.17 | 0.03 |
| AM dataset | Lin | 0.93 | 0.77 | 0.84 | 1 | 0.36 | 0.18 |
| | Lesk | 0.94 | 0.76 | 0.84 | 1 | 0.36 | 0.14 |
| | Path | 0.99 | 0.73 | 0.84 | 0.98 | 0.32 | 0.11 |

scores represent that there is a need for considering other similarity measures for accurate identification of corresponding pairs.

*Performance Variation Across Pairs.* The three graphs presented in Figs. 2 and 3 show a performance comparison of the techniques across the three types of pairs. From the figure it can be observed that the Recall for VB pairs is either exactly 1 or nearly 1. This indicates that all the three techniques successfully detected the VB pairs with a very high accuracy. It can also be observed from the graphs that the Recall drops significantly for MC pairs and it becomes extremely low for the HR pairs. This indicates that the similarity measures only identified a fraction of the corresponding pairs in which the constituent labels are substantially different. However, these measures completely failed in identifying the HR pairs. These dropping scores further represent that the enhancements to our dataset are in-line with our plan.

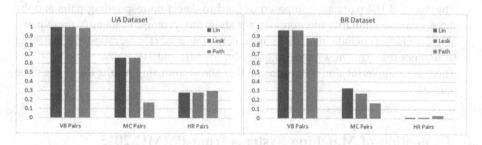

**Fig. 2.** Performance variation across pairs for UA and BR datasets

*Performance Variation Across Techniques.* To understand the performance variation across techniques, Fig. 4 plots the average of the Recall scores of the three datasets. From the graph it can be observed that there is no significant difference between performances of the three techniques for all the three types of pairs. This indicates there is no universally acceptable similarity measure that performs equally well for all the three datasets.

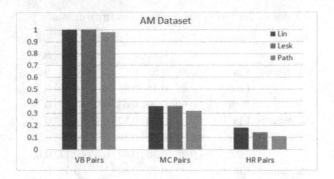

**Fig. 3.** Performance variation across pairs for AM dataset

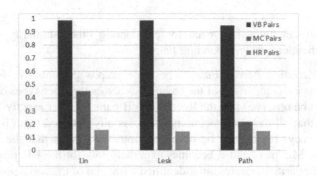

**Fig. 4.** Performance variation across techniques

Based on the results we conclude the following:

- The MC and HR pairs are composed of hard-to-detect corresponding pairs and the three semantic similarity measures do not show any promise to identify these pairs. We therefore conclude that there is a need for a next generation of matching techniques that can show promising results for MR and HR pairs.
- There is no universal similarity measure that show promising results for all the three datasets.

## 4    Evaluation of Matching Systems from PMMC 2015

This section presents our third contribution, a comprehensive evaluation of 12 matching systems that participated in Process Model Contest 2015. Similar to the evaluation of semantic similarity measures, we have used our enhanced PMMC'15 dataset for the evaluation of the matching systems. To that end, we mapped the publicly available results[3] to our enhanced dataset, and used it to generate the scores of the performance

---

[3] The results can be downloaded from https://ai.wu.ac.at/emisa2015/contest.php.

**Table 7.** Results of UA dataset

| | Overall | | | VB | MC | HR |
|---|---|---|---|---|---|---|
| | P | R | F1 | R | R | R |
| AML-PM | 0.56 | 0.70 | 0.62 | 0.93 | 0.47 | 0.64 |
| BPLang | 0.57 | 0.44 | 0.49 | 0.80 | 0.21 | 0.30 |
| NHCM | 0.88 | 0.44 | 0.58 | 0.92 | 0.28 | 0.22 |
| NLM | 1.00 | 0.29 | 0.45 | 0.99 | 0.00 | 0.00 |
| MSSS | 0.90 | 0.31 | 0.46 | 0.95 | 0.17 | 0.00 |
| OP-BOT | 0.76 | 0.37 | 0.49 | 0.71 | 0.28 | 0.21 |
| KMS | 0.77 | 0.52 | 0.62 | 0.99 | 0.70 | 0.23 |
| SMSL | 0.65 | 0.38 | 0.48 | 0.82 | 0.19 | 0.20 |
| TripleS | 0.56 | 0.34 | 0.42 | 0.99 | 0.13 | 0.05 |
| Knoma – Proc | 0.70 | 0.62 | 0.66 | 0.99 | 0.30 | 0.51 |
| VM2 | 0.41 | 0.58 | 0.48 | 0.86 | 0.51 | 0.44 |
| pPALMDS | 0.32 | 0.73 | 0.45 | 0.96 | 0.57 | 0.64 |

measures. For a thorough evaluation, we generated the scores of the performance measures using the complete datasets as well as for each type of pair, separately.

The results of all techniques for the three datasets are present in Tables 7, 8 and 9. Similar to the results of the semantic measures for the complete dataset, we have presented all the performance scores in the table. In contrast to that, for the three types of pairs we have only presented the Recall scores. Below, we present the *analysis of the results:*

*Overall Results of the Techniques.* For the UA dataset, overall highest $F_1$ score of 0.66 is achieved by Knoma-Proc, whereas pPALMDS achieved an $F_1$ score of 0.45. For the BR dataset, overall highest $F_1$ score of 0.68 is achieved by pPALMDS, whereas

**Table 8.** Results of BR dataset

| | Overall | | | VB | MC | HR |
|---|---|---|---|---|---|---|
| | P | R | F1 | R | R | R |
| AML-PM | 0.82 | 0.45 | 0.58 | 0.91 | 0.44 | 0.18 |
| BPLang | 0.94 | 0.35 | 0.51 | 0.77 | 0.34 | 0.11 |
| NHCM | 0.97 | 0.36 | 0.53 | 0.75 | 0.47 | 0.10 |
| NLM | 1.00 | 0.24 | 0.39 | 0.77 | 0.06 | 0.00 |
| MSSS | 1.00 | 0.22 | 0.36 | 0.68 | 0.09 | 0.00 |
| OP-BOT | 0.92 | 0.44 | 0.60 | 0.70 | 0.38 | 0.32 |
| KMS | 0.97 | 0.28 | 0.43 | 0.68 | 0.25 | 0.05 |
| SMSL | 0.72 | 0.37 | 0.49 | 0.78 | 0.37 | 0.15 |
| TripleS | 0.92 | 0.35 | 0.51 | 0.79 | 0.39 | 0.08 |
| Knoma – Proc | 0.86 | 0.37 | 0.52 | 0.78 | 0.46 | 0.11 |
| VM2 | 0.69 | 0.59 | 0.64 | 0.78 | 0.63 | 0.47 |
| pPALMDS | 0.85 | 0.57 | 0.68 | 0.77 | 0.58 | 0.46 |

Knoma-Proc achieved an $F_1$ score of 0.52. For the AM dataset, overall highest $F_1$ score of 0.82 is achieved by Knoma-Proc, whereas pPALMDS achieved an $F_1$ score of 0.44. These results indicate there is no universal system that achieved higher accuracy for all the three datasets.

From the results of the UA dataset it can be observed that KMS show promising results for MC pairs (R = 0.70). However, this technique performs poorly for HR pairs (R = 0.23). From the results of the BR dataset it can be observed that VM2 shows promising result for MC pairs (R = 0.63), and its performance reduces slightly for HR pairs (R = 0.47). Similar trends can be observed for the AM dataset. Based on these results we conclude that, a large majority of the techniques do not show comparable performance for MC and HR pairs.

**Table 9.** Results of AM dataset

|  | Overall | | | VB | MC | HR |
|---|---|---|---|---|---|---|
|  | P | R | F1 | R | R | R |
| AML-PM | 0.86 | 0.31 | 0.46 | 0.34 | 0.56 | 0.17 |
| BPLang | 0.79 | 0.29 | 0.42 | 0.32 | 0.40 | 0.16 |
| NHCM | 0.97 | 0.25 | 0.40 | 0.33 | 0.20 | 0.04 |
| NLM | 1.00 | 0.24 | 0.39 | 0.34 | 0.00 | 0.00 |
| MSSS | 0.91 | 0.23 | 0.37 | 0.33 | 0.04 | 0.00 |
| OP-BOT | 0.68 | 0.31 | 0.42 | 0.34 | 0.36 | 0.19 |
| KMS | 0.77 | 0.31 | 0.44 | 0.34 | 0.40 | 0.19 |
| SMSL | 0.79 | 0.13 | 0.22 | 0.15 | 0.12 | 0.06 |
| TripleS | 0.73 | 0.32 | 0.44 | 0.34 | 0.32 | 0.24 |
| Knoma – Proc | 0.85 | 0.79 | 0.82 | 0.97 | 0.60 | 0.28 |
| VM2 | 0.74 | 0.29 | 0.42 | 0.31 | 0.40 | 0.20 |
| pPALMDS | 0.52 | 0.38 | 0.44 | 0.34 | 0.56 | 0.47 |

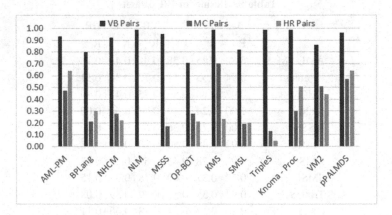

**Fig. 5.** Performance variation across pairs for UA dataset

Below, we further analyze the results of the matching systems.

*Performance Variation Across Pairs.* The three graphs in Figs. 5, 6 and 7 plots the Recall score across the 12 matching systems. From the figure it can be observed that the Recall scores for VB pairs are very high for UA and BR datasets. It can also be observed that the Recall scores drop significantly for the MC pairs. Furthermore, the Recall scores drop further for the HR pairs. These results indicate that majority of the matching systems fail to identify the HR pairs. However, there some exceptions (AML-PM, BPLang, Knoma-Proc, and pPALMDS) that achieve higher Recall score for HR pairs than MC pairs for one dataset, UA dataset. Among these, pPALMDS is the extraordinary matching system due to three reasons, (a) for the UA dataset, the matching system achieved higher Recall for the HR pairs than for the MC pairs (0.64 > 0.57), (b) for the BR dataset, the performance decline from MC to HR pairs is not substantial, i.e. 0.12, and (c) for the AM dataset, the performance decline from MC to HR pairs is not substantial, i.e. 0.09. Hence, we declare pPALMDS as the best performing system.

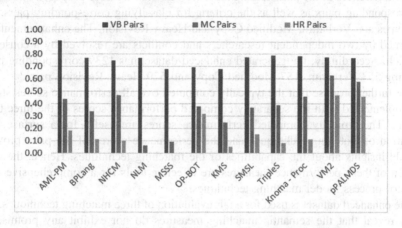

**Fig. 6.** Performance variation across pairs for BR dataset

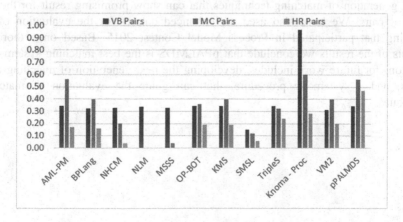

**Fig. 7.** Performance variation across pairs for AM dataset

# 5  Conclusion

A plethora of matching techniques have been developed. To evaluate the effectiveness of these techniques researchers typically use PMMC'15 datasets and the performance score of the three performance measures, Precision, Recall and $F_1$ score. However, our synthesis of the datasets and results of the matching techniques have revealed two issues, (a) the absence of trivial pairs in the datasets artificially inflates the performance scores, (b) the overall performance scores are useful for a surface level evaluation of a technique, however in the presence of diverse corresponding pairs it does not provide the necessary insights about the capabilities of the techniques. For instance, it does not answer important questions, such as how many trivial corresponding pairs are identified and many harder-to-detect corresponding pairs are identified.

In this paper, we address these two issues by enhancing the PMMC'15 datasets. For the enhancements, we have pre-processed the gold standards included in the PMMC'15 datasets and classified the corresponding pairs into three types, depending upon the level of differences in the participating labels. To do that, we have proposed three types of corresponding pairs as well as the criteria for classifying corresponding pairs. The three types are, Verbatim, Modified Copy and Heavy Revision. The enhancements are performed by two independent researchers and conflicts are resolved by a consensus approach. Accordingly, the generated enhanced dataset has 1239 corresponding pairs, including 553 Verbatim, 157 Modified Copy and 529 Heavy Revision pairs.

We further propose that the typically computed overall performance scores should be complemented with the separately computed performance scores of the three types of pairs. The typically computed performance scores are useful for a surface level evaluation of matching techniques and the performance scores of the pairs provides valuable insights about the capabilities of the matching techniques. Hence, the combination of these performance measures are effective tools for a comprehensive evaluation of process model matching techniques.

The enhanced dataset is used for a fair evaluation of three matching techniques. The results reveal that the semantic matching measures do not exhibit any promise for identifying Modified Copy and Heavy Revision Pairs. Hence, highlighting the need for a next generation of matching techniques that can show promising result for the two types of pairs. We have also used the enhanced dataset for the evaluation of the matching that participated in Process Model Contest 2015. Based on a thorough analysis of the results we conclude that pPALMDS is the best matching system. The directions for future work includes, developing the next generation of matching techniques, and a systematic procedure, that can guide the evaluation of matching techniques.

# References

1. Kuss, E., Leopold, H., van der Aa, H., Stuckenschmidt, H., Reijers, H.A.: Probabilistic evaluation of process model matching techniques. In: Comyn-Wattiau, I., Tanaka, K., Song, I.-Y., Yamamoto, S., Saeki, M. (eds.) ER 2016. LNCS, vol. 9974, pp. 279–292. Springer, Cham (2016). https://doi.org/10.1007/978-3-319-46397-1_22
2. Jabeen, F., Leopold, H., Reijers, Hajo A.: How to make process model matching work better? An analysis of current similarity measures. In: Abramowicz, W. (ed.) BIS 2017. LNBIP, vol. 288, pp. 181–193. Springer, Cham (2017). https://doi.org/10.1007/978-3-319-59336-4_13
3. Rodríguez, C., Klinkmüller, C., Weber, I., Daniel, F., Casati, F.: Activity matching with human intelligence. In: La Rosa, M., Loos, P., Pastor, O. (eds.) BPM 2016. LNBIP, vol. 260, pp. 124–140. Springer, Cham (2016). https://doi.org/10.1007/978-3-319-45468-9_8
4. Awad, A., Polyvyanyy, A., Weske, M.: Semantic querying of business. Process models. In: Proceedings of the 12th IEEE International Conference on Enterprise Distributed Object Computing Conference (EDOC 2008), pp. 85–94, Munich, Germany (2008)
5. Dumas, M., García-Bañuelos, L., La Rosa, M., Uba, R.: Fast detection of exact clones in business process model repositories. Inf. Syst. 38(4), 619–633 (2012)
6. La Rosa, M., Dumas, M., Uba, R., Dijkman, R.M.: Business process model merging: an approach to business process consolidation. ACM Trans. Softw. Eng. Methodol. 22(2), 11–42 (2012)
7. Meilicke, C., Leopold, H., Kuss, E.S., Reijers, H.: Overcoming individual process model matcher weaknesses using ensemble matching. Decis. Support Syst. 100(1), 15–26 (2017)
8. Antunes, G., et al.: The process model matching contest 2015. In: Kolb, J., Leopold, H., Mendling, J. (eds.) Proceedings of the 6th International Workshop on Enterprise Modelling and Information Systems Architecture (EMISA 2015), Innsbruck, Austria. LNI, pp. 1–29. Springer, Heidelberg (2015)
9. Kuss, E., Leopold, H., Aa, H., Stuckenschmidt Reijers, H.A.: A probabilistic evaluation procedure for process model matching techniques. DKE J. (2018, in press)
10. Sonntag, A., Hake, P., Fettke, P., Loos, P.: An approach for semantic business process model matching using supervised machine learning. In: Proceedings of the 24th European Conference on Information Systems, pp. 1– 12. AIS, Istanbul (2016)
11. Clough, P., Gaizauskas, R., Piao, S., Wilks, Y.: METER: MEasuring TExt Reuse. In: Proceedings of the 40th Annual Meeting on Association for Computational Linguistics (ACL 2002), Philadelphia, USA, pp. 152–159 (2002)
12. Clough, P., Stevenson, M.: Developing a corpus of plagiarized short answers. Lang. Resour. Eval. 45(1), 5–24 (2011)
13. Sameen, S., Sharjeel, M., Nawab, R.M.A., Rayson, P., Muneer, I.: Measuring short text reuse for the Urdu language. IEEE Access 6(1), 7412–7421 (2018)
14. Xiao, C., Wang, W., Lin, X., Yu, J.X.: Efficient similarity joins for near duplicate detection. ACM Trans. Database Syst. 36(3), 1–15 (2011)
15. Miller, A.G.: WordNet: a lexical database for English. Commun. ACM 38(11), 39–41 (1995)
16. Patwardhan, S., Banerjee, S., Pedersen, T.: Using measures of semantic relatedness for word sense disambiguation. In: Proceedings of the 4th International Conference on Intelligent Text Processing and Computational Linguistics, Maxico City, Mexico, pp. 241–257 (2003)
17. Budanitsky, A., Hirst, G.: Evaluating WordNet-based measures of lexical semantic relatedness. Comput. Linguist. 32(1), 13–47 (2006)

18. Lin, D.: An information-theoretic definition of similarity. In: Proceedings of the 15th International Conference on Machine Learning (ICML 1998), Madison, USA, pp. 296–304 (1998)
19. Lesk, M.: Automatic sense disambiguation using machine readable dictionaries: how to tell a pine cone from a ice cream cone. In: Proceedings of the 5th Annual International Conference on Systems Documentation (SIGDOC 1986), Toronto, Canada, pp. 24–26 (1986)
20. Niemann, M., Siebenhaar, M., Schulte, S., Steinmetz, R.: Comparison and retrieval of process models using related cluster pairs. Comput. Ind. 63(2), 168–180 (2012)
21. Sebu, M.L.: Similarity of business process models in a modular design. In: Proceedings of the Applied Computational Intelligence and Informatics (SACI 2016), Timisoara, Romania, pp. 31–36 (2016)

# Investigating the Applicability of the Normalized Systems Theory on IT Infrastructure Systems

Geert Haerens[1,2]([envelope])

[1] University Antwerp, Antwerpen, Belgium
geert.haerens@student.uantwerpen.be
[2] Engie, Brussels, Belgium
geert.haerens@engie.com

**Abstract.** The agile enterprise requires evolvability at all layers of the enterprise - business, application and infrastructure. IT infrastructure systems are at the heart of IT systems in general. Their evolution has a profound impact on applications and business capabilities. Normalized Systems Theory (NS) provides theorems to evaluate the evolvability of modular systems. As IT infrastructure systems can be represented by a modular structure, it is expected that NS can be used to study the evolvability of IT infrastructure systems. This paper demonstrates that NS can indeed be used to study the evolvability of IT Infrastructure systems. For this purpose, an artefact has been designed, made up of a 5-step method, to study the evolvability of a modular system representing an IT infrastructure system using NS. The artefact has been successfully applied to some IT infrastructure systems, but the method requires refinement and a more rigorous translation of the NS theorems into IT infrastructure equivalents is required. Although further research is required, the paper contributes to the growing number of domains on which NS can be applied.

**Keywords:** IT infrastructure systems · Normalised systems
Modularity · Evolvability

## 1 Introduction

The agile and morphogenic enterprise [1] requires the capabilities for an enterprise to cope with constant change. Enterprise organization, processes, applications and infrastructure need to cope with the required agility. IT infrastructure can be described as the Physical Infrastructure (PI) - processors, disks, network routers, switches and cables, and all other physical objects that are needed to run the software systems that constitute the business systems and software infrastructure layers - but it also includes the Software Infrastructure (SI) - software systems that are not specific for the organization, such as operating systems, database management systems, email servers, etc. (see [2]). No application will

© Springer Nature Switzerland AG 2018
R. Pergl et al. (Eds.): EOMAS 2018, LNBIP 332, pp. 123–137, 2018.
https://doi.org/10.1007/978-3-030-00787-4_9

run without IT infrastructure. During the last decades, massive changes have been observed in the evolution of IT infrastructure: from monolithic computer systems to distributed systems, from company owned data centers to a public cloud setup, from MB to PB's of storage, from Mb to Gb network speeds. Those evolutions have had a profound impact and one would expect IT infrastructure to be stable with respect to those anticipatable changes. Unfortunately, this is not the case. Based on the concept of stability from systems theory, the Normalized Systems Theory (NS) [5] investigates the necessary conditions for information systems to be stable with respect to a set of anticipated changes in order to exhibit high evolvability. This requires information systems to be free from Combinatorial Effects (CE). Combinatorial Effects (CE) occur when the impact of a change depends on the change itself and the size of the system. If this is the case, if CE occur, the system is considered unstable under change. To eliminate these Combinatorial Effects, the Normalized Systems Theory proposes four theorems that are constraints on the modular structure of the systems architecture. The theorems are prescriptive and ensure that stable information systems are built, thereby guaranteeing high evolvability. Although NS originates in software development, the concepts of modularity and the existence of CE can be observed and investigated in a much broader domain [8]. This paper aims at opening up NS to the domain of IT Infrastructure Systems.

If an IT infrastructure system could be represented by a relevant modular structure, then the NS theorems could be applied on this modular structure. By doing so, the evolvability of the IT infrastructure system could be evaluated.

In the proposal section of the paper, an artefact is being put forward, consisting of a 5-step method, to evaluate the compliance of a modular representation of an IT infrastructure system with the NS theorems. In the demonstration section, the artefact will be applied on 2 IT infrastructure hosting patterns, being physical and virtual hosting. In the evaluation section, the artefact will be scored based on the correctness of the applied method and the usefulness of the artefact. The conclusion section will elaborate on the main contribution - being that NS **can** be applied on IT infrastructure systems - and further required research.

## 2    Proposal

Design Science identifies a method, a step by step approach to address a problem, as a valid artefact to apply to a problem (see [9–11]). The problem has been identified as "Apply the NS theorems on a modular representation of an IT infrastructure system.". According to the Normalized Systems Theory (see [6,7]), a modular system is considered stable under change and thus evolvable, when the system is free of CE. NS postulates that the necessary conditions to have a CE-free system, is for the system to have a modular structure which respects 4 principles in all modules which make up the system: Separation of Concerns (SoC), Separation of State (SoS), Version Transparency (VT) and Instance Traceability (IT). The 4th NS theorem concerned with Instance Traceability is less relevant for evolvability and focuses on the isentropy or diagnosability of a system. A such, only the first 3 theorems will be considered. By applying the Normalized Systems theorems, the evolvability of the IT infrastructure system is being tested. The artefact resulting from the design process consists of the following 5-step method:

- **Step 1:** Create a relevant modular representation of the IT infrastructure system.
- **Step 2:** For each module of the modular representation, look for the manifestations of Concern, State and Version, as those are the primary aspects studied by NS in a modular system.
- **Step 3:** Check if the manifestations found in Step 2 are compliant with the relevant NS principles.
- **Step 4:** If there is non-compliance with one or more of the NS principles, describe changes to the system which will induce Combinatorial Effects (CE) - impact of the change depends on the change itself and the size of the system undergoing the change.
- **Step 5:** Summarize steps 1 to 4 in the artefact summary table (Fig. 1).

The artefact can also be used in the opposite direction, meaning that based on observed Combinatorial Effects, the violation of one or more of the NS principles can be identified and this violation can be associated with a manifestation of Concern, State and Version in a module representing a function and/or construction component of an IT infrastructure system. The next 5 subsections will elaborate more on each step of the artefact.

| Infrastructure System | Concern | State | Version |
|---|---|---|---|
| Module 1 | | | |
| Module 2 | | | |
| Module 3 | | | |
| Module 4 | | | |

| Compliance | SoC | SoS | VT |
|---|---|---|---|
| NS theorems respected Y/N | Y/N | Y/N | Y/N |

| Observed CE | 1. CE1 2. CE2 2. CE3 | 1. CE1 2. CE2 2. CE3 | 1. CE1 2. CE2 2. CE3 |
|---|---|---|---|

**Fig. 1.** Artefact summary table

## 2.1   Step 1: Modular Representation

ArchiMate [4] is being put forward to perform step 1 as it is a formal modelling language which addresses the IT infrastructure layer. A relevant ArchiMate compliant modular representation will combine ArchiMate IT infrastructure construction components (such as nodes, devices, system software - components which can be physically deployed) and ArchiMate IT infrastructure functional components (such as infrastructure function and infrastructure service -

components representing logical groupings, independent of physical implementation). IT infrastructure functional components are realised by a combination of IT infrastructure construction components. Those function and construction aspects are the modules which will be investigated in step 2 of the artefact.

## 2.2    Step 2: Manifestations of Concern, State and Version

For each module of the modular system, manifestations of Concern, State and Version must be looked for. In step 3, those manifestations will be tested against the 3 NS theorems. Concerns of a system are different aspects of the design of the system. Example, in the design of a house, the water network (plumbing) is one concern/aspect, while the electricity network is a second concern/ aspect. The Version of a system is an evolution of a concern/aspect which answers to new requirements. Example, in the design of a house, a new version of the water network is one that is connected to a descaling installation or a new version of the electricity network, is one that is connected to solar panels. State is the "uttering of the situation" of a system. Examples are the temperate of the water in the water network of the amount of current flowing thought the electrical network.

For IT infrastructure systems, a formalized method to detect and list Concern, State and Version (as defined above) is currently lacking and subject to further research. Detecting manifestations of Concern, State and Version must currently be performed based on domain-specific knowledge of IT infrastructure systems and the following rules of thumb:

- Different anticipated changes (add, replace, remove) to the modular structure represent different Concerns.
- Different infrastructure functions mean different Concerns.
- Infrastructure functions can be composed of other infrastructure functions – potential violation of Separation of Concern.
- Infrastructure construction component can realize more than one infrastructure function – potential violation of Separation of Concern.
- Infrastructure construction components can have a State which is persisted internally or externally to the component – potential violation of Separation of State.
- Infrastructure construction components can exchange data with other infrastructure components in a synchronous or asynchronous manner – potential violation of Separation of State.
- Infrastructure construction components can have different versions, and each version may address infrastructure functions differently or address different infrastructure functions – potential violation of Version Transparency.

## 2.3    Step 3: NS Theorems Compliancy Check

NS prescribes the conditions to which the modular structure of a system must adhere to in order for the system to the stable under change (free of CE). Checking the compliance with the NS theorems of the modular structure of an existing system will provide insight in the evolvability of the system. As explained in Sect. 2.1, 3 of the 4 NS theorems are taken into account. Those 3 theorems will be checked for each module making up the IT infrastructure system.

**Separation of Concern (SoC):** Are different concerns/aspects/functions address in different modules or are concerns/aspects/functions aggregated into modules? If they are, SoC is violated and changes (add, remove, replace) to the system (and the modules) will lead to CE and thus an unstable system under change (see [5–7] formal proof).

**Separation of State (SoS):** Do the different modules persist their state outside of themselves (and thus externally observable)? And do all modules exchange information with each other by first persisting the information outside of themselves? If they do not, SoS is violated and changes (add, remove, replace) to the system (and the modules) will lead to CE and thus an unstable system under change (see [5–7] formal proof.

**Version Transparency (VT):** Will different versions of the modules of the system behave in an idempotent way towards using modules? If they do not, VT is violated and changes (add, remove, replace) to the system (and the modules) will lead to CE and thus an unstable system under change (see [5–7] formal proof).

As indicated in step 2, Concern, State and Version have no formalized definitions in IT infrastructure systems. When a deeper understanding of Concern, State and Version in IT infrastructure systems is available (future research), it is expected that a transformation of the NS theorems into a set of infrastructure relevant theorems can be made, thus facilitating step 3.

### 2.4 Step 4: Describe CE in Case of Non-compliance with NS Theorems

When violations of the NS theorems are found, examples need to be provided which demonstrate that the violation leads to Combinatorial Effects - impact of the change depends on the change itself and the size of the system undergoing the change. CE can be expressed in IF A THEN B statements, where A is the change of an infrastructure component/function and B is the effect on the system. Sequences of IF THEN statements are possible.

### 2.5 Step 5: Fill Out the Summary Table

The results of steps 2 to 4 are summarized in Fig. 1. The current version of the artefact does not prescribe a semantic on how to fill out the summary table.

## 3 Demonstration

In [12], the artefact has been applied on 3 different IT infrastructure systems, being housing (data center facilities), hosting and network proxy. This paper will focus on demonstrating the artefact on the hosting IT infrastructure system as hosting is an elementary functionality required to run any application.

Two patterns of hosting will be discussed.

Hosting 1 is a pattern for physical hosting and Hosting 2 is a pattern for virtual hosting. These 2 patterns represent the dominant way in which hosting is set up. For example, hosting in a cloud infrastructure is nothing more than highly standardized and elastic virtual hosting with additional deployment facilities accessible via the Internet and standard Internet protocols (http/https). In addition, each virtual hosting platform is based on a physical hosting pattern as virtual hosts don't get their resources out of thin air but from physical hardware.

This paper does not focus on providing the most detailed and accurate model for a hosting IT Infrastructure system but on demonstrating that the NS theorems can be used to analyse the evolvability of IT infrastructure systems. Hosting is defined as the combination of a hardware platform and an Operating System (OS), offering the possibility to exploit the hardware resources (CPU, memory, disk, Input/Output) via an Operating System (OS). The presented model is a simplified version of a hosting IT Infrastructure system which is Operating System flavour agnostic [13].

### 3.1    Applying the Artefact to a Physical Hosting Pattern

**Step 1: Modular Structure**
Figure 2 is a modular representation of the Physical Hosting pattern using Archi-Mate as formal modelling language.

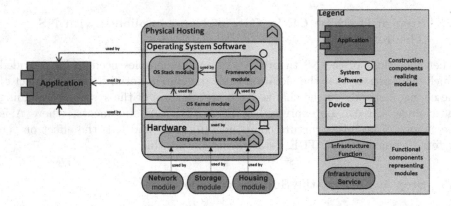

**Fig. 2.** Physical Hosting pattern

Note that the Physical Hosting pattern has couplings with other IT infrastructure systems such as network, storage and housing, and that an application has multiple ways to tap into the Physical Hosting resources.

A physical hosting IT Infrastructure system is made up of multiple modules. The first module of a hosting system is the Computer Hardware module which delivers processor power, memory and input/output control. All Computer Hardware functions are realised by physical devices, packed in a Hardware device. The Operating System Software, which is installed on the Hardware device, is composed of the OS kernel, OS stacks and Framework stacks.

The Operating System kernel module provides access to the Computer Hardware resources.

The Operating System stacks module is a collection of software running on top of the OS kernel module and installed with the OS kernel, which allow applications to get access to the network and storage resources, access to the graphical power of the hardware, access to the OS process and resource management capabilities.

The Framework stacks module consists of different software stacks which allow the exploitation of the computer resources by combining and packaging the functionalities offered by the OS kernel, network, storage, graphical, process and resource stacks (part of the OS stacks) in different software packages usable in different programming languages.

### Step 2: Manifestations of Concern, State and Version

Each of the modules making up the Physical Hosting pattern will now be investigated for manifestations of Concern, State, Version and Instance.

*Computer hardware* addresses multiple concerns - CPU, GPU (graphical CPU), memory, Input/Output. Computer hardware is a fine grained modular structure and has been a source of inspiration for the creation of the Normalized Systems Theory. The assumption is made that, although multiple concerns are addressed, they can be packaged in such way that these multiple concerns are not a source of Combinatorial Effects (CE). Computer hardware has manifestation of State. Computer hardware can persist its state outside the module and can be interrogated. An example is the ability to look up CPU and memory usage and the health status of hardware components. Some computer hardware will also persist state to transmit information. An example is the usage of buffers where one hardware module writes requests for instruction execution and another module will read those requests and execute them. Computer hardware has manifestation of Version - CPU versions, memory etc. Hardware vendors deliver compatibility matrices which prescribe which hardware versions are compatible with each other and other modules. Non-compliance with vendor-delivered compatibility can lead to serious malfunctioning.

*Operating System kernel* addresses multiple concerns such as pushing instructions to the CPU, transferring data from memory to buffers, reacting on interrupts, performing Input/Output. The OS kernel is an aggregation of functionalities. Operating System kernels have a state and will persist this state in logs. Operating Systems kernels work most of the time in synchronous mode. State is not used to transfer information between sub modules. Operating System kernels come in different versions, linked to the Operating System release and Operating System patch level. Version compatibility issues can occur.

*Operating System stacks* come in different forms and address multiple concerns. For instance, in the Network stack, the 7 OSI layers [14] are addressed to make sure data can be transferred from one computer to another. Each of the 7 layers of the OSI stack can be considered as a separate module at the conceptual level, but this does not mean that the OSI model is implemented as 7 loosely coupled modules. Not only will the OS stack address multiple concerns in each stack, but also within a stack, multiple concerns are present and depending on the implementation, even combined in modules. Operating System stacks will persist their state in logs. Calling functions of an Operating System stack happens synchronous, although the internal processing may be asynchronous. Operating System stacks come in different versions, linked to the Operating System release and Operating System patch level. Version compatibility issues can occur.

*Framework stacks* address multiple concerns. They can contain all kinds of combinations of calls towards the Operation System stacks and the Operating System kernel. Framework stacks may or may not persist their state. This will depend on the Framework. Frameworks come in different versions, linked to the Operating System release and patch level. Version Compatibility issues can occur.

**Step 3: Check NS Theorems Compliance**
Applying steps 1 and 3 to the Physical Hosting pattern leads to the conclusion that the pattern has serious evolvability issues as non of the 3 NS principles are respected in the modular structure. Operating Systems are packed with functionalities and the different modules do not respect Separation of Concern (SoC). According to NS, this will lead to Combinatorial Effects (CE) under change. Version Transparency will only amplify this issue. Backwards compatibilities is limited in time for commercial available Operating Systems. The non compliance with Separation of State (SoS) is more difficult to assess. NS identified synchronous communication as a root cause of CE and the vast majority of Operating Systems calls are implemented in a synchronous fashion. This becomes visible when an OS "freezes" - meaning no longer responds to commands or application calls - while seen from the external points of view, the cause of the freeze cannot be seen nor diagnosed. The non-compliance with both Separation of Concern (SoC) and Version Transparency (VT) has the largest impact in practice. There is no such thing as an impact-free OS upgrade, although it is an anticipatable change. During an OS upgrade, functions are added or removed or do not react in an idempotent fashion.

**Step 4: Describe Observed CE due to Non-compliance with the NS Theorems**
Let's consider the following anticipated changes to the modular structure: adding an application to a host and replacing a module of the host.

*Adding an Application.* The Hosting pattern is being used by a new application. The application may require a specific version of one of the host's modules. As a result, an upgrade/downgrade may be required. This upgrade/downgrade of an

OS module may result in the malfunctioning of the other applications running on the host. The more application running on the host, the more likely the impact and the more additional changes are required (making the other applications compatible). The impact of the change is thus proportional to the size of the system.

*Replacing a Host Module.* Let's assume that the host will connect to an IPV6 (TCP/IP version 6) network. The host requires a new network interface card (NIC) which supports the IPV6 protocol. But the network stack requires upgrading as well. The OS provider only supports this new network stack in his next major release and as such not only the network stack is upgraded but all other modules of the OS. This can lead to incompatibilities with all applications running on the host, leading to a full review of the application landscape and deployment. The introduction of a new technology - IPV6 - can lead to a full IT systems and landscape impact. The impact of the change is thus proportional to the size of the system.

The 2 examples above are real life examples. OS vendors pack their OS with functionalities which are spread over different modules and combined in different modules, leading to an OS which has a high degree of coupling and sometimes a low degree of cohesion (for instance cross cutting concerns like security and availability).

## Step 5: Complete Artefact Summary Table

The results of the analyses performed in the previous steps are summarized in Fig. 3.

| Infrastructure System Modules | Concern | State | Version |
|---|---|---|---|
| Computer Hardware | Aggregation of functions | hardware alerting | HW version dependencies and compatibilities |
| Operating System Kernel | Aggregation of functions | logging - synchronious message passing | OS Version dependencies and compatibilities |
| Operating System Stacks | Aggregation of functions | logging - synchronious message passing | OS Version dependencies and compatibilities |
| Framework Stacks | Aggregation of functions | unknown | OS Version dependencies and compatibilities |
| Compliance | SoC | SoS | VT |
| NS theorems respected | NO | NO | NO |
| Observed CE | Changes in one of the 4 modules have effect on applications using the system. | OS "Freeze" not externally visible | Compatibility issues with OS versions leading to the "one application = one host" |

**Fig. 3.** Applying artefact to Physical Hosting pattern

## 3.2    Applying the Artefact to Virtual Hosting Pattern

The practical implications of the non-compliance with the 3 principles is that one application is installed on one host and that all modules of the hosting pattern need to stay as unchanged as possible in order not to impact the functioning of the application. One application on one host [17] results in underutilization of the hardware resources. Transactional applications (such as SAP) have a spiky CPU usage profile, meaning the application will consume CPU during short burst - moments of user interaction with the system - and be dormant between bursts. Averaging this out over a period of a day results in an average CPU usage of 10 to 40% (depending on the application), while optimal CPU usage should be around 70–80%. Virtual hosting has been the trigger to solve this issue. Running multiple Operating Systems (called guest OS) on one piece of hardware containing a specialized OS (called Hypervisor or host OS) and having one application associated with each guest OS, results in more optimal resource utilization while maintaining application isolation. In addition, virtualization provides operational benefits such as lower cost of hosting computer hardware due to better resource utilization, lower energy consumption, reduced data center footprint, application isolation, faster deployment, increased uptime and reduced system administration burden. More information on virtualization can be found in [15,16].

**Step 1: Modular Structure**
Figure 4 is a modular representation of Virtual Hosting pattern using Archi-Mate as formal modelling language. The Virtual Hosting pattern contains a new module called the Hypervisor. A Hypervisor can be either a special Operating System (example VM ESX) or embedded in another OS (example HP UX and Windows Hyper V). It allows the installation of multiple Operating Systems on top of the Hypervisor. The Hypervisor virtualizes the hardware, transforming actual CPU's into virtual CPU's. The scope of virtualization does not stop at the CPU level. Memory, storage, I/O, all can and have been virtualized inside and outside of the Hypervisor.

**Step 2: Manifestations of Concern, State and Version**
The Hypervisor module is the only new module introduced in this pattern and is the only module that will be investigated in step 2. The analysis of the other modules is identical to the Physical Hosting pattern.

*The Hypervisor* addresses multiple concerns. Not only CPU and memory virtualization but also software implemented network layer (switches) and software implemented storage layer. The Hypervisor will persist its state in log files. The Hypervisor works in synchronous mode and does not use state to transfer information from one module to another. Hypervisors come in different versions which can lead to version compatibility issues.

**Step 3: Check NS Theorems Compliance**
The analysis of step 2 leads to the conclusion that virtual hosting still violates the principles related to Concern, State and Version. Although virtualization

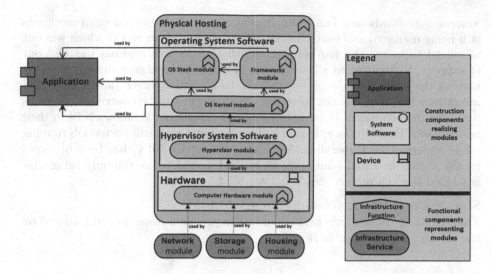

**Fig. 4.** Virtual Hosting pattern

has many operational benefits, it does not provide a solution for the evolvability issues related to the Physical Hosting pattern.

**Step 4: Describe Observed CE due to Non-compliance with the NS Theorems**

Let's consider the following anticipated changes to the modular structure: adding an application to a virtual host and replacing an OS module of the virtual host and Hypervisor.

*Adding an Application.* The possible cascade effect due to Version Transparency issues on OS modules is still present in a virtual host. Adding an application is thus best replaced by adding a new virtual host and adding the application on that host. This can trigger a lack of resources on the Hypervisor resulting in the need to install a new physical host with a Hypervisor and distributing the load over the different Hypervisors. This is still a CE but it grows at lower pace compared to adding an application to a physical host.

*Replacing a Host Module.* Evolutions in the Hypervisor have a more dramatic effect as those may require changes on all guest hosts (virtual hosts) running on the Hypervisor and this may required changes to the applications running on those hosts. Again, the impact of such a change is directly dependent on the size of the system. A real-life example is the issue of the usage of hosting in industrial environments. Some industrial equipment (machines, sensors, control systems) are managed by means of software running on COTS (Commercial Off The Shelf) Operating Systems, like Windows. The Windows NT4 OS found its way into the industrial environment around 1996. Most of this industrial equipment has a lifetime of 10 to 20 years, exceeding the lifetime of COTS Operating

Systems and hardware. The result is that, by 2005, industrial equipment was still being managed and controlled by software running on an OS which was out of official support. The hardware on which the OS was running was also out of support. Virtualization allowed to circumvent the hardware support issue by moving the server from a physical server to a virtual server (a so-called P2V migration) but that did not solve the OS support issue. Hypervisors evolve as well, and the vendors of Hypervisors stopped supporting Windows NT4 in their new releases. By 2010 the situation had evolved into an unsupported OS running on an unsupported Hypervisor. A project called "Kill NT4" has been observed by the author in 2 multi-nationals he worked in and twice, the only thing that got killed was the project, not Windows NT4.

**Step 5: Complete Artefact Summary Table**
The results of the analysis performed in the previous steps are summarized on the artefact summary table (Fig. 5).

| Infrastructure System Modules | *Concern* | *State* | *Version* |
|---|---|---|---|
| *Computer Hardware* | Aggregation of functions | hardware altering | HW version dependencies |
| *Hypervisor* | Aggregation of functions | logging - monitoring of Guest OS - synchronous message passing | Hypervisor and Guest OS Version dependencies and compatibilities |
| *Operating System Kernel* | Aggregation of functions | logging - synchronous message passing | OS Version dependencies and compatibilities |
| *Operating System Stacks* | Aggregation of functions | logging - synchronous message passing | OS Version dependencies and compatibilities |
| *Framework Stacks* | Aggregation of functions | unknown | OS Version dependencies and compatibilities |
| **Compliance** | SoC | SoS | VT |
| **NS theorems respected** | NO | NO | NO |

| | Changes in one of the 5 modules have effect on applications using the system. | OS "Freeze" not externally visible | Compatibility issues with OS versions leading to the "one application = one host" Compatibility issue between Hypervisor and Guest OS. |
|---|---|---|---|
| *Observed CE* | | | |

**Fig. 5.** Applying artefact to Virtual Hosting pattern

# 4    Evaluation

The design science refers to a "Knowledge Base" [9] against which each step of the design process can be checked. As the Normalized Systems Theory has not been applied yet on IT infrastructure systems, such a "Knowledge Base" does not exist. This motivated the creation of an expert team. The team was used to evaluate the whole design process and the end result, effectively evaluating the correctness and usefulness of the artefact. The expert team was made up of 13 IT infrastructure professionals with at least 10 years of experience in IT infrastructure. The team also included 2 people who have knowledge of NS, one of which has implemented NS in software development. The expert team was requested to score the artefact based on 3 questions. More information on the composition of the expert team can be found in [12].

The first question - "Are the models a good representation of reality?" - serves to score the correctness of the modular representation of the IT infrastructure system.

The second question - "Are the found Combinatorial Effects (CE) in line with your expectations and experience?" - serves to score the correctness of the found Combinatorial Effects (CE) based on the found manifestations of Concern, State, Version and Instance in the modular representation.

The last question - "Has the artefact given you extra insight?" - serves to score the usefulness of the analysis made via the artefact. The results of the evaluation can be found in Fig. 6.

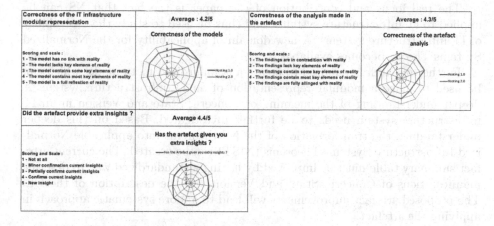

**Fig. 6.** Artefact evaluation results

The expert team did not limit itself to scoring and checking but also provided feedback on Combinatorial Effects (CE) they observed and were now able to link these effects to the non-compliance with one or more of the NS principles. The expert team contained 2 CIOs stating that "The artefact provides a meta model which is in line with practical decision making" and "The artefact provides a theoretical model explaining why infrastructure is so tricky". In [12], the evaluation of the application of the artefact on 2 additional IT infrastructure systems (housing and network proxy) can be found.

## 5    Conclusion

IT infrastructure systems are packed with hidden couplings. Changes and evolutions often result in the most bizarre Combinatorial Effects. The results of the application of NS on the Hosting IT infrastructure system (physical and virtual pattern) are no surprise. What is interesting is that thanks to the NS theorems, the most fundamental root cause of the evolvability issues become clear - the non-compliance with the NS theorems which are the necessary conditions for evolvability.

When the NS theorems are applied in a rigorous way, the resulting modular structure of the system will be a fine-grained modular structure. Each module will address 1 concern, will separate its state, will be version transparent. The modules making up and constructing a Hosting IT Infrastructure system do not have such fine grained modular structure at all. Although not the focus of this paper, it is worth mentioning that with the introduction of micro services and containerisation, Hosting is moving toward a more fine grained modular structure. For instance, a Docker container will run a stripped down version of the OS, containing only the functions required by the application running in the container.

The real focus and contribution of the paper is the fact that NS can be applied to IT infrastructure systems, and thus be used to study the evolvability of IT infrastructure systems. A new domain of applicability for the Normalized Systems Theory becomes available.

Further research is required to create a standardized meta model which can be used to make a modular representation of an IT infrastructure system. A deeper understanding of the meaning of Concern, State and Version in an IT infrastructure system needs to be further investigated. Based on this deeper understanding, the transformation of the NS theorems into applicable Normalized Infrastructure Systems Theorems (NIST) can be created. The current artefact summary table must be improved by having a standardized way to describe manifestations of Concern, State and Version and the description of the CE. The proposed artefact improvements will lead to a more systematic approach in applying the artefact.

The domain of IT infrastructure systems is changing rapidly. The times of complex IT Infrastructure systems with intertwined hardware, firmware, OS and software, are changing towards a domain where IT infrastructure systems become more fine grained available in the cloud where they are assembled by means of calling API's (Application Programming Interfaces). IT infrastructure becomes Software Defined. Once the transformation of the NS theorems into applicable Normalized Infrastructure Systems Theorems (NIST) is available, the research can shift towards ways of assembling Software Defined IT infrastructure components respecting the NIST such that the resulting IT infrastructure system has ex-ante proven evolvability. The enforcement of the NIST should be automated by means of an expander which will generate code which can be deployed on a Software Defined Infrastructure Platform (like AWS, Azure, Google), resulting in deployable and evolvable IT infrastructure systems.

# References

1. Hoogervorst, J.A.P.: Enterprise Governance and Enterprise Engineering. Springer, Heidelberg (2009). https://doi.org/10.1007/978-3-540-92671-9
2. Zarvic, N., Wieringa, R.: An Integrated Enterprise Architecture Framework for Business-IT Alignment (2006)
3. Wieringa, R., van Eck, P., Steghuis, C., Proper, E.: Competences of IT Architects (2009)
4. ArchiMate: The Open Group, February 2017. http://www.opengroup.org/subjectareas/enterprise/archimate
5. Mannaert, H., Verelst, J., De Bruyn, P.: Normalized Systems Theory: From Foundations for Evolvable Software Toward a General Theory for Evolvable Design (2016)
6. Mannaert, H., Verelst, J., Ven, K.: The transformation of requirements into software primitives: studying evolvability based on systems theoretic stability. Sci. Comput. Program. **76**(12), 1210–1222 (2011)
7. Mannaert, H., Verelst, J., Ven, K.: Towards evolvable software architectures based on systems theoretic stability. Softw. Pract. Exp. **42**(1), 89–116 (2012)
8. Huysmans, P., Oorts, G., De Bruyn, P., Mannaert, H., Verelst, J.: Positioning the normalized systems theory in a design theory framework. In: Shishkov, B. (ed.) BMSD 2012. LNBIP, vol. 142, pp. 43–63. Springer, Heidelberg (2013). https://doi.org/10.1007/978-3-642-37478-4_3
9. Johannesson, P., Perjons, E.: An Introduction to Design Science. Springer, Cham (2014). https://doi.org/10.1007/978-3-319-10632-8
10. Hevner, A.R., March, S.T., Park, J., Ram, S.: Design science in information systems research. MIS Q. **38**(1), 75–105 (2004)
11. Peffers, K., Tuunanen, T., Rothenberger, M.A., Chatterjee, S.: A design science research methodology for information systems research. J. Manag. Inf. Syst. **24**(3), 45–77 (2007)
12. Haerens, G.: Applying the generalized normalized systems theory to the Engie IT reference architecture library. Master thesis (2016). https://www.linkedin.com/in/geerthaerens/ under the "Education" section
13. Tanenbaum, A.S., Bos, H.: Modern Operating Systems, 4th edn. Prentice Hall Press, Upper Saddle River (2015). Global Edition
14. Zimmermann, H., Day, J.D.: The OSI reference model. Proc. IEEE **71**(12), 1334–1340 (1983)
15. https://www.vmware.com, February 2017
16. Portnoy, M.: Virtualization Essentials, 2nd edn. Wiley, Hoboken (2016)
17. Bhathal, G.B., Singh, G.N.: A comparative study of application portability with virtualization softwares. Int. J. Comput. Sci. Commun. **1**(2), 83–85 (2010)

# The DEMO Co-creation and Co-production Model and Its Utilization

Frantisek Hunka[1]([⊠]), Steven J. H. van Kervel[2], and Jiri Matula[1]

[1] University of Ostrava, Ostrava, Czech Republic
{frantisek.hunka, jiri.matula}@osu.cz
[2] Formetis Consultants BV, Boxtel, The Netherlands
info@formetis.nl

**Abstract.** Co-creation and Co-production in production chains is the typical way of cooperation one observes in high value industrial production chains. The DEMO (Design Engineering Methodology for Organization) co-creation and co-production (CC-CP) model is based on the DEMO methodology and the DEMO Enterprise Ontology. This model enables modeling paired transactions applications. The paired transactions mean that the core of the application is formed by two different kinds of transactions, where one kind of transactions is in consideration of the other kind of transactions. This is the fundamental aspect of e.g. accountancy systems, or various applications that utilize a contract. The paper describes and explains the main features of this model and then shows the model's application on a Rent-A-Car example. This is an example in which service (services) is exchanged for money. The paper also discusses various possibilities that the DEMO CC-CP model provides to properly capture modeling reality, and also mentions future research in this area.

**Keywords:** DEMO Enterprise Ontology (DEO) · DEMO methodology
Co-creation Co-production

## 1 Introduction

A transaction is a formalism, by which it is possible to capture human's communication in organizations. This term is also used in database technologies and other areas. Actually, it represents a set of operations that have to be performed all or a transaction is invalidated. Incomplete transactions that inevitably occur are solved by revoking operations that enable to roll back the performed operations at the beginning of the transaction.

DEMO (Design Engineering Methodology for Organization) [1] on the basis of the *transaction axiom* declared in the DEO (DEMO Enterprise Ontology), provides three different forms of transaction pattern; the basic, the standard and the complete transaction patterns. These forms contain the common transaction core and differ in the extension of this basic pattern. The complete transaction pattern is the highest extent of the DEMO transaction and captures all human's communication in the modeling reality including revoking operations.

© Springer Nature Switzerland AG 2018
R. Pergl et al. (Eds.): EOMAS 2018, LNBIP 332, pp. 138–152, 2018.
https://doi.org/10.1007/978-3-030-00787-4_10

The *composition axiom* enables DEMO transactions to be arranged in a tree structures. These structures provide a parent-child relationship between transactions. Child transactions are enclosed in the corresponding parent transaction and together form a business process; arranged as a tree of transactions. Business processes may be related to each other by information links (interstriction relationships). In this way, the DEMO methodology is able to capture all the things that happen in reality with great empirical evidence.

However, paired transactions, which have their origin in accountancy systems, assume relationships in which one kind of transactions is in consideration of the other kind of transactions. A prime example may be e.g. transactions in REA model [5], which apart from others, deals with accountancy systems. There are no parent-child relationships between these transactions, transactions are placed in parallel. In other words, there is no decomposition – construction kind of relationship - between the production facts of these transactions. However, there are conditions – business rules – that control the sequence in time of various transactions. Example: a contract must be signed first, and then can it be executed.

The current DEMO methodology doesn't provide any mechanism for supporting the pair transaction arrangement. The parent-child relationship, in which the DEMO transactions are arranged doesn't support this arrangement. The DEMO CC-CP model [6], which is based on DEMO Enterprise Ontology, and extended by the FAR (Fact Agenda Rule) ontology [8], is not only able to model paired transactions but has capability to do it in a truthful and appropriate way.

A Rent-A-Car example, as described in [3], differs from traditional examples, in which a product is usually exchanged for money (or possibly for other product). This example addresses a service which is exchanged for money. A service is a time-bound activity, during which a customer can utilize provided service such as renting a car, visiting a theatre, or lending books. The beginning and the fulfillment of a service has to be taken into account during modeling. Features of abstract services have to be captured.

The structure of the paper is as follows. Section 2 shortly describes the main features of the DEMO methodology. The DEMO CC-CP model, its structure, and the Fact Model [7] are depicted in Sect. 3. The main features of the Rent-A-Car example solved in standard DEMO methodology are depicted in Sect. 4. Section 5 brings the DEMO CC-CP model and its possibilities to solve the Rent-A-Car example. Results evaluation is depicted in Sect. 6. Section 7 deals with discussion and future research.

## 2   DEMO Enterprise Ontology

DEMO is an engineering methodology to derive conceptual models of enterprises, based on an ontological theory, DEMO enterprise ontology (DEO) [1, 2]. DEO is comprised of four axioms and a theorem. DEMO is part of the emerging discipline of 'enterprise engineering' (EE) [2]. EE is founded on the same kind of theories as more mature engineering disciplines such as civil engineering, aviation and electronics. A claim for the quality of the applied methodology is guaranteed by the underlying theories, methodologies, formal methods [2, 9, 10] and a good body of empirical cases in many domains.

According to DEMO methodology [1], an organization is composed of people (social individuals) that perform two kinds of acts, *production* acts and *coordination* acts. By performing production acts, people fulfill the aims of the organization. A production act can be either material or immaterial. By a material production act we mean a tangible act such as a manufacturing or transportation act. By an immaterial act we mean an intangible act such as the approval of an insurance claim or delivery of a judgment. By performing coordination acts human beings enter into and comply with commitments. They initiate and coordinate production acts. Abstracting from the particular subject that performs the action, the notion of the *actor role* is introduced. A subject in his/her fulfillment of an actor role is called an actor.

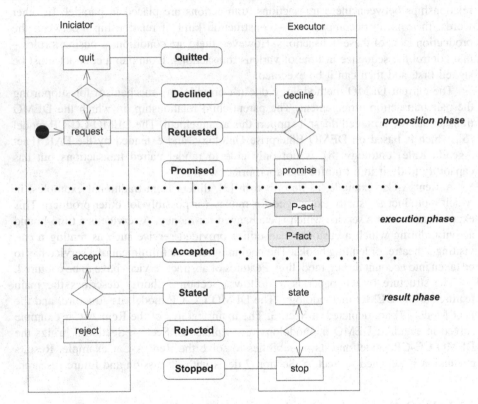

**Fig. 1.** The standard DEMO pattern (Source [1])

The result of successfully performing a production act is a *production fact*. An example of a production fact may be that the payment has been paid or an offered service was accepted. All realization issues are fully abstracted. Only the facts as such are relevant, not how they are achieved. The result of successfully performing a *co-ordination act* is a *coordination fact*. Examples of coordination acts are *requesting* and *promising* a production fact. Coordination facts are usually denoted as business events in other business methodologies.

The diagram in Fig. 1 shows the standard transaction pattern (transaction). It contains two actor roles, the initiator and the executor and coordination and production acts between them. Each transaction starts with a *request* coordination act made by the initiator. In response to the *request*, the executor performs either a *promise* or *decline* coordination act. In short, a *decline* means the end of a transaction. The *promise* goes on in a *production act* which results in a *production fact*. The production fact is *stated* to the initiator who can either *accept* it or *reject* it. The standard transaction pattern can be extended to the complete transaction pattern. In this case, the transaction pattern also contains four cancellation patterns that enable revoking of an act and thus faithfully model real conditions. For the purpose of the paper, only the standard transaction pattern will be used.

In general, DEMO transactions are arranged in a tree structure with a parent-child relationship between them (utilizing the *composition axiom*). The parent-child relationship is very effective and natural, but in some cases it is unable to capture all real world phenomena. By this is meant the case when the transactions are placed in parallel (with no parent-child relationship between them). This case is an inseparable part of so called paired transactions, in which one kind of transactions is in consideration of the other kind of transactions. These paired transaction model is typical for accountancy systems but it can be also find in applications with a contract. A contract entity controls the paired transactions processing and in the course of time it is precisely in one of its states (phases). The model of contract implicitly covers different kinds of transactions with no parent-child relationship. In order to solve the above described issues, the DEMO co-creation and co-production (CC-CP) model was conceived [6, 7].

## 3 The DEMO CC-CP Model

Generally, the purpose of the proposed DEMO CC-CP model [6, 7] is to be a generic specification of any financial or business transaction between our enterprise of interest and any external stakeholders such as customers, suppliers, personnel staff and taxation or other governmental institutions. It can be said that the DEMO CC-CP model represents a *generic pattern of interaction,* equivalent to the DEMO transaction. Its main benefits rest on (i) the possibility to explicitly express relationships between different kinds of transactions and (ii) capture partial deliveries and partial payments. The possibilities to explicitly express relationships between different kinds of transactions mean distinction between individual phases of the contract. Here, a contract is modelled by two independent DEMO transactions, from which individual object classes representing a contract are derived.

In execution of that enterprise model, factual knowledge must be provided for information systems. This model is claimed to capture any interactions between an enterprise and any stakeholder. However, the current DEMO Enterprise Ontology does not enable us to explicitly express (deal with) all communication facts or to deal with any logic aggregated facts or dependent facts. Currently, the Fact Model only addresses production facts in the form of object classes, property types, and attribute types. In order to capture all phenomena, the Fact Model should be able, for instance, to explicitly address these new specific requirements.

All these issues are proposed in the FAR (Fact, Agenda, Rule) Ontology [4, 8], which is an extension to the current DEMO Enterprise Ontology. The FAR Ontology affects further modeling possibilities, primarily of the Fact Model, represented in the Object Fact Diagram, and of the Action Model, represented in the Action Rule Specification.

The FAR ontology [8] specifies that a fact is a proposition that may have a logic relation with other facts in a recursive way. A fact is a proposition that may have three values; true | false | undefined. To illuminate the previous, let us consider the following example.

Fact: "the invoice (xyz) has been paid". Value true: the invoice has been paid, which can be validated empirically by checking the bank statement. Value false: the invoice has not been paid, also as shown by the bank statement. Value undefined: it is not known, probably because there is no access to any bank statements for empirical validation.

While the meaning of the values true and false are clear, the value of "undefined" reflects a situation in which, for some unknown reason, factual information is not available. In the FAR ontology, four kinds of facts exist:

1. Communicative (coordination) facts; as defined by the DEMO *transaction axiom*.
2. Infologic and datalogic production facts. An example is the text of the contract of the DEMO CC-CP model. It is precisely the "text only", without any actor commitments.
3. Facts about the world of phenomena not captured by the DEMO ontology, kinds 1 and 2. Example: the exchange rate dollar − euro = 0.85. The value of this proposition can be true | false | undefined.
4. Any logic aggregated facts, or dependent facts, composed of logic relations (AND | OR | NOT relations) of other facts. Evaluation laws for the three-state logic.

### 3.1 Co-creation Co-production Between an Enterprise and Its Stakeholders

Many highly specialized enterprises 'Contractors' do not have a well-defined portfolio of products with fixed prices but offer their capabilities to meet the specific requirements of their Principals. We define: co-creation captures the principal and the contractor(s) working together on the engineering of an acceptable artifact; co-production captures the shared production of the engineering artifact by both principal and contractor(s), including matching financial transactions. The co-creation co-production model is composed of three phases, each of which contains two generic transactions.

*The Co-creation Phase*
Transaction T-1 represents a production fact the definition of *what* the production to be delivered by the Contractor must be. Typically production specifications with quality criteria, materials used, testing procedures to be followed. The initiator of T-1 is the Principal who issues T-1.Request to the executor, Contractor, to provide appropriate production specifications. Usually this transaction encapsulates other transactions for engineering, product development etc. If T-1 is Stated and Accepted then there is a

shared agreement, without any ambiguity, between Principal and Contractor about *what* the co-production must be.

Transaction T-2 represents as production fact the definition of the price, including specific payment terms and conditions, etc. precisely applied to the production defined by the transaction result of T-1. The Principal is the initiator who issues a T-2.Request to the Contractor for a price for the production defined in T-1. This implies the condition that T-1.Accepted must be true before T-2.Request can be issued by the Principal. T-2.Accepted means that the two actors agree that there is a well-defined price for the production. It does not mean yet that the two actors have decided to commit to a delivery and payment.

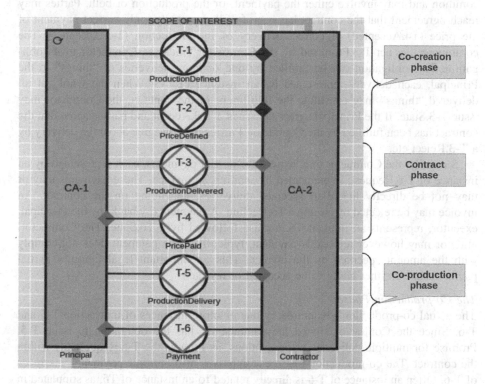

**Fig. 2.** The CC-CP construction model (Source [6, 7])

*The Contract Phase*
At this stage, with T-1.Accepted and T-2.Accepted, represent the situation that there is a well-defined but yet unsigned contract on the table. The contract is composed of two directly related mutually binding obligations; defined by the two transaction results of T-1 and T-2. It is important to realize that a contract is a *binding commitment to deliver* goods/services/payments in both directions, depending on certain defined conditions. The Principal requests the Contractor a commitment to deliver the production, T-3, by issuing T-3.Request. The Contractor requests the Principal a commitment to pay the

price, T-4, by issuing T-4.Request. The two signatures on the contract are represented by T-3.Promised and T-4.Promised. Transaction T-3 represents the commitment, an *obligation* that the production has to be delivered by the Contractor, executor, to the Principal, initiator. At some moment the Contractor may issue T-3.State, meaning that the Contractor thinks that the contractual agreement to deliver the product has been fulfilled.

If the Principal agrees then the Contractor may issue T-3.Accept, the contractual obligation for the production has been fulfilled. Similarly, transaction T-4 represents the obligation to pay the price to be paid by the Principal, executor, to the Contractor, initiator. If both actors agree, they will issue T-4.State and T-4.Accept, the contractual obligation to pay the correct price has been fulfilled. Contract disputes are very common and may involve either the payment, or the production or both. Parties may reach agreement that the contract has been fulfilled partially, only correct payment of the price (T4.Accepted) or correct delivery of the production (T-3.Accepted). The communicative act T-3.Promised by the Contractor binds the Contractor to its obligation. This obligation can be fulfilled by one or more deliveries of "things" to the Principal, each delivery represented by an instance of T-5. When the whole of all delivered "things" may constitute the fulfillment of the contract, the Contractor may issue T-3.State. If the Principal agrees he issues a T-3.Accept and parties agree that the contract has been fulfilled by the Contractor. Parties may disagree about the delivery by a T-3.Reject etc.

Similarly, the Contractor may request for partial payments, each represented by an instance of T-6.Request, implemented by sending an invoice. These payments may or may not be directly linked to accepted deliveries, depending on the contract. An invoice may be rejected by issuing a T6.Decline. A payment (by bank) by the Principal, executor, represents an implicit T6.Promise followed by a T6.State. The Contractor, initiator may however reject this payment, typically if the payment does not comply with the amount specified by the invoice. This an important legal figure, a partial payment that is either going to be accepted or rejected.

*The Co-production Phase*
The actual co-production is captured by one or more instances of transaction T-5 and T-6. Since the Contractor signed the contract, he has the obligation to issue T-5. Promise for multiple deliveries of productions, as long as the T-5.Request fits within the contract. The co-production phase encompasses also multiple payments, instances of T-6. Often an instance of T-6 is directly related to an instance of T5, as stipulated in the contract. The co-production phase ends when the Principal and the Contractor have fulfilled their obligations defined in T-3 and T-4. The fulfilment of the obligation of goods/services delivered by instances of T-5 will result in T-3 being Stated and Accepted. Similarly, the fulfilment of the obligation of PricePaid delivered by instances of T-6 will result in T-4 being Stated and Accepted. The contract has been fulfilled by both parties.

The structure of the CC-CP Construction Model, shown in Fig. 2, is based on observation of reality, in which the production of a document (T-1) specifies the Pfact of T-5. Similarly, it holds for T-2 and T-6 transactions. Parties may agree to produce these one or two documents, without any commitments (obligations, intentions) for actual later production (by execution of T-3 and T-4 transactions). If we embed the co-creation transactions (T-1, T-2) as child transactions of T-5 and T-6 transactions then we assume that there is an intention to produce T-5 and T-6. However, this observation is not always the case.

## 3.2   The CC-CP Fact Model

The three phases stated in the DEMO CC-CP Construction Model will also be used in the description of the DEMO CC-CP Fact Model [7].

The *co-creation phase* is formed by the ensuing object classes: CONTRACT, PRODUCTION_LINE, PRICE_LINE, PRODUCTION_KIND, MONEY_KIND and the external object class ENTERPRISE. The object class CONTRACT is the core object class in the whole CC-CP Fact Model.

The *contract phase* is formed by the object classes CONTRACT_SIGNED and CONTRACT_FULFILLED. The object class CONTRACT_SIGNED is an extension of the result kinds "[production_agreement] was contracted and [price_agreement] was contracted". This object class represents the signing of a contract. The object class CONTRACT_SIGNED is a specialization of the object class CONTRACT.

The object class CONTRACT_FULFILLED is an extension of the result kinds "[production_agreement] was fulfilled and [price_agreement] was fulfilled". This object class represents the fulfilment of the contract. The object class CONTRACT_ FULFILLED is a specialization of the object class CONTRACT_SIGNED. This phase includes production and coordination facts of T-3 and T-4 transactions mentioned in the CC-CP Construction Model.

The result kind "[production agreement] was fulfilled" is an existentially inde-pendent unary fact kind which is the result of a T-3 transaction. It means that all sub production deliveries were fulfilled. The result kind "[price agreement] was fulfilled" is an existentially independent unary fact kind which is the result of a T-4 transaction. It means that all part payments were concluded.

The *co-production phase* is formed by the object classes PRODUCTION_DE-LIVERY, PRODUCT (KIND), PAYMENT and MONEY_KIND.

The property type between the object classes CONTRACT_SIGNED and PRO-DUCTION_DELIVERY indicates that a *contract signed* can have more *production deliveries,* which is in compliance with the modeling reality.

The object class CONTRACT and its subclasses play a crucial role in the Fact Model and are necessary for any production of an enterprise. It is a production of the commercial department, it represents value and costs have been made (Fig. 3).

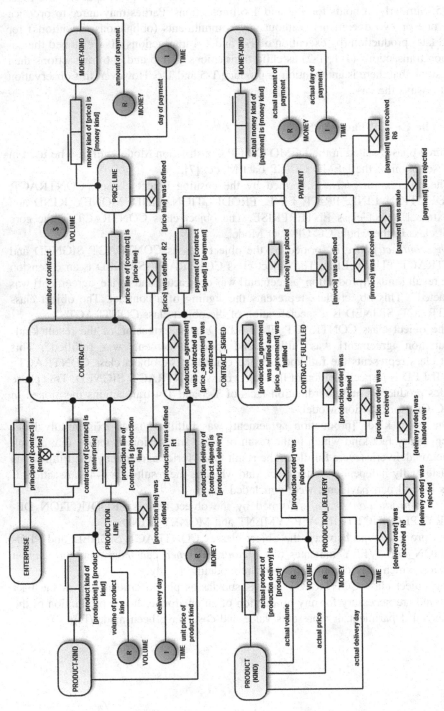

**Fig. 3.** The CC-CP fact model (Adapted [7])

## 4  Rent-A-Car Example in the DEMO Methodology

This practical and probably familiar example can elucidate the differences and common issues of both models (the DEMO methodology model [3] and the DEMO CC-CP model). Specifics of this example are in providing not a particular product but a specific service, which is time-bound. It is necessary to cope with the beginning of the service and the termination of the service in the process of modeling. The whole example utilizing the DEMO methodology was described in [3]. Therefore, the description in this paper is restricted only to fundamental features of the example. To introduce the problem a short narrative description follows. Rent-A-Car (RAC) is a service which is provided either to walk-in customers or customers who make a rental reservation by telephone, fax or email. A car may be rented on the same day or may be reserved for a specific term in the future after a contract between an employee of the rental company and a customer has been signed. The company which rents out cars has many branches around the country. So the rented car may be picked up and dropped off at different branches. The rental payment depends directly on the number of days of rental and kind of rented car. The signed contract states the period of the rental, the kind of rented car, and the name of the branch where the car will be dropped off. If the period of rental or/and the drop off branch do not coincide with the conditions in the signed contract, the customer is liable for a penalty payment. The contracted payment must be made by the starting day of the rental at the latest. Additional penalty payments must be made at the drop off point. The Construction model is shown in Fig. 4.

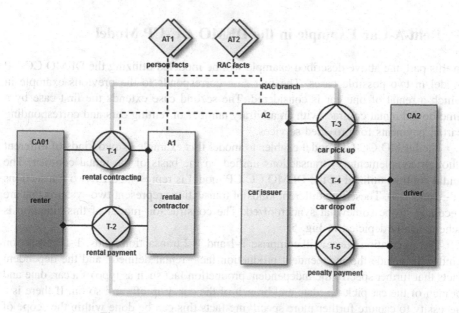

**Fig. 4.** Rent-A-Car construction model (Source [3])

This solution comprises the Construction model as it is fully in compliance with the necessity of both models comparison. The Construction model requires identification of the actor roles, transaction kinds and product kinds. In terms of actor roles there are actor roles A1 and A2 representing employees of the rental company. The other actor roles represent a renter and a driver respectively. As it is not a complex example, it is not difficult to identify essential transactions. The first transaction T-1 - rental contracting covers signing a contract to rent a car. The next transaction T-2 – rental payment is enclosed in T-1 transaction and both transactions form a business process. The rental payment must be promised before the contract is signed and this must be made by the first day of the rental at the latest.

The car pick-up transaction T-3 includes the promise of the driver to drop off a car according to the rental contract and the pick-up of a car. T-4 transaction is thus enclosed in T-3 transaction. The car drop-off transaction T-4 covers dropping of the car and in case of breaching the rental contract, it also includes the penalty payment, which is done through the penalty payment transaction T-5. This transaction is an optional transaction which is executed if the driver exceeds conditions agreed in the rental contract. T-5 transaction is thus enclosed in T-4 transaction. Transactions T-3, T-4, and T-5 comprise the second business process.

Rental contract is not, in this case, a real contract represented by two kinds of different transactions but it is represented only by T-1 transaction, in which renter promise and state rental conditions and the driver accept these conditions. By accepting the rental conditions the driver is bound to follow by these conditions as well as renter is bound by the conditions as a renter.

## 5   Rent-A-Car Example in the DEMO CC-CP Model

In this part, the above described example will be modeled utilizing the DEMO CC-CP model in two possible cases. The first case corresponds to the previous example in which a rental of one car is considered. The second case extends the first case by a time-bound rental contract with an arbitrary number of renting cars and corresponding partial payments for provided services.

The DEMO CC-CP model enables to model this example as two kinds of different (though complementary) transactions unified on the basis of the rental contract. The rental contract utilized in the DEMO CC-CP model is represented by two transactions (T-3, and T-4). These two different kinds of transactions represent two systems that are necessary to be somewhat synchronized. The construction model of this situation is schematically depicted in Fig. 5.

The co-creation phase will comprise T-1 and T-2 transaction kinds. T-1 transaction kind will include the independent production fact "rental defined" and the dependent facts that further specify the independent production fact such as type of a car, date and branch of the car pick up, date and branch of the car drop off, and so on. If there is a necessity to capture further more specifying facts this can be done within the scope of an additional child transaction kind of T-1 transaction kind. Similarly, T-2 transaction kind will include the independent production fact "payment defined" and other dependent facts specifying particular condition of rental payment including a penalty payment. If necessary, an additional child transaction kind of T-2 transaction kind can contain all necessary details in the same way as T-1 child transaction kind.

T-3 and T-4 transaction kinds will constitute the contract phase. Their function remains the same as was described in Sect. 3.1. In short, a contract is composed of two balanced transactions.

T-5 and T-6 transaction kinds will comprise the co-production phase. T-5 transaction kind represents the service delivery, which means a car pick up and a car drop-off independent production facts. As can be seen, the service is represented by a couple of the independent production facts, one of which represents the start of the service and the other of which stands for the end of the service. Generally, a service should be represented only by one transaction similarly as a product delivery.

There are two possibilities how to cope with this problem. The first one is that the DEMO CC-CP model would contain only one T-5 transaction kind, in this case one T-5 transaction (instance) would represent the car pick up production fact and the other transaction (instance) T-5 would represent the car drop off production fact. The other solution rests on the fact that T-5 transaction kind will have two child transactions marked for example T-51 and T-52, which would record the car pick up and the car drop-off production facts. Both solutions are possible.

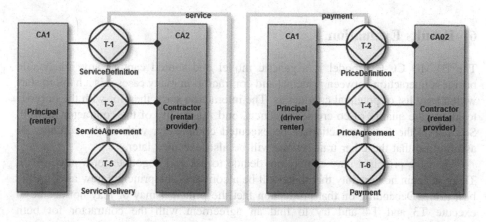

**Fig. 5.** Rent-A-Car construction model (using CC-CP model)

The second case represents the possibility, in which the DEMO CC-CP model deals with a contract which is time-bound what means that during, in the contract specified time, a number of rent a car can happen as well as a number of partial payments can occur. In the scope of the co-creation phase the definition of car's renting is done. It can be done in one T-1 transaction or it is possible, in case of different services, consider multiple T-1 transaction instances; for instance, renting a personal car, renting a van, or renting a motorcycle. In this example, three T-1 transaction instances will have to be declared. In terms of T-2 transaction, different kinds of payments have to be distinguished. Each payment kind requires individual T-2 transaction instance. In case that there is necessary to specify further facts (properties) a child transaction can be defined.

In case of T-1 transaction, it would be T-11 and similarly in the case of T-2 transaction, it would be T-12 transaction. The contract phase remains the same as in the first case.

The co-production phase will record individual renting a car and partial payments for the service. As was mentioned earlier, a service is considered to be an equivalent of a product delivery. For this reason, a car pick-up will be captured by T-51 transaction and a car drop-off will be processed by T-52 transaction. Both these transactions are enclosed in T-5 transaction. Partial payments can be modelled either by more T-6 transaction instances or by T-61 transaction instances which are enclosed in T-6 transaction.

Both models differ in modeling the service. In the traditional model (Fig. 4) the service itself is modelled by two transactions; T-3 car pick up and T-4 car drop off. The executor of T-3 is the car issuer and the executor of T-4 is the driver. The DEMO CC-CP model utilizes for starting and ending the service T-5 service delivery transaction kind, in which starting and ending of the service is modelled either by two different instances of T-5 or by two child transactions of T-5. The executor is the rental provider. To clarify the distinct executors in models it can be argued that T-3 car pick up and T-4 car drop off are not typical DEMO transactions with clear requester and clear executor. In general, both transactions must agree to have accepted the production fact which illuminates the distinct executors in the models.

## 6  Results Evaluation

The DEMO CC-CP model is a generic model and should capture any imaginable business interaction between principal and contractor. In many cases it is a habit to start with a long list of potential contractors. The interaction starts therefor with the purpose to assess the quality of co-created products, and the quality of the contractor as well. So, T-1 is the first transaction to be executed completely, without the certainty or assumption that the other transactions will be also executed later.

Then the principal may or may not decide to ask and negotiate for a price (T-2). There is again no certainty that there will be a contract. The principal now asks for the best price. Depending on that production fact the principal may or may not decide to execute T3 and T4 and try to find an agreement with the contractor for both transactions.

Since T-3 and T-4 represent important facts, signed contracts, notably for accounting systems, T-3 and T-4 execution must be synchronized. Contract signing *T-3.pm and T-4.pm* must be achieved before any delivery of products or payments can be made. Therefor in the DEMO CC-CP model there are no links, dependencies, conditional or causal rules between T-1–T-6 transactions, other than a sequential execution. The only exception is *T-3.pm and T-4.pm* that must be both issued for a contract to be valid in accounting and legal terms.

For a specific implementation of the DEMO CC-CP model, to capture a specific case, any causal and conditional rules can be applied.

The DEMO CC-CP model doesn't explicitly mention penalty payment because it is a part of T-2 and T-4 transactions. Only the amount or the applicability of the penalty is not yet known but a penalty does exist otherwise it can never be imposed later.

The complexity issue of transaction roll-back in case of the DEMO CC-CP model is completely solved in theory and in software implementation.

# 7 Conclusion and Future Research

The aim of the paper is to claim and prove that the DEMO CC-CP model is a suitable for applications, in which there are explicitly two parties with different but somewhat complementary interests. These different interests are managed by a contract, which is in the traditional solution utilizing the DEMO methodology modelled by one DEMO transaction because the presented model represents one system. The DEMO CC-CP model stands for two systems (two different kinds of transactions), in which one system represents a car rental (service) and the other system stands for customer (payment). Two different kinds of transactions properly represent states and state transitions of the contract in a way which is closer to modeling reality. Object classes of the contract are derived from these two transaction kinds subsequently. The contract itself ensures synchronization between two different kinds of transactions.

The presented example is also specific in that it deals with services, which are time and place bound. In general, a service may be composed of more parts and these parts have to be completed before the whole service is fulfilled. In the modeling example only the beginning and the fulfilment of the service are distinguished.

This requires a specific approach in the form of further transaction instances or further child transactions. In the traditional solution this is done explicitly by two different kinds of transactions with a parent-child relationship between them. The DEMO CC-CP model utilizes two transaction instances or two child transactions for this purpose.

Utilizing the DEMO CC-CP model can be beneficial mainly in the following cases. Firstly, when the contract conditions are more complex, and require detailed specification on both sides of the contract. Secondly, when the exchange between parties covers more product kinds or more time-bound services. Finally, when there are partial deliveries of the production, or service, or partial payments for the delivered products, or provided services.

In spite of promising results which were achieved, much future research is needed to validate our generally careful claims: (i) more empirical appropriateness case studies to support the claim that the DEMO CC-CP model captures any enterprise - enterprise co-creation and co-production operation; (ii) in this perspective, many implementation-specific extensions of the DEMO CC-CP model; (iii) progress in the application of the GSDP-MDE approach and in conceptual modeling; the fact that one application - the DEMO engine - works well does not guarantee its generic applicability.

**Acknowledgements.** The paper was supported by the grant provided by Ministry of Education, Youth and Sports Czech Republic, reference no. SGS05/PRF/2018 and the grant provided by city of Ostrava.

# References

1. Dietz, J.L.G.: Enterprise Ontology: Theory and Methodology. Springer, Heidelberg (2006). https://doi.org/10.1007/3-540-33149-2
2. Dietz, J.L.G., Hoogervorst, J.A.P.: The discipline of enterprise engineering. Int. J. Organ. Des. Eng. **3**(1), 86–114 (2013)
3. Dietz, J.L.G.: The Essence of Organization. An Introduction to Enterprise Engineering. Sapio bv, Voorburg (2012)
4. Dudok, E., Guerreiro, S., Babkin, E., Pergl, R., van Kervel, S.J.H.: Enterprise operational analysis using DEMO and the enterprise operating system. In: Aveiro, D., Pergl, R., Valenta, M. (eds.) EEWC 2015. LNBIP, vol. 211, pp. 3–18. Springer, Cham (2015). https://doi.org/10.1007/978-3-319-19297-0_1
5. Hruby, P.: Model-Driven Design Using Business Patterns. Springer, Heidelberg (2006). https://doi.org/10.1007/3-540-30327-2
6. Hunka, F., van Kervel, S.J.H., Matula, J.: Towards co-creation and co-production in production chains modeled in DEMO with REA support. In: Aveiro, D., Pergl, R., Gouveia, D. (eds.) EEWC 2016. LNBIP, vol. 252, pp. 54–68. Springer, Cham (2016). https://doi.org/10.1007/978-3-319-39567-8_4
7. Hunka, F., van Kervel, S.J.H.: The REA model expressed in a generic DEMO model for Co-creation and Co-production. In: Pergl, R., Lekkerkerk, H., Aveiro, D., Guizzardi, G., Almeida, J.P., Magalhaes, R. (eds.) EEWC 2017. LNBIP, vol. 284, pp. 151–165. Springer, Cham (2017). https://doi.org/10.1007/978-3-319-57955-9_12
8. Skotnica, M., van Kervel, S.J.H., Pergl, R.: Towards the ontological foundations for the software executable DEMO action and fact models. In: Aveiro, D., Pergl, R., Gouveia, D. (eds.) EEWC 2016. LNBIP, vol. 252, pp. 151–165. Springer, Cham (2016). https://doi.org/10.1007/978-3-319-39567-8_10
9. van Kervel, S.J.H., Dietz, J.L.G., Hintzen, J., van Meeuwen, T., Zijlstra, B.: Enterprise ontology driven software engineering. In: Proceedings of International Conference on Software Paradigm Trends (2012)
10. van Kervel, S.J.H.: Ontology driven enterprise information systems engineering. Ph.D. thesis, University of Technology Delft (2012)

# The Intellectual Dimension of IT-Business Alignment Problem: Alloy Application

Marina Ivanova and Pavel Malyzhenkov[✉]

Department of Information Systems and Technologies,
National Research University Higher School of Economics,
Bol. Pecherskaya 25, 603155 Nizhny Novgorod, Russia
miivanova_1@edu.hse.ru, pmalyzhenkov@hse.ru

**Abstract.** Information technologies have evolved from its traditional back office role to a strategic resource role able not only to support but also to shape business strategies. For over a decade IT-business alignment has been ranked as a top-priority management concern and is widely covered in literature. However, conceptual studies dominate the field, while there is little research on practical ways to achieve the alignment. The aim of this paper is to formalize and verify the alignment assessment model developed in the previous research by integrating the traditional Strategic Alignment Model and EA framework TOGAF in an attempt to provide a practical approach to the alignment evaluation and implementation. The Alloy Language and Analyzer are used as a means of model formalization and verification.

**Keywords:** IT-business alignment · Enterprise Architecture · SAM
TOGAF · Alloy Analyzer

## 1 Introduction

The strategic alignment of business and information technologies has consistently been reported as one of the key CIO concerns across various industries. According to *The Global IT Trends Survey* [26] the alignment issue has held its position in the top three IT management concerns since 2007 along with business agility and business cost reduction (Fig. 1).

These data prove the need for alignment which enables organizations to leverage IT, enhance business flexibility and maximize return on IT investments, leading to increased profitability and sustainable competitive advantage [4, 8, 11, 12, 14].

Conceptual studies on the nature of IT-business alignment dominate the literature, most of them are focused on the alignment from the strategic perspective, addressing the compliance of business and IT strategies, but giving little attention to the functional side of alignment and lacking practical instruments and approaches to its implementation [6, 7].

The aim of this paper is to formalize and verify the alignment assessment model developed in [19] by integrating the traditional Strategic Alignment Model [12, 30] and EA framework TOGAF [28] in an attempt to provide a practical approach to the alignment evaluation and implementation. The Alloy Language and Analyzer [25] were chosen as a means of model formalization and verification.

© Springer Nature Switzerland AG 2018
R. Pergl et al. (Eds.): EOMAS 2018, LNBIP 332, pp. 153–168, 2018.
https://doi.org/10.1007/978-3-030-00787-4_11

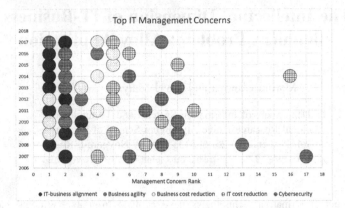

**Fig. 1.** Top IT management concerns (based on the data provided in [26])

The rest of the paper is organized as follows. Section 2 summarizes theoretical background relevant for the proposed approach and analyzes the linkage between the main components of SAM and TOGAF. Section 3 formalizes and verifies the proposed approach using the structural modeling language Alloy. Finally, in Sect. 4 the conclusions are drawn and the future research directions are identified.

## 2   Theoretical Background

### 2.1   The Alignment and Approaches to Its Achievement

There is an extensive research conducted on the nature of IT-business alignment, approaches to its assessment and enhancement. IT-business alignment can be determined as "the extent to which the IS strategy supports and is supported by the business strategy" [17] or as "the degree to which the IT mission, objectives and plans support and are supported by business mission, objectives and plans" [21]. Terms like fit, harmony, fusion, linkage and bridge [12] are often used referring to the alignment.

However, many researchers consider alignment to be not a static state that can be measured at a single point in time but rather a continuous process of adjustment of business and IT domains [2, 3, 12, 18].

In [21] two dimensions of the IT-business alignment, intellectual and social, are distinguished. Intellectual dimension is concerned with the consistency, interrelation and validity of IT and business plans. Social dimension is related to the mutual understanding and commitment between business and IT managers with respect to each other's missions, objectives and plans [19].

The proposed research is focused on the intellectual dimension of IT-business alignment, attempting to provide a formalized approach to the detection of violation of IT and business components consistency, interrelation and validity. The literature provides multiple approaches to the alignment evaluation [13, 15], many of them are questionnaire-based.

Though, bridging the IT-business gap and providing shared alignment estimation, questionnaire-based methods depend on subjective judgement of IT and business managers. Moreover, few of them provide the guidance on the alignment assessment results interpretation and further misalignment elimination.

The Strategy Alignment Model (SAM) [12, 30], one of the most cited alignment frameworks, drawing a distinction between the external (IT strategy) and internal (IT infrastructure and processes) components of IT, thus acknowledging its potential not only to support but also to shape business strategy. Figure 2 is a schematic representation of the SAM illustrating an integration of business domain, consisting of business strategy and organizational infrastructure and processes, and IT domain represented by IT strategy and IS infrastructure and processes.

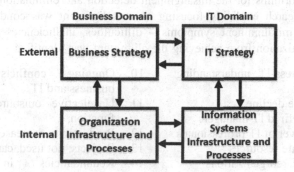

**Fig. 2.**  Strategic Alignment Model (adapted from [12, 30])

In order to ensure the right balance between the choices made across all four domains it is vital to review multivariate cross-domain relationships. SAM distinguishes between four dominant cross-domain relationships (called alignment perspectives) based on the premise that strategic alignment can only be attained when three of the four domains are aligned. These perspectives are divided into two groups according to what strategy (business or IT) is considered as a driving force [19].

After alternative strategic choices within four dominant alignment perspectives have been analyzed and evaluated, one or more perspectives should be selected and adopted as the driving force of organizational transformation towards strategic alignment.

Despite the clear vision and strong theoretical background, some researchers argue that SAM is too broad and does not provide practical tools to the alignment achievement and sustainment, especially for those organizations lacking formal, structured strategy formulation and decision-making processes. Therefore, the model extensions were later proposed [4, 14, 18]. However, there is still little literature covering activities that should be applied within each SAM domain to enhance the level of alignment as well as the literature on practical application of the model.

## 2.2    The Misalignment and Approaches to Its Elimination

When analyzing IT-business alignment, two general perspectives may be taken: focus on its presence (alignment) or its absence (misalignment). And while there is a consistent research on the nature of alignment and approaches to achieve it, the literature seems to be less concerned with an inverse concept – misalignment, which is characterized as a state where organization's strategy, structure and business processes are not harmonized with information systems and technologies used within an organization. However, companies stay in the state of misalignment most of the time, at least until they try to approach the alignment. Thus, misalignment analysis should be taken in order to understand where the company stands and what are the barriers holding it back from the desired state of alignment.

The literature suggests several approaches to the alignment assessment from the misalignment perspective. Most of them are symptom-based [5, 16, 20], whereas others focus on the algorithms for the misalignment detection and elimination [9].

The first research explicitly focusing on misalignment was conducted in [16], where a set of misalignment symptoms – difficulties, inefficiencies and inabilities preventing organization from achieving the alignment was identified:

1. Poor business-IT understanding and rapport
2. Competitive decline
3. Frequently fired IT managers
4. High turnover of IT professionals
5. Inappropriate resources
6. Frequent IT reorganizations
7. Lack of executive interest in IT
8. Lack of vision/strategy
9. No communication between IT and users
10. Ongoing conflicts between business and IT
11. Unselective outsourcing of IT function
12. Productivity decrease
13. Projects: not used, canceled, late
14. Redundancies in systems development
15. Absent systemic competencies
16. Systems integration difficulties
17. Unhappy users/complaints

Following that, several other misalignment symptom collections have been proposed. In [20] alignment heuristics are developed, representing sets of rules to check when aligning Enterprise Architecture components such as Business Architecture, Information Architecture, Application Architecture (Technical Architecture is omitted for the reason of its dependency on the technology itself). An inverse of those rules may be used as a set of misalignment symptoms. However, heuristics presented deal with the technical issues, rather than with the specific alignment problems between EA components. In [5] a basic collection of misalignment symptoms and signs, that can be found in organizations, accompanied with their etiology (factors that may be the cause of the proposed misalignment symptoms), is presented.

There are two most recognized misalignment models: Business IT Alignment Method, BITAM [9] and Business and Information Systems Misalignment Model, BISMAM [5]. The BITAM model describes a process consisting of twelve steps for managing, detecting and correcting misalignment from the business model level down to the business architecture level, followed by the IT architecture level. The BISMAM model addresses the alignment problem through the misalignment concept combined with the medical sciences perspective, based on an analogy between the misalignment and disease. The BISMAM model establishes a nomenclature and semantics for misalignment and defines a misalignment classification scheme, divided into three dimensions – organ system, symptom/sign, etiology, based on the nosology discipline, dealing with the systematic classification of diseases.

According to the BISMAM approach, the general process of managing the misalignment follows three steps:

- detecting misalignment by mapping the current organization state with the symptoms and signs provided by the classification scheme, and using other techniques such as questionnaires and tests
- correcting misalignment by establishing realignment initiatives, alleviating and eliminating the misalignment symptoms, addressing their etiology
- preventing misalignment using the BISMAM library of misalignment prophylaxis techniques.

Despite providing wide variety of misalignment symptoms and techniques for its elimination, these models are quite informal due to (1) being based on subjective judgement of the stakeholders involved in the symptoms detection process (for example, misalignment symptoms might sound like "I do not have the required information to support decision-making"); (2) providing misalignment correction techniques that are very broad suggesting general actions such as "Implement data integrity, data consistency and data quality controls".

## 2.3  The SAM and TOGAF Integration-Based Alignment Framework

As stated above SAM suggests the alignment of four domains: business strategy, organizational infrastructure and processes, IT strategy, IS infrastructure and processes. Unfortunately, in practice, enterprises lack formal definition of business strategy [22]. IT strategy is often not even present or is restricted by internally-oriented view [12]. Moreover, the organizational structure is rarely stable in many companies [31] and the ever-increasing complexity of IT applications and infrastructure is referred to by CIOs as a major concern. Therefore, there is a need for an instrument providing a holistic enterprise view.

EA frameworks implicitly ensure the achievement of a specific IT-business alignment level. However, they do not distinguish between different alignment perspectives allowing only for the classic business-to-IT alignment scheme. Whereas diverse misalignment situations require different design approaches. And IT may and should be used in an innovative way as an enabler for renewed or even completely new business strategies, products and services, organization forms and processes.

In the previous research [19] the alignment framework based on the integration of traditional Strategic Alignment Model and EA framework TOGAF was proposed. Different alignment perspectives were incorporated into the EA design process and integrated with the methodologies, tools and techniques provided by EA framework.

The choice of TOGAF as an EA framework to employ within the approach proposed is based on several reasons: firstly, it describes a detailed EA development algorithm, called ADM, and provides a strong documentation support to each of its phases; secondly, the framework is quite flexible, it allows changes in the ADM phase order; thus, may be tailored to fit a specific alignment perspective.

**Table 1.** Linking the main components of the SAM and TOGAF

| SAM business domains | | SAM IT domains | | | | |
|---|---|---|---|---|---|---|
| Business strategy | Organizational infrastructure and processes | IT strategy | IS infrastructure and processes | | | |
| **TOGAF** architecture domains | | | | | | |
| Business architecture | | IS architecture | Application architecture | Data architecture | Technology architecture | |
| **ADM A** | **ADM B** | **ADM C** | **ADM C** | **ADM C** | **ADM D** | |
| • Stakeholder map matrix<br>• Value chain diagram<br>• Driver/Goal/ Objective Catalog | • Business service/function catalog<br>• Business footprint diagram<br>• Business service/ information diagram<br>• Goal/objective/ service diagram | • **IT strategy** | • Application portfolio catalog<br>• Application/function matrix<br>• Application interaction matrix | • Data dissemination diagram<br>• Data entity/business function matrix<br>• Application/data matrix | • Technology portfolio catalog<br>• Application/ technology matrix<br>• Platform decomposition diagram | |

Table 1 represents the linkage between the main components of SAM (four integration domains) and TOGAF (architecture domains, ADM phases and artifacts). The set of artifacts delivered by TOGAF ADM phases is limited to the most substantial within the current research due to their interchangeability and redundancy.

External and internal business domains of SAM correspond to the TOGAF's Business Architecture domain. SAM's internal IT domain matches TOGAF's Application, Data and Technology Architecture domains. Finally, SAM's external IT domain does not seem to have a clear match because TOGAF does not explicitly determine the IT strategy or its essential components such as IT vision, goals and objectives, justification of IT investments etc. However, it is reasonable to assume that the IT strategy is formulated and implemented as a part of the overall TOGAF's Information Systems Architecture domain.

Each TOGAF's architecture domain is covered by some ADM phases. Phases A and B/C (Application)/C (Data)/D are used to develop baseline and target Business/Application/Data/Technology Architectures and analyze the gap between them. Thus, ADM phases A-B may be used to detect the misalignment between SAM's business and IT domains and identify the target aligned architectures. The alignment assessment is done by identifying interrelationships and establishing correspondence between artifacts delivered by ADM phases in different SAM's integration domains.

## 3    The Alloy Application to the Proposed Alignment Framework

The formalization and verification of our proposal may be realized by means of Alloy which is [10, 25]:

- a structural modelling language, based on first-order logic, for expressing complex structural constraints and behavior of relational models;
- a constraint solver that provides fully automatic simulation and checking of relational models.

An Alloy model is a collection of constraints that describes a set of structures. Alloy's tool, the Alloy Analyzer, is a constraint solver which may be used both to explore the model by generating sample structures, and to check properties of the model by generating counterexamples.

Alloy has been developed by the Software Design Group at MIT in 1997, and since then it has been used to model and analyze all kinds of systems: network configuration protocols, access control, scheduling, document structuring, cryptography, filesystem synchronization, semantic web. In [1] Alloy is used to analyze the consistency of EA models. However, its application to the field of IT-business alignment is almost entirely unexplored. The only instance we encountered is the use of Alloy in the Systemic Enterprise Architecture Methodology (SEAM) project, which is an EA design methodology allowing organizational modeling from market position down to the IT services and infrastructure for the purpose of IT-business alignment [32]. The application of Alloy to the SEAM has been considered by several studies in the context of the overall model logic verification limiting the use of Alloy to the SEAM model formalization and simulation [23, 33, 34]. The employment of Alloy for the misalignment detection *automatization* has not been explored.

The use of Alloy within the approach proposed is organized as follows. First, the metamodel representing the components of artifacts, delivered by the TOGAF ADM phases, relationships and dependencies between them is designed. Second, sets of alignment rules pertaining to the SAM perspectives are developed. Third, the standard case study, provided by The Open Group, is represented in terms of the metamodel designed. Finally, the case study model is checked against the alignment rules defined.

## 3.1 Metamodel Design

The gross structure of an Alloy model consists of:

- Some signature declarations, labeled by the keyword *sig*, representing sets of atoms and (optionally) introducing relations whose domain is a subset of the signature;
- Some constraint paragraphs, recording various forms of constraints and expressions:
  - a fact, labeled by the keywords *fact*, is a named constraint that is assumed always to hold;
  - a function, labeled by the keyword *fun*, is a named expression with zero or more declarations for arguments and an expression bounding for the result;
  - a predicate, labeled by the keyword *pred*, is a named constraint with zero or more declarations for arguments;
- Some assertions, labeled by the keyword *assert*, that are constraints expected to follow from the facts of the model;
- Some commands, representing instructions to the analyzer to perform particular analyses:

- a *run* command tells the analyzer to search for an instance of a predicate;
- a *check* command tells the analyzer to search for a counterexample of an assertion.

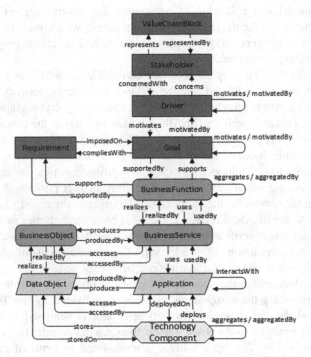

**Fig. 3.** The metamodel

Figure 3 illustrates the metamodel representing the components of artifacts, delivered by the TOGAF ADM phases, and relationships between them. For example, the declaration of motivational components contained in the artifact "Driver/Goal/ Objective Catalog" is the following:

```
abstract sig Motivation {
motivates: set Motivation,
motivatedBy: set Motivation
}
sig Driver extends Motivation{
concerns: set Stakeholder
}
sig Goal extends Motivation {
compliesWith: set Requirement,
supportedBy: set BusinessFunction
}
```

Along with the signature and relation declarations the model contains some fact constraints ensuring its logical validity, such as:

- **no** @motivates **&** ~^@motivates: the *motivates* relation is acyclic
- **all** g: Goal | **some** g.motivatedBy: goals are always motivated by some drivers, whereas drivers may be standalone (external)
- **no** @aggregates **&** ~^@aggregates: the *aggregates* relation is acyclic
- **no** realizes **&** uses: business functions do not use services they realize
- **no** iden **&** @interactsWith: the *interactsWith* relation is irreflexive
- mutual relations (allow to apply different alignment perspectives):

  - o   motivates = ~motivatedBy
  - o   (supports :> Goal) = ~ (Goal <: supportedBy)
  - o   (supports :> Requirement) = ~ (Requirement <: supportedBy)
  - o   (BusinessFunction <: realizes) = ~ (BusinessService <: realizedBy)
  - o   ● (DataObject <: realizes) = ~ (BusinessObject <: realizedBy)
  - o   etc.

## 3.2   Alignment Rules Design

The IT-business alignment rules within different SAM perspectives have been identified as assertions. For example, some of the rules comprised by the "Strategy Execution" perspective are:

*Business Strategy (ADM Phase A) → Organizational Structure (ADM Phase B)*

- Every value chain block may be decomposed into a set of business functions:

  ```
  assert P1_rule1 {
  all vc: ValueChainBlock |
  some vc.representedBy.concernedWith.^motivates.supportedBy
  or some vc.representedBy.concernedWith.^motivates.compliesWith.supportedBy
  }
  ```
- Every business object should be produced by exactly one business service:

  ```
  assert P1_rule5 {
  all bo: BusinessObject | one bo.producedBy
  }
  ```

*Organizational Structure (ADM Phase B) → IS Infrastructure (ADM Phases C, D)*

- Every business object should be realized by data object (electronic document management #1):

  ```
  assert P1_rule7 {
  all bo: BusinessObject | some bo.realizedBy
  }
  ```

- Business services use applications to produce business objects (electronic document management #2):

  ```
  assert P1_rule8 {
  all s: BusinessService, bo: BusinessObject, do: DataObject | (bo in s.produces and
  bo in do.realizes) implies (do.producedBy in s.uses)
  }
  ```

- Every data object produced/accessed by an application should be stored on the technology component deploying this application or aggregating or aggregated by such technology component, or aggregated by the same node as such technology component:

  ```
  assert P1_rule10 {
  all do: DataObject, a: Application |
  (a in (do.producedBy + do.accessedBy)) implies (some do.storedOn •&
  (a.deployedOn + a.deployedOn.^aggregates + a.deployedOn.^aggregatedBy)
  or some do.storedOn.^aggregatedBy & a.deployedOn.^aggregatedBy)
  }
  ```

Among rules contained in the "Service Level" perspective are:
*IT Strategy (ADM Phase C) → IS Infrastructure (ADM Phases C, D)*

- Every data object should be produced by exactly one application (data redundancy & consistency #1):

  ```
  assert P4_rule1 {
  all do: DataObject | one do.producedBy
  }
  ```

- Every data object should be stored on exactly one technology component (data redundancy & consistency #2):

  ```
  assert P4_rule2 {
  all do: DataObject | one do.storedOn
  }
  ```

*IS Infrastructure (ADM Phases C, D) → Organizational Structure (ADM Phase B)*

- Every application should be used by some business service:

  ```
  assert P4_rule3 {
  all a: Application | some a.usedBy
  }
  ```

### 3.3  Case Model Design

To verify the approach proposed the classic case study [27], developed by The Open Group to illustrate the use of ArchiMate enterprise modeling language in the context of the TOGAF framework, has been chosen. The case study describes the baseline business, application, data and technology architectures for the fictitious organization and then proceeds with the possible change scenarios depicting target architectures.

The ArchiSurance organization described in the case is the result of a recent merger of three previously independent insurance companies:

- *Home & Away*, specializing in homeowners' insurance and travel insurance
- *PRO-FIT*, specializing in auto insurance
- *Legally Yours*, specializing in legal expense insurance.

The new company consists of three divisions with the same names and head-quarters as their independent predecessors and offers all the insurance products of the three pre-merger companies, selling directly to customers. The merger has resulted in a number of integration and alignment challenges for the new company's business processes and information systems.

Based on the data provided in the case study we designed the ArchiSurance model representation as an extension of the metamodel developed. For example, the "General CRM System" application entity is expressed as:

```
sig A2_GeneralCRMSystem extends Application {} {
usedBy = S2_RequestHandling
produces = DO1_CustomerProfile + DO2_InsuranceRequest
accesses = DO1_CustomerProfile + DO2_InsuranceRequest + DO5_Invoice + DO6_Payment
interactsWith = A4_HomeAwayPolicyAdministration + A5_AutoInsuranceApplication
deployedOn = T5_FrontOfficeServer
}
```

### 3.4  Alignment Assessment Using Alloy

Finally, we successively checked the case model against the alignment rules defined. Partially, the results are summed up in the tables below (Table 2).

**Table 2.** The results of alignment assessment using Alloy

| | |
|---|---|
| **Violated rule** | *P1_rule6:* every business service producing/accessing business object should use applications<br>*P1_rule7:* every business object should be realized by data object |
| **Illustration** | 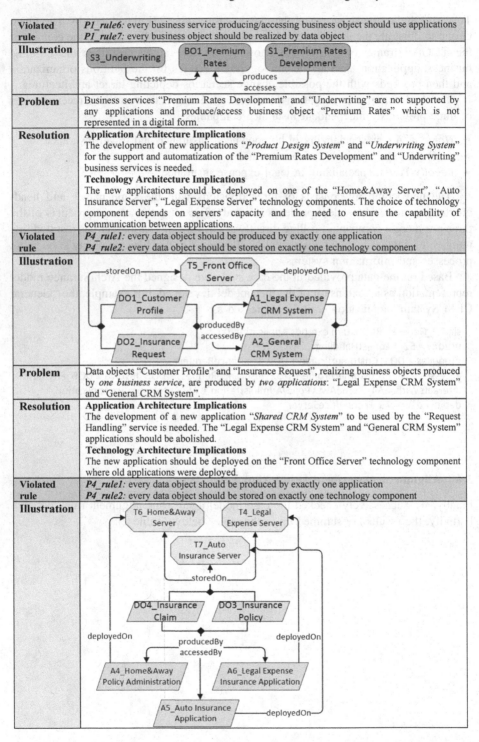 |
| **Problem** | Business services "Premium Rates Development" and "Underwriting" are not supported by any applications and produce/access business object "Premium Rates" which is not represented in a digital form. |
| **Resolution** | **Application Architecture Implications**<br>The development of new applications *"Product Design System"* and *"Underwriting System"* for the support and automatization of the "Premium Rates Development" and "Underwriting" business services is needed.<br>**Technology Architecture Implications**<br>The new applications should be deployed on one of the "Home&Away Server", "Auto Insurance Server", "Legal Expense Server" technology components. The choice of technology component depends on servers' capacity and the need to ensure the capability of communication between applications. |
| **Violated rule** | *P4_rule1:* every data object should be produced by exactly one application<br>*P4_rule2:* every data object should be stored on exactly one technology component |
| **Illustration** | |
| **Problem** | Data objects "Customer Profile" and "Insurance Request", realizing business objects produced by *one business service*, are produced by *two applications*: "Legal Expense CRM System" and "General CRM System". |
| **Resolution** | **Application Architecture Implications**<br>The development of a new application *"Shared CRM System"* to be used by the "Request Handling" service is needed. The "Legal Expense CRM System" and "General CRM System" applications should be abolished.<br>**Technology Architecture Implications**<br>The new application should be deployed on the "Front Office Server" technology component where old applications were deployed. |
| **Violated rule** | *P4_rule1:* every data object should be produced by exactly one application<br>*P4_rule2:* every data object should be stored on exactly one technology component |
| **Illustration** | |

| Problem | Data objects "Insurance Policy" and "Insurance Claim", realizing business objects produced by *one business service*, are produced by three applications: "Home&Away Policy Administration", "Auto Insurance Application", "Legal Expense Insurance Application", and therefore stored on several technology components deploying these applications. |
|---|---|
| Resolution | **Application Architecture Implications**<br>The development of a new applications "*Shared Policy Administration*" and "*Shared Claim Administration*" to be used by the "Policy Issuing" and "Claim Processing" services accordingly is needed. The "Home&Away Policy Administration", "Auto Insurance Application", "Legal Expense Insurance Application" applications should be abolished.<br>**Technology Architecture Implications**<br>New applications should be deployed on one of the "Home&Away Server", "Auto Insurance Server", "Legal Expense Server" technology components where one of the old applications was deployed. The choice of technology component depends on servers' capacity and the need to ensure the capability of communication between applications. |

# 4   Discussion

We compared the results derived from the alignment assessment using Alloy Analyzer with those provided by The Open Group in the case solution. They turned out to be quite similar (Table 3).

**Table 3.** Comparison of the case study solution and results obtained using Alloy

| Architecture changes defined in the case | Architecture changes derived using Alloy |
|---|---|
| *Application architecture* | |
| Development of new CRM system replacing "Legal Expense CRM System" and "General CRM System" | Analog of the new "*Shared CRM System*" application propose |
| Development of "P-CONFIG", a product configurator management system used to define all insurance products | Analog of the new "*Product Design System*" application proposed |
| Development of "AUTO-U", an automated underwriting system | Analog of the new "*Underwriting System*" application proposed |
| Development of "P-ADMIN", a packaged policy administration system which also handles customer accounting and billing replacing "Home&Away Policy Administration", "Home&Away Financial Application", "Auto Insurance Application", "Legal Expense Insurance Application" | Analog of the new "*Shared Policy Administration*" application proposed with the exception for the billing functionality which might be realized by the new "*Shared Billing System*" application proposed (omitted in the in the results table represented above) |
| Development of "VERSA-CLAIM", a packaged claims system replacing "Home&Away Policy Administration", "Auto Insurance Application", "Legal Expense Insurance Application" | Analog of the new "*Shared Claim Administration*" application proposed |
| Development of "BRIMS", a business rule management system | No analogs proposed |

*(continued)*

**Table 3.** (*continued*)

| Architecture changes defined in the case | Architecture changes derived using Alloy |
|---|---|
| *Technology architecture* | |
| CRM system is deployed on the "Front Office Server" technology component | Analog of the solution proposed |
| Technology components "Auto Insurance Application", "Legal Expense Insurance Application" are removed | One of the possible variations of the solution proposed |
| Applications "P-CONFIG", "AUTO-U", "P-ADMIN", "VERSA-CLAIM", "BRIMS" are deployed on the "Home&Away Server" | One of the possible variations of the solution proposed |
| New technology component "Back-up Server", deploying applications' replicas, is introduced to ensure data availability and protection in case of the failure at primary location | No analogs proposed |

The obtained results show that alignment assessment may be partly automated by means of Alloy: the recommendations for the Application and Technology Architecture changes derived from the use of Alloy coincided with those defined by the experts in the case study solution. So, it permits us to speak about the creation of a solid base for the formal IT-business alignment reference model which can be extended to other business cases. It also constitutes the main direction for the further research.

# 5    Conclusions

The issue of IT-business alignment has consistently been reported as one of the key CIO concerns for the last two decades. In the previous research [19] the integration of classic Strategic Alignment Model and The Open Group Architecture Framework was proposed as an attempt at providing a practical guidance for IT-business alignment as well as a strategic guidance for EA development. The current study formalizes and verifies the approach proposed using the structural modeling language Alloy. Three Alloy modules were defined. First, the metamodel representing the components of artifacts, delivered by the TOGAF ADM phases, relationships and dependencies between them was designed. Second, sets of alignment rules pertaining to the SAM perspectives were developed. Third, the standard case study, provided by The Open Group, was represented in terms of the metamodel designed. Finally, the case study model was checked against the alignment rules defined using the Alloy Analyzer tool as a mean of partial automatization of alignment assessment process.

# References

1. Babkin, E.A., Ponomarev, N.O.: Analysis of the consistency of enterprise architecture models using formal verification methods. Bus. Inform. **3**(41), 30–40 (2017)
2. Baets, W.: Aligning information systems with business strategy. J. Strateg. Inf. Syst. **1**(4), 205–213 (1992)
3. Broadbent, M., Weill, P.: Improving business and information strategy alignment: learning from the banking industry. IBM Syst. J. **32**(1), 162–179 (1993)
4. Byrd, A., Lewis, B.R., Bryan, R.W.: The leveraging influence of strategic alignment on IT investment: an empirical examination. Inf. Manag. **43**(3), 308–321 (2006)
5. Carvalho, G., Sousa, P.: Business and information systems misalignment model (BISMAM): an holistic model leveraged on misalignment and medical sciences approaches. In: Proceedings of the International Workshop on Business/IT Alignment and Interoperability (BUSITAL 2008), vol. 336, pp. 104–119. CEUR (2008)
6. Cataldo, A., McQueen, R.J., Hardings, J.: Comparing strategic IT alignment versus process IT alignment in SMEs. J. Res. Pract. Inf. Technol. **44**(1), 43–57 (2012)
7. Chan, Y.E., Reich, B.H.: IT alignment: what have we learned? J. Inf. Technol. **22**(4), 297–315 (2007)
8. Chan, Y.E., Sabherwal, R., Thatcher, J.B.: Antecedents and outcomes of strategic IS alignment: an empirical investigation. IEEE Trans. Eng. Manag. **53**(1), 27–47 (2006)
9. Chen, H.M., Kazman, R., Garg, A.: BITAM: an engineering-principled method for managing misalignments between business and IT architectures. Sci. Comput. Program. **57** (1), 5–26 (2005)
10. Daniel, J.: Software Abstractions: Logic, Language, and Analysis. The MIT Press, Cambridge (2011)
11. Gerow, J.E., Grover, V., Thatcher, J.B., Roth, P.L.: Looking toward the future of IT-business strategic alignment through the past: a meta-analysis. MIS Q. **38**(4), 1059–1085 (2014)
12. Henderson, J.C., Venkatraman, N.: Strategic alignment: leveraging information technology for transforming organizations. IBM Syst. J. **38**(1), 4–16 (1993)
13. Kearns, G.S., Lederer, A.L.: The effect of strategic alignment on the use of IS-based resources for competitive advantage. J. Strateg. Inf. Syst. **9**(4), 265–293 (2000)
14. Kearns, G.S., Sabherwal, R.: Strategic alignment between business and information technology: a knowledge-based view of behaviors, outcome, and consequences. J. Manag. Inf. Syst. **23**(3), 129–162 (2007)
15. Luftman, J.N.: Assessing IT/business alignment. Inf. Syst. Manag. **20**(4), 9–15 (2003)
16. Luftman, J.N.: Competing in the Information Age: Align in the Sand. Oxford University Press, New York (2003)
17. Luftman, J.N., Lewis, P.R., Oldach, S.H.: Transforming the enterprise: the alignment of business and information technology strategies. IBM Syst. J. **32**(1), 198–221 (1993)
18. Luftman, J.N., Papp, R., Brier, T.: Achieving and sustaining business-IT alignment. Calif. Manag. Rev. **42**(1), 109–122 (1999)
19. This entry is known to the authors, but is omitted here for anonymization reasons. It will be re-added for the final submission of the paper
20. Pereira, C.M., Sousa, P.: Enterprise architecture: business and IT alignment. In: Proceedings of the ACM Symposium on Applied Computing (ACM SAC 2005), pp. 1344–1345 (2005)
21. Reich, B.H., Benbasat, I.: Measuring the linkage between business and information technology objectives. MIS Q. **20**(1), 55–81 (1996)
22. Reich, B.H., Benbasat, I.: Factors that influence the social dimension of alignment between business and IT objectives. MIS Q. **24**(1), 81–113 (2000)

23. Rychkova, I., Regev, G., Wegman, A.: Using declarative specifications in business process design. Int. J. Comput. Sci. Appl. **5**(3b), 45–68 (2008)
24. Tan, F.B., Gallupe, R.B.: Aligning business and information systems thinking: a cognitive approach. IEEE Trans. Eng. Manag. **53**(2), 223–237 (2006)
25. The Alloy: A language & tool for relational models. http://alloy.mit.edu/alloy/
26. The Global IT Trends Survey (2017). http://www.globaliim.com/
27. The Open Group ArchiSurance Case Study. https://publications.opengroup.org/y163
28. The Open Group Architecture Framework (TOGAF Version 9.1). http://www.opengroup.org/
29. The Standish Group, Chaos Report (2015). http://www.standishgroup.com/
30. Venkatraman, N., Henderson, J.C., Oldach, S.: Continuous strategic alignment: exploiting information technology capabilities for competitive success. Eur. Manag. J. **11**(2), 139–149 (1993)
31. Wang, X., Zhou, X., Jiang, L.: A method of business and IT alignment based on enterprise architecture. In: Proceedings of IEEE International Conference on Service Operations, Logistics and Informatics, vol. 1, pp. 740–745 (2008)
32. Wegmann, A.: On the systemic enterprise architecture methodology (SEAM). In: Proceedings International Conference on Enterprise Information Systems (ICEIS 2003), pp. 483–490 (2003)
33. Wegmann, A., et al.: Requirements modeling in SEAM: the example of a car crash management system. In: Comparing Requirements Modeling Approaches Workshop (CMA@ RE) (2013)
34. Wegmann, A., Le, L-S., Hussami, L., Beyer, D.: A tool for verified design using alloy for specification and CrocoPat for verification. In: Jackson, D., Zave, P. (eds.) Proceedings of First Alloy Workshop (2006)

# Invited Workshop Notes

# Methods for Evaluating the Quality of Process Modelling Tools

Josef Pavlicek[1]([⊠]) and Petra Pavlickova[2]([⊠])

[1] Faculty of Information Technology,
Department of Software Engineering, CTU,
Zikova 4, Prague 6 - Dejvice, 166 27 Prague, Czech Republic
`josef.pavlicek@fit.cvut.cz`
[2] Faculty of Economics and Management, Department of Systems Engineering,
Czech University of Life Sciences, Kamycka 959, 165 00 Prague,
Czech Republic
`pavlickovap@pef.czu.cz`

**Abstract.** This invited workshop **Methods for evaluating the quality of process modelling tools** was a part of EOMAS 2018. Workshop dealt with the comparison of BPMN and BORM process modelling tools in the form of Usability study. We practically presented the methods used to compare, defined the appropriate equipment of the laboratory and proposed the CASE study model. We hired participants (from the audience) and we used Tobii Glasses for eyes tracking and recording the participants focus. This technology has been used by authors in previous years to find a measure of quality of process models, and this year has been demonstrated and applied on BPMN and DEMO models.

**Keywords:** BPMN · BORM · Usability study · Process modelling tools
TOBII Glasses

## 1 Introduction

In the past years, our team has dealt with the design of appropriate measures to determine the quality of design of the process models. Our experience has been published not only at the EOMAS conference [1, 2], but also in the journals and scientific papers [3–8]. During the determination of the appropriate measures of the process models we focused primarily on the BPMN notation [9, 10]. This notation is currently very well sophisticated, it can be considered as a standard tool in the modelling of the business processes in a wide group of process-controlled organizations [3]. During the panel discussion at the EOMAS 2017 conference in Essen, Germany, we were directed to solve another, nowadays burning problem.

The issue is undoubtedly a discussion about:

- Applicability
- Overview
- General user friendliness

of the tools designed for the business processes modelling. Indeed, BPMN [9, 10] and BORM [11] compete with the notion of the favors of process designers. An interesting

© Springer Nature Switzerland AG 2018
R. Pergl et al. (Eds.): EOMAS 2018, LNBIP 332, pp. 171–177, 2018.
https://doi.org/10.1007/978-3-030-00787-4_12

work dealing with the quality of process models and the implementation of the DEMO methodology is the "Empirical Study of Applying the DEMO Method for Improving BPMN Process Models in Academic Environment" [14]. It is clear from the authors' work that streamlining process models is desirable for a number of reasons. A similar problem is currently undergoing conceptual modeling tools such as OntoUML [12] and UML [13].

If the problem is deeper under our examination, probably we come to the conclusion that the important attributes such as usability, clarity, user friendliness compete with factors:

- availability of the information to the appropriate methodology,
- custom of the environment in which we implement the solution (corporate culture),
- the size of the community using the technology.

Usability attributes (based on the work of Jacob Nielsen and his scientific educational company Nielsen Group [16, 17]) have demonstrably influenced users of SW tools [17]. It is therefore worth paying attention to them. The aim of this work is to propose the method of testing the quality of the process models, based on the basics of the work of Jacob Nielsen [16, 17] and our practical experience [1–8, 18].

## 2 Materials and Methods

### Eye Tracking System
As we have already mentioned, our team has carried out a wide range of process models with a eye-catching camera [1–7]. This technology allows us to monitor both the orientation of the participant's view on the presented process model and the time spent by reading or trying to recognize the element displayed [1]. Last but not least, it is possible to track the direction of movement, iterations over model elements, abandoning models and loss of attention.

### Models
For the purpose of the required workshop, we designed a set of four process models designed to select an employee for a chosen university position. The models were presented to conference participants and the TOBII Glasses technology captured their responses during reading the models.

In order to define the hypothesis under consideration, it is necessary first to define the term Applicability of the model. Under this concept, we understand the model's ability to be user-friendly, the orientation in the model is no longer than 7 s after it is read, the reader understands within 7 s the basic (but not hidden) meaning of the elements used, i.e.:

Definition of usability of BPMN:

- Circle and circle with center for the beginning and end of the process model.
- Rectangle for aktivity.
- Diameter for decision making and process branching.
- Arrow as a transition line.
- Swimlines as the area of responsibility for the process (Fig. 1).

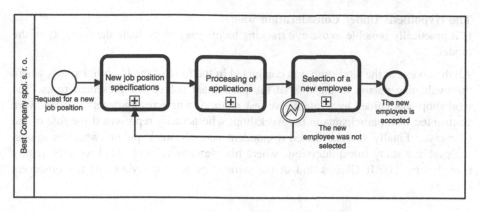

**Fig. 1.** Request for a new job position BPMN

Definition of usability of DEMO:

- Recognizing the basic elements of the process (Fig. 2).

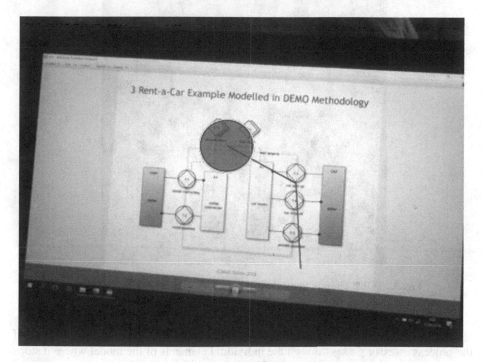

**Fig. 2.** DEMO model during the usability test

**The Hypothesis Under Consideration was:**
Is it practically possible to use eye tracking technology to evaluate the usability of the model?

All the course of the workshop was conducted in the form of the Usability study, where the evaluating person in the role of the participant solved the presented tasks. The workshop was guided by a qualitative test method, where respondents' answers were confronted with participants in the workshop, who actually represented the role of the Obeserver. Finally, the questioned respondent was still made public (which is against the usability study rules) interview, where his views were confronted with the reality recorded by TOBII Glasses and at the same time with the views of the observers (Fig. 3).

**Fig. 3.** TOBII Glasses focus during explanation the model by the authors

During this workshop, it was practically demonstrated how the user in the role of the process assessor passes through the individual elements of the model where it stops and how it responds to the process elements, i.e. primarily the arrows. The purpose of the workshop was also to demonstrate how the implementation of the process model affects the reader's attention, which elements are distracting, and what is the real correlation between the eye movement and the evaluator's final response. Each evaluator had the task of answering 3 questions arising from the process model. He had the time to answer, during which he went through the process model. TOBII Glasses technology enabled the respondent's eye to capture and quantitatively capture the eye.

During the workshop, we have experienced typical graphical and multimedia problems while reading the model (Figs. 4, 5, 6 and 7).

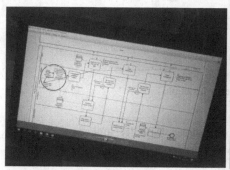

**Fig. 4.** The TOBII Glasses focus during the usability test BPMN model

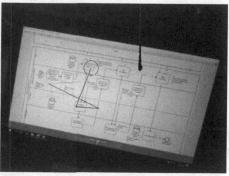

**Fig. 5.** The TOBII Glasses focus during the usability test BPMN model

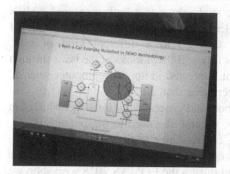

**Fig. 6.** The TOBII Glasses focus during the usability test DEMO model

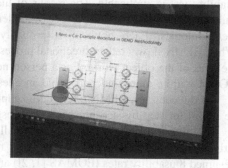

**Fig. 7.** The TOBII Glasses focus during the usability test DEMO

## 3  Results

The technology used has been shown and we demonstrated that it can be used to evaluate the quality of process models in terms of their clarity - i.e. usability. It is obvious that a process designer may not want to disassemble his working model (usability) or to design it "readable" without having to retreat from maintaining all the required functional requirements for the process. Just the structure of the individual objects, the insensitive sequence of decisions, see Fig. 8 or a number of iterations etc.

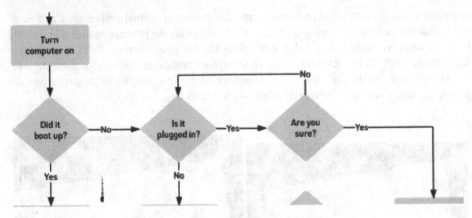

**Fig. 8.** IF sequence example

The process model makes it unclear, and sometimes formally logical, nonsensical. These conclusions of the work in the EOMAS group have shown a in a practical form.

## 4   Conclusion

The method of verifying the quality of process modelling tools in the form of a usability test is applicable. The results of the study show that both measured BMPN and BORM notations bring process modellers the benefits defined by authors of methodologies. Each notation is probably targeted to a different kind of user. While BPMN shows rather directional process flows, BORM looks at the issue through the eyes of the object world. For a person not interested in applied computer science, BORM will be more understandable and descriptive than BPMN.

On the contrary, BPMN offers OMG support and process flow tracking, which can be useful for step-by-step process-by-process, without the need to understand it.

Usability testing methods and, above all, collaborative testing allows us to qualitatively verify the usability of the process model. Based on these findings, we have designed 8 usability rates (EOMAS [1, 2]) and during the EOMAS 2018 workshop we have demonstrated the performance of the test. The aim of the authors is to extend the process model community with the ability to perceive the process model's readability as a user-friendly value for the user, thus leading modellers to comply with the principles of clarity and usability without limiting or omitting functional requirements for the model.

# References

1. Pavlicek, J., Hronza, R., Pavlickova, P., Jelinkova, K.: The business process model quality metrics. In: Pergl, R., Lock, R., Babkin, E., Molhanec, M. (eds.) EOMAS 2017. LNBIP, vol. 298, pp. 134–148. Springer, Heidelberg (2017). https://doi.org/10.1007/978-3-319-68185-6_10. ISBN 978-3-319-68184-9
2. Pavlicek, J., Hronza, R., Pavlickova, P.: Educational business process model skills improvement. In: Pergl, R., Molhanec, M., Babkin, E., Fosso Wamba, S. (eds.) EOMAS 2016. LNBIP, vol. 272, pp. 172–184. Springer, Heidelberg (2016). https://doi.org/10.1007/978-3-319-49454-8_12. ISBN 978-3-319-49454-8
3. Hronza, R., Pavlíček, J., Náplava, P.: Míry kvality procesních modelů vytvořených v notaci BPMN. Acta Inform. Pragensia **4**(2), 140–153 (2015)
4. Jelínková, K.: Návrh měr kvality obchodních procesních modelů. Czech Technical University in Prague (2017)
5. Lassaková, M.: Návrh a tvorba měr pro výpočet kvality procesních modelů. Czech Technical University in Prague (2016)
6. Neumann, M.: Míry kvality procesních modelů. Czech Technical University in Prague (2016)
7. Hronza, R., Pavlíček, J., Mach, R., Náplava, P.: Míry kvality v procesním modelování. Acta Inform. Pragensia **4**(1), 18–29 (2015)
8. Mach, R.: Návrh a tvorba nástroje pro optimalizaci procesů na základě analýzy BPM modelů. Czech Technical University in Prague (2015)
9. Bruce, S.: BPMN Method and Style. Cody-Cassidy Press, Aptos (2011)
10. OMG: Business Process Model & Notation (BPMN) (2016). http://www.omg.org/bpmn/index.htm. Accessed 21 Mar 2017
11. Knott, R., Merunka, V., Polak, J.: The BORM methodology: a third-generation fully object-oriented. Knowl.-Based Syst. **16**(2), 77–89 (2003). https://doi.org/10.1016/S0950-7051(02)00075-8
12. Bassetto, L.: OntoUML Specification. http://ontology.com.br/ontouml/spec/
13. OMG: Unified Modeling Language (UML) (2008). http://www.uml.org
14. Náplava, P., Pergl, R.: Empirical study of applying the DEMO method for improving BPMN process models in academic environment. In: Proceedings of the 17th IEEE Conference on Business Informatics, pp. 18–26. IEEE Operations Center, Piscataway (2015). ISBN 978-1-4673-7340-1
15. Nielsen Norman Group: Evidence-Based User Experience Research. https://www.nngroup.com/
16. Nielsen, J.: Why you only need to test with 5 users. Jakob Nielsens Alertbox **19**, 1–4 (2000)
17. Pavlicek, J., Bock, R.: Collaborative usability lab design and methodology to use that, part of HUBRU. https://katedry.czu.cz/en/hubru/home. Accessed 7 Jul 2018
18. Tobii Tech: Eye tracking. https://www.tobii.com/tech/technology/what-is-eye-tracking. Accessed 7 Jul 2018

# Author Index

Ali, Muhammad   107
Arzumanyan, Maxim   76

Bork, Dominik   16

Depaire, Benoît   49

Eybers, Sunet   16

Gerber, Aurona   16
Gordeeva, Tatiana   63

Hadar, Ethan   91
Haerens, Geert   123
Hunka, Frantisek   3, 138

Ivanova, Marina   153

Jans, Mieke   49
Jouck, Toon   49

Karagiannis, Dimitris   16
Kudryavtsev, Dmitry   76

Lieben, Jonas   49

Malyzhenkov, Pavel   63, 153
Masi, Maurizio   63
Matula, Jiri   3, 138
Miron, Elena-Teodora   16

Pavlicek, Josef   171
Pavlickova, Petra   171
Pergl, Robert   31

Rybola, Zdeněk   31

Shahzad, Khurram   107
Sumereder, Anna   16

Van der Merwe, Alta   16
van Kervel, Steven J. H.   138
van Deventer, Phil   16

Zaramenskikh, Evgeny   76

Printed in the United States
By Bookmasters